The Philosophy of Merleau-Ponty

The
Philosophy
of
MERLEAU-PONTY

JOHN F. BANNAN

Loyola University

HARCOURT, BRACE & WORLD, INC.

New York / Chicago / San Francisco / Atlanta

COVER ART BY J. P. TREMBLAY

Library of Congress Catalog Card Number: 67-17509

Printed in the United States of America

To my wife, Rosemary

Preface

Merleau-Ponty's philosophy belongs in the movement of phenomenology and existentialism that dominates European philosophy today. Like Husserl, Heidegger, Sartre, and Marcel, Merleau-Ponty possesses a man-centered perspective, an acute sense of the complexity of the world, and the stubborn determination to deal with this complexity in its most concrete forms. In France phenomenological existentialism has displaced the tradition of intellectualism, which reaches back to Descartes, and the more recent Bergsonian vitalism—both of which were prevalent during the first third of this century. What Merleau-Ponty has contributed to phenomenological existentialism (and what he has helped establish in France) is a revised understanding of perceptual consciousness—an understanding that allows perception to stand as the primary human function and the perceiving human to take his place as central reference point in philosophy.

In its original statement Merleau-Ponty's philosophy is difficult. His view is unusual; his terminology is neither familiar nor completely consistent. His thought develops in an orderly way, but the order is complex and not easy to follow. Finally, many of the important things that he had to say are to be found in articles and lectures. These have now, for the most part, been collected and translated, but because they are articles and lectures, they do not reveal the coherence of his position. Such complaints are justified in the cases of Husserl, Heidegger, and Marcel, and this is another characteristic that he shares with them. It is doubtful that any movement of thought has found introduction and commentary as useful in expediting its assimilation into philosophy as phenomenological existentialism has. It is to the promotion of familiarity with Merleau-Ponty's position among English-reading philosophers and students that this book is devoted.

Merleau-Ponty must, of course, be presented in his own terms. This is basic, for, like every significant philosophical achievement, his work carries its own meaning with it. In the pages that follow, then, we shall not aim at locating him among the classic positions in the history of philosophy but shall center upon his more immediate context—for example, his relations with Husserl's work, with Sartre, and with Marxism. Neither shall we strain to find in him connections with what we may assume to be the philosophical experience of many readers: linguistic analysis. If he is to be presented in his own terms, he must be accepted in these same terms. We shall attempt to convey the tone and style of this philosophy by declaring its themes in a distinct and measured way and by inviting the reader to join in its movement.

We shall attentively discuss what Merleau-Ponty has written, noting the structure of his arguments, their documentation, and what it is they strive to accomplish. Thus the four chapters that follow the Introduction will offer a close analysis of his two major works (*The Structure of Behavior* and *Phenomenology of Perception*). They contain his treatment of the relationship of consciousness and nature. After this we shall consider his less organized (but no less serious) discussions of the relation of consciousness with one form or another of consciousness. Such problems as the nature of philosophy, the existence of an Absolute, and the nature of history are treated here, as is Merleau-Ponty's relation with Sartre. In a final chapter we review his later work, calling attention to his return to the question of the relations of consciousness and nature.

My attention was first drawn to the philosophy of Merleau-Ponty by Monsignor Albert Dondeyne, who is now Rector of L'Institut Supérieur de Philosophie at the University of Louvain in Belgium. I owe him a very special debt for this and for his help in the early stages of my work. I am grateful also to the American Philosophical Society for research grants that allowed me to devote the necessary time to the manuscript and to the four persons on whose recommendations the Society advanced its funds: Professor Paul Weiss of Yale University; Professor James Collins of St. Louis University; Dr. Jordan Scher, editor of *Existential Psychiatry* and founder of the American Onto-analytic Association; and the Reverend Robert W. Mulligan, S. J., of Loyola University.

JOHN F. BANNAN

Contents

The Philosophy of Merleau-Ponty

Introduction

CONTEMPORARY AND CLASSIC

Rarely has a philosopher been as intimate with his times as Maurice Merleau-Ponty. Phenomenologist, existentialist, Marxist, he derived his ideas from each of the three dominant modes of twentieth-century European philosophy. If we are to understand him we must know something about them. He did not, of course, simply submit to their influence but imposed his own style upon their themes, eliciting from them quite unforeseen capacities for coexistence, exchange, and development. If we are really to appreciate them, we should understand him. His philosophical approach was humanistic in that comprehensive sense that takes man as the central reference point in the posing and solving of fundamental problems. The philosophical problem of the time, he once said, is "to explore the irrational and to integrate it with an enlarged reason."[1] It is as if the enlargement of reason would be accomplished when it could accommodate man and the rest of reality in relation to him. In their best moments, phenomenology, existentialism, and Marxism share this emphasis, and this is the ground for the reciprocity between himself and them. In Merleau-Ponty, then, we must expect to encounter their themes but to find them integrated distinctively in his remarkable philosophical life.

---

1. Maurice Merleau-Ponty, "L'Existentialisme chez Hegel," *Les Temps Modernes,* I (Ap., 1946), p. 1311.

But we must also look beyond the twentieth-century context, for Merleau-Ponty was a philosopher in the full and classic sense of the term. The questions that occupy him—questions about the meaning of man, the nature of consciousness, truth, freedom, and coexistence— have always been the distinctive concern of philosophers. When he attempts to formulate a conception of consciousness, he struggles with the perennial demands of unity and multiplicity; his work on the nature of history clearly recognizes the need for a balance between process and stability. He is at ease drawing together the results of his first extended phenomenological treatment of man in a restatement of the body-soul relationship.[2] He turns regularly to Descartes for help in posing the problem of the nature and unity of consciousness, and Descartes is his partner in the dialogue that seeks to solve it.[3] Philosophers in every age share certain concerns, however differently they reduce them to problems: *contemporary* and *classic* are names for concentric, not juxtaposed dimensions of philosophy and of the life of the philosopher who, because he is a philosopher, attempts "to conceive the world, others, and himself, and their interrelations."

BIOGRAPHICAL NOTE

Merleau-Ponty was born in 1908. His father died prior to World War I, and he and a brother and sister were raised in Paris by their mother. His education followed a familiar pattern: secondary education at the Lycée Louis-le-Grand, and then L'Ecole Normale, from which he graduated in 1930. During the next five years he taught in a lycée at Beauvais, held a grant for research from the Caisse de la Recherche Scientifique for a year, and then taught again—this time at the lycée in Chartres. In 1935 he returned to Paris as a junior member—*agrégé répétiteur*—of the faculty at L'Ecole Normale. In the

---

2. See M. Merleau-Ponty, *La Structure du comportement* (Paris: Presses universitaires de France, 1942), Ch. IV. The work is available in English translated by Alden Fisher: *The Structure of Behavior* (Boston: Beacon Press, 1963). Hereafter, this book will be referred to as *Structure*.
3. See *Structure*, Ch. IV. Cf. also M. Merleau-Ponty, *Phénoménologie de la Perception* (Paris: Gallimard, 1945), Part III, Ch. I. English translation by Colin Smith: *Phenomenology of Perception* (London: Routledge and Keegan Paul, 1962). Hereafter, M. Merleau-Ponty will be abbreviated in the footnotes as M. M-P and *Phenomenology of Perception* as *Phenomenology*.

winter of 1939 he entered the army and served as a lieutenant in the infantry. After demobilization and during the German occupation he taught again and labored over what was to be his major work: *Phenomenology of Perception*. With the end of the occupation he joined the faculty of L'Université de Lyon and at the same time became co-editor with Sartre of the periodical *Les Temps Modernes*. By 1950 his reputation was established, and he came to the Sorbonne as Professor of Psychology and Pedagogy. He was to remain in this post—not at all well suited to him—for only two years. In 1952 he was appointed to the Collège de France, to the chair that had been left vacant by the death of Louis Lavelle and that had previously been occupied by Henri Bergson and Edouard LeRoy. He was the youngest philosopher ever to hold this position—one of the more exalted in French academic life —and he retained it until his death in May, 1961.

EARLIEST WORK

There seems never to have been a time when Merleau-Ponty's philosophy was not *existentialist* in the sense that it centers upon a finite human consciousness caught up in a world, rather than simply observing its world from a distance. Neither was there a time when he was not attentive to the meaning of human history in a way that made practically inevitable his prolonged and sympathetic sounding of *Marxism*. Above all, there seems never to have been a time when he doubted that philosophy meant *phenomenology*.[4] What attracted him to phenomenology was the prospect that he felt it offered for a renewal of philosophy. Husserl, who was the founder of phenomenology, called it a return "to the things themselves," which the already established philosophies had lost sight of. This return was accomplished primarily by beginning with a careful description of *things* as they appear and of the *consciousness* in which they appear—a description sensitive to the richness and complexity that characterize both things and consciousness before they are refined by philosophical analysis. It is this richness, the phenomenologist feels, that previous philosophies have let slip away by attempting to analyze reality as if it were fashioned according to some mechanical, biological, or spiritual model. In his earliest writings

---

4. Cf. Alphonse DeWaelhens, "Situation de Merleau-Ponty," *Les Temps Modernes,* Vol. XVII, pp. 184–85 (Numéro spécial, 1961), p. 377.

Merleau-Ponty protests this abuse and advances phenomenology as its corrective.

His first publication was an article entitled "Christianity and Resentment," which appeared in a June, 1935, issue of the Catholic bimonthly *La Vie Intellectuelle*.[5] In it he reviewed *Über Ressentiment und Moralisches Werturteil* by Max Scheler, a German phenomenologist and student of Husserl, which had just been published in a French translation. In October, 1936, he reviewed Gabriel Marcel's *Being and Having* in the same periodical.[6]

In the first of these two books Scheler defends Christianity against the attack that Nietzsche launched against it. For Nietzsche, Christianity is essentially resentment, and the Christian, a man who is too weak to participate joyfully in life by triumphant self-assertion. Hence, Christianity rejects human values and constructs an antihuman morality exalting pain, poverty, sacrifice, and love. Scheler maintains that such a view of Christianity results from Nietzsche's naturalism, which reduces all values to a biological level and knowledge to sensation. But such priorities are only prejudices unless they can be justified philosophically, and for Scheler philosophical justification begins with phenomenological description. For this reason Merleau-Ponty endorses Scheler, saying that every philosophy should begin with "an inventory, a description of consciousness . . . as it appears immediately, the 'phenomenon' of consciousness in all its original variety."[7] Such description will find in consciousness the many and varied emotional, volitional, and affective components for which Nietzsche's biological point of view left too little room. It will discover that Christian love is far richer and more worthy than Nietzsche was willing to admit: not failure and weakness at all, Scheler insists, but a positive spiritual overflow. It will also reveal that consciousness is, in its very structure, *intentional*—that is, oriented toward objects. This orientation places consciousness in direct touch with moral and religious values along with perceptual objects and opens the way to the description with which philosophy should begin its work.

In addition to defending Christianity against naturalism, phenome-

---

5. M. M-P., "Christianisme et ressentiment," *La Vie Intellectuelle*, XXXVI, 2 (June 10, 1935), pp. 278–306.
6. M. M-P., "Etre et avoir," *La Vie Intellectuelle*, Vol. XLV (Oct., 1936), pp. 98–109.
7. "Christianisme et ressentiment," p. 288.

nology can provide it with a tenable picture of its own relation with human life, both collective and personal. Acknowledging that he may be criticized for pulling Scheler's thought "toward the left," Merleau-Ponty suggests that Christianity's "other worldliness" can be understood as the means by which Christianity maintains its power to commit itself freely where it is needed. Its refusal to identify itself with particular social or political institutions, then, can actually favor its presence in the world.[8] Finally, he simply disagrees with Scheler's identification of the moral act with the intention of the one who performs it. The situation in which the performer finds himself and the consequences of what he does cannot be ignored and have always been important to Christianity.[9]

In concluding his review of Scheler's book Merleau-Ponty turns to the intellectual scene in France. Here, too, he feels, a reductionism threatens the variety in consciousness and in things. It is not Nietzsche's biological naturalism, instinctively held and displayed in vivid literary terms, but an intellectualism with enough affinities with physical science to regard itself as a scientific naturalism. Intellectualism turns perception, art, sentiment, and religious behavior into rigid and uniform objects of scientific observation. Jean Wahl and Gabriel Marcel had already asserted the incompetence of such a view to deal with the fullness of what exists.[10] What is needed, and what Merleau-Ponty feels phenomenology can supply, is another philosophical act—one which "becomes conscious of the objects of thought and follows the articulations which they impose on us [and] describes existence in all its forms.[11]

In his review of Marcel's work Merleau-Ponty offers us a glimpse of the specific emphases and reversals of perspective that a phenomenological description of "existence in all its forms" might offer. He

---

8. "To insist upon the intemporal character of the religious act, to refuse to have it adhere to any form of social or political organization, is in no sense to relieve it from the demands of the present. It is, perhaps, to prepare it to be more faithful to them." (*Ibid.*, p. 297.)

9. "However decisive the importance of the intention and even if justification is never 'felt,' it is nonetheless characteristic of Christianity to admit that there are acts which affect the 'spiritual person' . . . a substantial connivance of 'spiritual person' with sensible consciousness." ("Christianisme et ressentiment," pp. 303–04.)

10. Wahl did this in his *Vers le concret* (Paris: Vrin, 1933) and Marcel in his *Journal Métaphysique* (Paris: Gallimard, 1923).

11. "Christianisme et ressentiment," p. 305.

confronts the intellectualist position, describing its distinctive subject-object relation: "Everything occurs as if common sense and the philosophers had long ago accepted as their type and ideal of human knowledge our contemplation of inanimate objects, things which are indifferent and which do not *touch* us." Marcel had pointed out that such a manner of knowing cannot do justice to our experience of the other person whose *presence* we know, nor of our *bodies*, which are so much a part of our own presence. The classic analysis of perception—treating one's own body and the other person as objects with various properties that give rise to certain impressions that consciousness deciphers—simply dissolves what most needs explaining about them: their "human," subjective character. As usual, the point at which one analysis founders becomes the starting point of the one that challenges it. Marcel concentrates on the human body and the other person, and Merleau-Ponty says of this effort: "It becomes more and more apparent that the analyses of the human body and the 'thou' were the first attempts at a new general method, the first examples of a new kind of knowledge . . . phenomenology." Marcel reflects on the great variety of things and values that present themselves directly to our consciousness and does so through his direct encounter, his *intuition* of them. Consciousness becomes central and the relation between it and "objective" categories is *reversed*. Thus, "presence and absence should no longer be thought of as modes of spatial and temporal distance and proximity; on the contrary, one must derive the latter from the former. The theory of time, in particular, needs to be reworked." Though Merleau-Ponty accepts this attention to the body and the reversal of perspective between subject and object, he has several serious reservations about Marcel's position. These arise from the problem of distinguishing among intuitions. For example, both what is real and what is illusory, present themselves in consciousness; how does one decide which is which? Merleau-Ponty feels that *in the experience* where they are encountered and taken to be real or illusory—that is, where the problem of the real and the illusory arises in the first place—there are to be found certain describable *structural* features that distinguish one from the other. By studying these structural features we can regulate intuition without destroying its valuable immediacy.[12]

---

12. Cf. *Etre et avoir*, pp. 107–08.

Description, intentionality, the recovery of the concrete, the incarnation of personal consciousness in the body, the incarnation of social consciousness in institutions that respond to the needs of the great masses of mankind, the humanist reversal of perspectives in classic philosophical problems, the fruitfulness of reflection on structure: all these were present in Merleau-Ponty's first efforts. All endure throughout his career. There are, however, important early changes in the structure of the philosophical dialogue in which these themes are worked out. Merleau-Ponty did not prolong his relationship with Scheler and Marcel. Early in his philosophical career he turned to Husserl, both to grasp phenomenology at its source and to seek the best balance of intuition (with its advantages in producing evidence) and analysis (with its advantages for distinct philosophical statement). His apparent confidence in the Catholic Church's relevance to society soon yielded to the conviction that Marxism's insight into the meaning of human history was the most sure. Sartre, too, exercised considerable influence on Merleau-Ponty. Both exploited the same basic themes. Because philosophy is never simply the struggle of a solitary individual with one or more problems or positions, but is rather a community activity involving the philosopher in a web of relations with his peers, the development of Merleau-Ponty's thought is the history of his exchanges with Husserl, Sartre, and various Marxists, and of his extending, refining, revising, and at times dramatically altering these relations. With this in mind we focus our attention on Merleau-Ponty's relations with his contemporaries.

HUSSERL AND PHENOMENOLOGY

The dialogue with Husserl was in all probability the most important in Merleau-Ponty's career. He returns to it regularly throughout his life, and his profound respect for the German thinker never wavers. Husserlian themes more than any others structure his most important works.

Husserl often distinguished his philosophy from that of Descartes.[13] This was necessary because they shared much, particularly in those

---

13. Cf. E. Husserl, *Ideas: General Introduction to Pure Phenomenology*, trans. by W. R. Boyce Gibson (New York: The Macmillan Co., 1931), pp. 107–09; and E. Husserl, *Cartesian Meditations* (The Hague: Martinus Nijhoff, 1960), pp. 1–26. Hereafter, the former work will be referred to as *Ideas*.

aspects of their work most easily delivered for public observation. Each declared himself repelled by the confusion of the philosophical scene that he faced, and each reacted with that remarkable combination of naiveté and self-confidence that distinguishes so many great thinkers, who decide to resolve the confusion by rethinking philosophy systematically themselves. For Husserl, philosophy was to be a rigorous science, as well as a return to the things themselves.[14] He shares Descartes' conviction that one must turn toward the subject if he is to find the unchallengeable evidence that philosophy as a rigorous science demands.[15] If the turn toward the subject in the interest of rigor seems to contradict the return to the things themselves (most of which do not lie in the direction of the subject), Husserl can feel that he is able to avoid the contradiction and reconcile the two contrasting movements by having philosophy begin with the description of *phenomena*.

We must be careful to distinguish what Husserl meant by the term phenomena from what Kant meant by it, particularly since the Kantian meaning seems to have become firmly established in the conventional usage of philosophers. For both of these thinkers the term phenomena designates what appears to consciousness. But for the phenomenologist there is no unknowable world behind the appearances, no noumenal ballast to guarantee against the absorption of phenomena into the consciousness with which it is essentially related. Whatever counts in any way can appear "in person" and be available for description. This is a richer and more promising conception of phenomena than that of Kant because the structures that underwrite its coherence and integrity are integrated in it. For Husserl, then, the return to the things themselves and the focus upon phenomena are really one and the same movement: the things to which he returns are *appearing* things. Description can take a firm grip on them and can even reveal the very essence of what appears. Husserl said that phenomenology, a study of phenomena, is at the same time to be "a science which aims exclusively at establishing the 'knowledge of essences.' "

We do not normally consider our surroundings as phenomena. It is natural for us to assume that the things around us are independent existences, each functioning according to its own laws, and we assume this in both our common sense behavior and in science. If he is to see

14. Cf. *Cartesian Meditations*, pp. 7–14.
15. Cf. *Ideas*, pp. 107–09.

things simply as they appear, then, the phenomenologist must take up some vantage point other than our "natural" attitude. Husserl calls this philosophical vantage point the *transcendental attitude* and refers to the movement by which one adopts this attitude as the *reduction*. The reduction, unlike Descartes' methodic doubt, is not an attempt to deny the existence of the natural world. Rather, in it one suspends his spontaneous belief in the world with the result that the world's initial claim to be accepted as independent is neutralized.[16] Its status, then, is phenomenal: its being is a being-for-consciousness.

The consciousness to which the world appears is, for its part, intentional, and this means (as was pointed out earlier) that it is always consciousness *of* something. Thus, if the things with which the phenomenologist deals are things-for-consciousness, the consciousness with which they are related is essentially bound to them. This relation to what appears helps stave off an idealist overemphasis on consciousness and also offers Husserl a structure that guides the application of his method. The phenomenological analysis in any given area—perception, for example, or imagination—begins with a description of what appears. This description seeks out what essentially characterizes any perceived object or any imagined object. After uncovering the essence of the objective or *noematic* pole of consciousness, the analysis turns to the subjective or *noetic* pole. In our examples this would mean a shift in attention from the thing perceived to the perceiving and from the thing imagined to the imagining. Here, too, the essence would be sought: what must necessarily characterize any perceiving or any imagining? *Noema* and *noesis*—what appears and the consciousness in which it appears—stand in a symmetrical relationship, as the search for an essential structure continues on the basis of a direct description of a concrete perceiving or imagining.

However, the balance between consciousness and its object is eventually disrupted in favor of the former. Husserl regards consciousness as the condition for the appearing of anything—that is, as the condition of all phenomena. By examining the kinds of consciousness involved in

---

16. "Unlike Descartes, we shall plunge into the task of laying open the infinite field of transcendental experience. . . . This field is completely unique and separate, since it relates likewise to all the world and all the objective sciences, yet does not presuppose acceptance of their existence." (*Cartesian Meditations*, p. 31.)

the various kinds of phenomena, he feels that one could lay hold of what underlies the appearing of everything that does or could present itself. Thus he could consider the reduction not as a diminishing of the amount of reality available for analysis, but as a great extension of it. When, however, phenomenology passes from the examining of particular regions of consciousness and phenomena to a discussion of the basic nature of all phenomena and all consciousness, the idealist tendency takes over. For much of his career he took consciousness as an absolute and its most basic intentionality as creating the empirical reality that was described in the various regions of being.[17]

This position not only contains all the classic difficulties of idealism, it contradicts Husserl's own clearly expressed concern for the concrete; to trace all particular entities to an absolute consciousness that creates them is to leave them very little independence or self-consistency. The status of the individual consciousness is compromised, and this was particularly troublesome for Husserl. To his credit, he did not let his passion for rigor overcome his sense of the importance of the concrete, and if he had difficulty reconciling these, he never let go of either. As time went by, he seems to have allowed the emphasis on an absolute and transcendent consciousness to fade in the face of the relentless presence "in person" of things and other conscious subjects. This had to affect the other phenomenological themes. Intentionality became less a stroke of creation and more an involvement of consciousness in an obscure and shifting world. This involvement was a matter of *direct* experience—sensible, emotional, affective—that led to its being regarded not as a knowing of the world but as a generalized living of it. In this *Lebenswelt* or *lived world* perspective, meanings could not be traced to a stroke of pure creativity; therefore, the matter of their genesis becomes important, and a genetic phenomenology takes its place beside the pursuit of essences. The way has been opened, and steps have been taken in the direction of an "existentialist" phenomenology. Enter the French School and with it Maurice Merleau-Ponty.

---

17. "Consciousness . . . must be reckoned as a *self-contained system of Being*, as a system of *Absolute being*, into which nothing can penetrate and from which nothing can escape . . . . On the other side, the whole spatio-temporal world, to which man and the human ego claim to belong as subordinate singular realities, is *according to its own meaning mere intentional Being*, a Being, therefore, which has the merely secondary, relative sense of a Being *for* a consciousness." (*Ideas*, p. 153.)

Merleau-Ponty regarded his own philosophy as a prolongation of the *Lebenswelt* philosophy of Husserl.[18] He frequently commented on the work of his German predecessor but never more significantly than in the preface to *Phenomenology of Perception*. This short section, bearing the title "What Is Phenomenology?" focuses on the conception of the subject as lived engagement in a world and treats the major phenomenological themes as philosophical expressions and amplifications of this conception. *Of these themes Merleau-Ponty regards as Husserl's most important discovery the generalized version of intentionality connecting not an explicit act of consciousness and a particular object but consciousness in its entirety and the world as a whole or, as it is more frequently stated, the world-in-general.* This intentionality is *perception* in Merleau-Ponty's most basic use of that term. It is the

> consciousness, through which from the outset a world forms itself around me and begins to exist for me. To return to the things themselves is to return to that world which precedes knowledge, of which knowledge always *speaks*.[19]

Taking up phenomenological *description* first, he contrasts it as Husserl did with scientific analysis. He establishes the contrast by placing analysis in the context of the general scientific attitude of which it is an essential feature and then outlines his view of the relation between this attitude and the lived experience of the world:

> Scientific points of view . . . are always both naive and at the same time dishonest, because they take for granted without explicitly mentioning it, that other point of view, namely that of the consciousness, through which from the outset a world forms itself around me and begins to exist for me.[20]

---

18. In *Phenomenology of Perception* Merleau-Ponty indicates that he has made use of all the works by Husserl then published as well as three works not yet published (cf. *Phenomenology*, p. 458). The latter were *Ideen zu einer Phänomenologie und Phänomenologischen Philosophie, II; Umsturz der Kopernikanischen Lehre; Die Krisis der Europäischen Wissenschaften und die Transzendentale Phänomenologie, II* and *III*. The first and last of these have since been edited at the Husserl Archives in Louvain by Mme. Marley Biemel and M. Walter Biemel, respectively, and published by Nijhoff in 1952 and 1954, respectively. For a closer look at Merleau-Ponty's use of Husserl's unpublished works, compare H. Van Breda, "Maurice Merleau-Ponty et les Archives-Husserl à Louvain," *Revue de Métaphysique et Morale*, No. 4, 1962.
19. *Phenomenology*, Preface, p. ix.
20. *Ibid.*

The consequences of this position are no less serious for the way in which one understands philosophy than for the way in which one understands science. Merleau-Ponty considers these as he discusses the *reduction*. The reduction is not a return to a transcendental ego in any idealist sense: no such definitive vantage point exists. What the reduction affects is a conversion of attitude from one of attention to the world to one of attention to the primary intentional bonds between self and world. Philosophy too is bound to the world. However much it may pursue the goal of making its reflection equivalent to the non-reflective life of consciousness,[21] it can turn to no "thought which embraces all our thought," nor can it outstrip "its own dependence upon an unreflective life which is its initial situation, unchanging, given once and for all." When at its most extreme point philosophy attempts to understand itself, it finds a problem and another beginning, not a vantage point beyond which no further vantage point can be sought.

As one might suspect, the priority of the engagement for Merleau-Ponty strongly influences his concept of essences. They become a means for understanding engagement:

> The need to proceed by way of essences does not mean that philosophy takes them as its object, but, on the contrary, that our existence is too tightly held in the world to be able to know itself as such at the moment of its involvement, and that it requires the field of ideality in order to become acquainted with and to prevail over its facticity.[22]

Seeking an essence is a process of clarification or rediscovery carried out with regard to what the primordial and antepredicative life of consciousness—that is, its unreflective life—proposes. In this process the essence itself loses a good deal of its ideality. When the search for essence turns to perception—that primordial life itself—it seems to transcend itself and to become a declaration of both fact and principle: "perception is . . . defined as access to truth." The *evidence* that this communication with the world offers is *never* exhaustively clarified, then. Its merit seems to lie in that dense, coercive presence that is characteristic of the evidence of empiricism, rather than in the transparency that idealist evidence claims. It makes of *Lebenswelt* phenomenology "a phenomenological positivism which bases the possible on the real." As we indicated above, the theoretical—and inherited—foundation for

---

21. Cf. *Phenomenology*, Preface, p. xvi.
22. *Ibid.*, p. xv.

this immersion in the real is a general intentionality that Husserl called *Fungierende Intentionalität* and that he distinguished from the particular intentionality of the explicit act. Merleau-Ponty says that it "produces the natural antepredicative unity of the world and of our life, being apparent in our desires, our evaluations, and in the landscape we see more clearly than in objective knowledge, and furnishing the text which our knowledge tries to translate into precise language." This general and basic intentionality leaves room for the genesis of particular meanings that, though not created according to a preexistent pattern, are nonetheless not haphazard. These take the form of styles of behavior and address that characterize things, persons, doctrines, and even historical periods. To comprehend each, one must grasp its style. While not completely accomplished, the styles are sufficiently established to give every act—even the seemingly fortuitous ones—a significant place. Meaning, in short, is inevitable, and we are condemned to it.

The phenomenologist will seek the root—the genesis—of meaning as he carries out his task, which is "to reveal the mystery of the world and of reason." The coincidence of this description of phenomenology and his description of the work of the philosopher as an attempt "to conceive the world, others, and himself and their interrelations . . ." emphasizes once again the point of the entire preface: philosophy is phenomenology.[23]

The Structure of Behavior was the first step in Merleau-Ponty's phenomenological program. It was his most decisive exercise in the phenomenological reduction, and it climaxes in his assertion of the philosophical primacy of perception. Because Merleau-Ponty operated the reduction against the natural attitude as it had become institutionalized in the philosophical presuppositions of experimental psychology, *The Structure of Behavior* also stands as a critique of these schools. The result of the critique (and its consequence, the assertion of the philosophical primacy of perception) is the rejection of that conception of the relation of consciousness and nature maintained by scientific naturalism.

Phenomenology of Perception, published some three years after *The*

---

23. "The phenomenological world is not the bringing to explicit expression of a pre-existing being, but the laying down of being. Philosophy is not the reflection of a pre-existing truth, but, like art, the act of bringing truth into being. . . . True philosophy consists in relearning to look at the world . . . . Phenomenology, as a disclosure of the world, rests on itself." (*Phenomenology,* Preface, p. xx.)

Structure of Behavior, continues this reflection on consciousness and nature in the interest of constructing a positive phenomenological theory. Once the reduction has led to the recognition of the primacy of perceptual engagement, one must show how meanings arise from this most fundamental dimension. Merleau-Ponty conceives intentionality in a way that allows it to be the foundation of a being-for-me of what appears with all the fullness and integrity that the things that appear seem to have. He must tread carefully here to avoid both the conception of intentionality as pure creativity, which Husserl held for so long, and its opposite, a passive consciousness irreconcilable with any kind of engagement. In *Phenomenology of Perception* intentionality is conceived as the giving of meaning, an *act* of signification. The body is construed as its vehicle and is transformed by its role in the giving of meaning and by its resulting intimacy with consciousness into a distinctly "subjective" dimension. Things and the world are the body's correlates— the former, of its explicit activity and the latter, of its possibilities. The most profound comprehension of this intentionality as an act of signification is achieved by connecting it to the concept of time. Consciousness thus emerges as a present, generating and recapitulating its past and projecting itself toward a future. Consciousness is the dynamic possibility of situations, and the ultimate dimension of its giving of meaning is the deployment of past, present, and future.

SARTRE AND EXISTENTIALISM

Such a human consciousness—the free and finite giving of meaning— is the principal characteristic of existentialism and is nowhere more forcefully displayed than in the works of Sartre. In the final chapter of *Phenomenology of Perception* Merleau-Ponty measures off his position against that of his colleague. Unlike Husserl and Marx, Sartre is not an earlier source of a particular trend now integrated with others in Merleau-Ponty's work. He is a contemporary, but also a phenomenologist, existentialist, and Marxist of sorts. Merleau-Ponty and Sartre knew each other somewhat as students and better as associates during the resistance; finally, they worked together editing *Les Temps Modernes,* one of France's major periodicals. *Les Temps Modernes* has from the beginning carried Sartre's name as editor-in-chief, although during the first seven years the journal's political posture was determined by Merleau-Ponty. Constantly compared, the two were keenly aware of each other's position. Their relationship varied widely, from mutual support to opposition and polemic. The source of their disagreements (and agreements) were personal and political, but they were also fundamentally philosophical. Each advanced the phenomenological impulse in a different direction.

Sartre's position on consciousness was made famous by the publication of *Being and Nothingness*.[24] Like Merleau-Ponty, Sartre seems to have begun with a phenomenological conception of consciousness and to have developed from this the notions of engagement, freedom, and the absurd, which the postwar public became accustomed to calling "existentialist." This development took place from 1936 to 1940 while Merleau-Ponty was completing *The Structure of Behavior* and working on *Phenomenology of Perception*. During this period Sartre wrote a series of essays sketching out phenomenological conceptions of the imagination, the ego, and the emotions.[25]

In the very first of these—*L'Imagination*—we find the distinctive Sartrian handling of intentionality that is to dominate his work up to and well beyond *Being and Nothingness* and that is at the philosophical root of his eventual clash with Merleau-Ponty. Sartre insists upon the extreme opposition between the terms that intentionality relates: "There naturally follows from [intentionality] a radical distinction between consciousness and that of which it is conscious." He makes this distinction an "ontological law": "It is an ontological law that there are only two kinds of existence: existence as thing and existence as consciousness." Prevailing theories of imagination, ego, and emotion run afoul of this law by treating consciousness as thing: taking the image as a "representation," the ego as a distinct entity, and emotion as the composite of the elements into which experimental psychology analyzes it. Sartre insists that the image is not a representation, but an *act* of

---

24. Jean-Paul Sartre, *L'Etre et le néant* (Paris: Gallimard, 1943). English translation by Hazel Barnes, *Being and Nothingness* (New York: Philosophical Library, 1956).

25. *L'Imagination* (Paris: Presses Universitaires de France, 1936). "La Transcendance de l'égo," *Recherches Philosophiques*, Vol. VI, 1936–37. *Esquisse d'une théorie des émotions* (Paris: Hermann, 1939). *L'Imaginaire* (Paris: Gallimard, 1940). These are often lost to view because of the novels that he was writing at the same time—*La Nausée*, for example, or the monumental *L'Etre et le néant*, which came later, or both. They are, however, an excellent introduction to his thought and to phenomenology.

awareness of an absent object and that to become emotional is to alter the world-for-me according to the laws of consciousness. In each case consciousness ceases to be thing and becomes relation and spontaneity. *Things,* opposite in nature to consciousness, are isolated and inert: they fit the description of the elements in the most crudely mechanist system imaginable.

In *Being and Nothingness* the ontological law operates as ultimate philosophical framework, and its terms are driven to their limit: things and consciousness are the being and nothingness of the title. In being *en soi* the inertness and opaqueness of things reach a point where they are a fullness of being beyond all meaning. Being *pour soi* is consciousness and also nothingness in the sense of a spontaneous act of negation. Sartre's view of these becomes more intelligible when we recognize that in *Being and Nothingness* he takes knowledge as the model for the relations between the terms of intentional consciousness. In knowledge consciousness tends to efface itself before what it knows. With this in mind he says that knowledge has "for its original structure not-being-what-is-known." This self-effacement of consciousness seems necessary to the object's presenting itself as independent and meaningful. It is thanks to consciousness, Sartre says, that there is being—not because consciousness gives rise to being but because it supplies the *there is.* Consciousness is so completely given over to negation that even in its unreflective awareness of itself it is unreflectively self negating. Out of this self-negation Sartre draws a conception of consciousness as temporality, at every instant negating its present in an ecstatic movement that is at once a retreat from a past and a projection toward a future. Like Merleau-Ponty, Sartre makes consciousness a source of meaning by having it introduce a temporal dimension into being. For Sartre, however, consciousness pursues a goal of realizing itself by becoming the foundation of all meaning. It wishes, in short, to be God. But however vehemently it is pursued, this goal and God are contradictory—an impossible union of *en soi* and *pour soi.*

Such a consciousness is incredibly agile. Because it negates whatever it is related to, it is not determined by the world or even by itself. This undetermined character of consciousness is, of course, the freedom with which the existentialist identifies man. The impossibility of things "weighing" on man is such that one's situation cannot even act as motive in moral action. This is the root of the absurdity in human existence: the giving of meaning is unmotivated. But it is only with the greatest difficulty that the consciousness described in *Being and Nothingness* can be conceived as taking hold in the world and of itself. Though it never breaks free from the *en soi* or itself, its attachment is still simply negation, and it is difficult to see this negation as an act that can give sufficient meaning to provide the variety that the relief and complexity in the world and self seem to demand. Sartre has difficulty in making the body share the intimacy of consciousness and even more in developing a theory of the other person and of society on the basis of a consciousness that treats everything else as object. He does insist upon the *facticity* of consciousness—that is, its contingent character, the fact that I did not choose my situation and might be in the world in a radically different way.[26] It is hard, however, to reconcile this feature of the subject with the other elements of Sartre's ontology.

Where Sartre insists upon an agile, mercurial consciousness lying on the surface of the world, Merleau-Ponty affirms an intentionality that takes hold in the world and of itself and that is heavy with this engagement and with the body and with its past. For Sartre the model is knowledge, and the attitude one of great confidence in reflection and in its lucidity. In *L'Imaginaire*, for example, he said that "we must repeat here what has been known since Descartes: a reflective consciousness gives us absolutely certain data." But for Merleau-Ponty the decisive experience is perception, and reflection is never allowed to be sure of itself. A remark by Sartre reflects, as much by its tone as by its content, the difference in style that has grown out of these two developments: "I have always thought, I still think that the Truth is one . . . . Merleau-Ponty, on the contrary, found his security in the multiplicity of perspectives."[27]

MARXISM

In his article presenting *Les Temps Modernes* to the public Sartre said, "We loudly affirm that man is the absolute," and added, "Our intention is to contribute to producing certain changes in the society around us." In carrying out this intention *Les Temps Modernes* became the existen-

---

26. Cf. *Being and Nothingness*, pp. 79–84.
27. Jean-Paul Sartre, "Merleau-Ponty vivant," *Les Temps Modernes*, No. 184–85 (Numéro spécial, 1961), pp. 307–08.

tialist voice in the three-cornered contest among those determined to generate the *humanism* that would command postwar French thinking. The other two were the communists and the Catholics. The former, more vocal, closer to the great mass of workers and so clearly associated with one of the victorious powers, drew the most attention. For Merleau-Ponty, determined in 1945 to fashion a view of history based upon an inventory of his time (just as he had previously fashioned his view of perception on the basis of an inventory of consciousness), the communists were bound to be of central importance.

Merleau-Ponty's interest in Marxism was not born at the end of World War II. During the 1930's, the period of his intellectual formation, everyone watched the Russian experiment with intense interest. In France socialism was a practical political alternative that reached a climax in 1936 with the election of Leon Blum, a socialist, as Prime Minister.[28]

Most of Merleau-Ponty's reflections on history are contained in two volumes, *Humanisme et terreur*[29] and *Les Aventures de la dialectique*.[30] The first, subtitled *Essai sur le problème communiste*, was published in 1947 and is a collection of essays, most of which had appeared in 1946 and 1947 in *Les Temps Modernes*. In it Merleau-Ponty assumes a position that he called "Marxist anticipation" (*l'attentisme marxiste*)—a qualified acceptance of Marxism as a philosophy of history and a refusal to disapprove the lines of communist politics in the hope that their advance might bring about an awakening of the proletariat. *Les Aventures de la dialectique,* which appeared in 1955, records his complete disillusionment with communist politics and the consequent dismissal of Marxism as a philosophy of history. It also made public his break with Sartre, which had occurred three years earlier when disagreement over the attitude of *Les Temps Modernes* toward communism crystallized the differences in philosophy that had up to that time been passed over in silence. With the exception of *Les Aventures de la dialectique* (itself a collection of essays) Merleau-Ponty's work in the philosophy of history and in politics took the form of articles, most of which are

---

28. Merleau-Ponty comments on this period in his article "Pour la vérité," *Les Temps Modernes*, I, 4 (Jan., 1946).
29. M. M-P., *Humanisme et terreur* (Paris: Gallimard, 1947). This work is discussed in detail in Chapter 8.
30. M. M-P., *Les Aventures de la dialectique* (Paris: Gallimard, 1955). This work is discussed in detail in Chapter 8 and again in Chapter 9.

occasional, as one might expect from a thinker conducting an inventory of his time.[31]

At first Merleau-Ponty was optimistic about Marxism's susceptibility to partnership: "That concrete thought which Marx calls critical in order to distinguish it from speculative philosophy is what others propose under the name of existential philosophy."[32] But one can dispute whether Marxism is a philosophy at all.[33] To the extent that it is a philosophy, it is a materialism, proud of its partnership with the physical sciences and understanding man on the basis of a theory of economic determinism. In connection with the latter, Marx said that "the mode of production in material life determines the general character of the social, political and spiritual process of life."[34] Meanwhile, existentialism is not only a philosophy, but a philosophy of subjectivity, where consciousness gives meaning and the freedom of the individual is exalted. Merleau-Ponty labors to find ground for a dialogue with Marxism by uncovering those features in the work of Marx, Lenin, and others that are reconcilable with the existentialist themes. In "Autour du marxisme" and "Marxisme et philosophie"[35] Merleau-Ponty treats Marxism according to its more general lines and pays particular attention to the primitive expression of these in Marx's early works.[36] Philosophy, he says,

---

31. The studies in *Les Aventures de la dialectique* were not previously published, while those in *Humanisme et terreur* were, as we have just said. In addition, articles bearing on the problem of history are included in his collection *Sens et non-sens* (Paris: Nagel, 1948), and *Signes* (Paris: Gallimard, 1960).

32. M. M-P., "Marxisme et philosophie," *Revue Internationale*, Vol. VI (June–July, 1946). This article is also included in *Sens et non-sens*, where the remark quoted is found on page 271.

33. In one of his theses on Feuerbach Marx himself protested that "the philosophers have only interpreted the world in various ways: the point, however, is to change it." ("Theses on Feuerbach" in *Marx and Engels*, Lewis Feuer (ed.) (New York: Doubleday, 1959), p. 245.) Engels also remarked that "with Hegel philosophy comes to an end." ("The End of Classical German Philosophy" in *Marx and Engels*, p. 202.)

34. Karl Marx, "A Contribution to a Critique of Political Economy," in *Marx and Engels*, p. 44.

35. We have already mentioned the latter. "Autour du marxisme" is dated August, 1945, and was first published in *Fontaine* (Jan.–Feb., 1946), pp. 304–31. It, too, is included in the collection *Sens et non-sens* to which we shall refer henceforth as *Sens*, and from which we shall cite both articles.

36. The latter emphasis is particularly evident in "Marxisme et philosophie." Though he does not declare any intention of concentrating on the early works, the texts by Marx that he cites or refers to are almost all drawn from

need not be considered as having come to an end with Hegel despite what Engels said. This was philosophy as ideology in the classic Marxist sense: "occupation with thoughts as with independent entities, developing independently and subject only to their own laws."[37] The protest against a philosophy separated from human activity is something that phenomenological existentialism will gladly echo. Merleau-Ponty proposes another version, however, in which the philosopher "gives up the illusion of contemplating the totality of completed history and takes himself to be, like the rest of men, caught up in it and standing before a future to be accomplished [*à faire*]. Then philosophy can be fulfilled by suppressing itself as separate philosophy."[38] Such a statement seems applicable to both existentialist and Marxist commitment and reconcilable with Marx's intention, for he too accepted a transformed notion of philosophy when he said that "as philosophy finds its material weapon in the proletariat, so the proletariat finds its spiritual weapon in philosophy."[39]

The materialism in such a philosophy is of a very special sort: historical or dialectical rather than mechanical. Metaphysical or classical materialism was a materialism of *things* or *objects*, while dialectical materialism as Marx conceived it was a materialism of human practice and relation. Merleau-Ponty feels that contemporary Marxists—and communists in particular—have tended more toward mechanical materialism than toward this original man-centered position. He reminds them of the effort by Marx and Engels to distinguish their materialism from mechanism. Thus the latter said: "It is not that the economic situation is the *cause, solely active,* while everything else is only a passive effect."[40] And Marx complemented this with an acknowledgment of human initiative: "Men make their history themselves, only they do so in a given environment."[41] Such assertions encouraged Merleau-

the period prior to the *Communist Manifesto*—that is, before 1848 (when Marx was thirty). Most frequently cited are the texts *Political Economy and Philosophy* of 1844, *Toward a Critique of Hegel's Philosophy of Right* (also 1844), and *The German Ideology*, which Marx and Engels wrote in 1846.

37. Engels, "The End of Classical German Philosophy," in *Marx and Engels*, p. 237.
38. *Sens,* p. 271.
39. Karl Marx, "Toward a Critique of Hegel's Philosophy of Right," in *Marx and Engels*, p. 265.
40. "Letter to Starkenburg" written by Engels in *Marx and Engels*, p. 411.
41. Karl Marx, "The Eighteenth Brumaire of Louis Bonaparte," in *Marx and Engels*, p. 32.

Ponty to see original Marxism as a position in which man "the concrete human intersubjectivity" is the motive force of history and the bearer of its meaning. There is room in Marxism for man's initiative, which in turn indicates the presence of the contingent and the unforeseen. If history has a logic, then it cannot be a completely determined unfolding, an inexorable march toward a classless society. Merleau-Ponty does not deny history a logic; he accepts the notion that its events in some way constitute a single drama that moves toward a conclusion. But the instruments of this logic, he maintains, are not fixed laws or clear ideas but "political complexes and anonymous projects which give a group of individuals a certain common style." The movement of history so understood can deviate in its direction or otherwise fail to be realized. There are indeed many departures from the original vision of Marx that can be interpreted as such deviations. For example, the revolution was established in only one nation rather than throughout the world simultaneously; capitalism proved much more resilient than anticipated, and the proletariat developed in consciousness and initiative at such a slow pace that the apparatus of Party and leadership came into being to control and discipline the masses; the individual came to participate in history by submitting to this political leadership.

After a favorable reading of Marx in "Autour du marxisme," Merleau Ponty singles out the question of contingency as the major Marxist problem and asserts that on the historical scene "marxism could only be proposed in the form of negative propositions." By this he means that only with the socialization of property and the realization of other proletarian values can society be organized in a truly human way but that there is no guarantee that this will in fact be achieved. He commits himself to what he calls at one time a "marxism without illusions, quite experimental and voluntary." The class struggle is obscure, and the proletariat—which Merleau-Ponty sees as the only hope of a renewal of human values—undeveloped. Perhaps it will never develop. But "we must be careful that nothing in our action contributes to restricting the proletarian movement should it be reborn . . . . [We should] carry out the effective politics of the Communist Party. Rebuild with the proletariat—there is nothing else to do for the moment."[42]

French communists were not in the least attracted by such qualified

<hr>

42. *Sens,* p. 348. This remark is taken from his "Pour la vérité," *Les Temps Modernes,* I, 4 (Jan., 1946). In *Sens* we learn that it was completed in November, 1945.

endorsement. This was still the Stalinist period, when anything other than a clear "yes" to official Marxism was to be taken as a clear "no." Their response to Merleau-Ponty's work ranged from objection to violent abuse. For his part he devoted the years following 1945 to a careful appraisal of communist behavior for its relevance to the awakening of the proletariat. His discouragement grew as the Stalinist character of that behavior made the continued oppression of the proletariat more likely than its awakening. By 1950 he was ready to close out his expectations for communism, and when the Korean War broke out he did so, feeling that it had been in Soviet power to prevent this.

LATER WORKS

The reflection on history was only one of Merleau-Ponty's during his last years. He also worked at the traditional duties of the philosopher who has become well known, explaining what he had already done, testing out his perspective in new areas, and prolonging the line of development of his original work. He summarizes and explains his position in articles such as "Le Primat de la perception et ses conséquences philosophiques"[43] and the frequently quoted "La Métaphysique dans l'homme."[44] There are also occasional articles on art, the novel, the cinema, sociology, and religion. All attest the fruitfulness of his particular vision. At the same time, he faces the questions of the nature of philosophy and the meaning of the absolute. These, particularly the first, are points at which most formal criticism of his philosophy is directed: can one emphasize perception, as Merleau-Ponty has done, and keep philosophy at its historical task of dominating and comprehending what is perceived? His attack on the question is spread through books and articles, but the two articles on language are most important.[45] Merleau-Ponty discusses the question of the absolute in many of

---

43. "La Primat de la perception et ses conséquences philosophiques," *Bulletin de la Société Française de Philosophie* (Oct.–Dec., 1947). This was originally given as a lecture to the Société.

44. "La Métaphysique dans l'homme," *Revue de Métaphysique et Morale* (Oct., 1947), pp. 290–307. This is included in the collection *Sens*.

45. M. M-P., "Sur la Phénoménologie du langage" in *Problèmes actuels de la phénoménologie* (Bruxelles: Desclée de Brouwer, 1951); and "Le Langage indirect et les voix du silence," *Les Temps Modernes* (July, 1952), pp. 2113–44; (Aug., 1952) pp. 70–94. Both are to be found in his collection *Signes*.

his later works, particularly "La Métaphysique dans l'homme," "Foi et bonne foi,"[46] and *Eloge de la philosophie.*[47]

In *Eloge de la philosophie* Merleau-Ponty seems to have reached a decisive point in his intellectual career. Having abandoned Marxism as a preferred mode of social thought and having broken with Sartre, he turns to a reexamination of his own basic commitment. His inauguration as member of the Collège de France provides the occasion, and in his acceptance address he reflects on the nature of philosophy as, eight years earlier in *Phenomenology of Perception*, he had meditated on the nature of phenomenology. Commenting on his predecessors Bergson, LeRoy, and Lavelle, Merleau-Ponty sees philosophy as an endeavor of free inquiry, the authenticity of which is to be found more in the process of questioning than in any explicit system of responses. Reflecting on the life of Socrates, Merleau-Ponty notes that the philosopher must be radically independent of the interests of his world and that his detachment constitutes the most effective critical presence to these interests.

In *Les Aventures de la dialectique*, published in 1955, Merleau-Ponty rejected Marxism and Sartre's existentialism. He also indicated the future direction of his own thought on the nature of history.

In 1956 he edited a book of essays on important philosophers, *Les Philosophes célèbres.*[48] Each section opens with Merleau-Ponty's reflection on some major area of philosophy. Later, he comments again on Husserl in an important article, "The Philosopher and his Shadow."[49]

This article and a number of others—some of which we have already cited—were published in 1960 in book form under the title *Signes*, to which we have already alluded. Its preface is serene and hopeful about the prospects for philosophers and for history, although the title of the work stresses his view that human accomplishment—philosophical and other—is still in the form of disparate and disconnected successes. His final publication was an article entitled "L'Oeil et l'esprit"[50] and constituted a return to the problem of perception.

---

46. "Foi et bonne foi," *Les Temps Modernes*, Vol. I (Feb., 1946), pp. 769–82.
47. *Eloge de la philosophie* (Paris: Gallimard, 1953). This work is considered in detail in Chapters 7 and 10.
48. M. M-P. (ed.), *Les Philosophes célèbres* (Paris: Editions d'Art Lucien Mazenod, 1956).
49. M. M-P., "Le Philosophe et son ombre," in *Edmund Husserl 1859–1959* (The Hague: Nijhoff, 1959), pp. 195–220.
50. "L'Oeil et l'esprit," *Art de France*, No. 1, 1961. This article was also included in *Les Temps Modernes*, No. 184–85 (Numéro spécial, 1961).

Part **I**

*THE
RELATIONSHIP
OF
CONSCIOUSNESS
AND
NATURE*

Chapter 1

The Structure
of Behavior

The introduction to *The Structure of Behavior* is brief, its opening remark abrupt and clear:

> Our goal is to understand the relations of consciousness and nature: organic, psychological or even social. By nature we understand here a multiplicity of events external to each other and bound together by relations of causality.[1]

The issue is as old as philosophy and yet as recent as the thinking that phenomenology expects to replace:

> among contemporary thinkers in France, there exist side by side a philosophy, on the one hand, which makes of every nature an objective unity constituted vis-à-vis consciousness and, on the other, sciences which treat the organism and consciousness as two orders of reality and, in their reciprocal relation, as "effects" and "causes."[2]

The "contemporary thinkers" to whom Merleau-Ponty refers were those of the 1930's. The philosophy of that period was the intellectualism of men like Brunschvicg and Lachelier, both strongly influenced by Kant. The sciences of the period were represented primarily by psychologists, particularly those of the stimulus-response and gestalt schools. The "critical thought" of the first group and the "realist analysis" of the second both accept and refine the natural attitude to

---

1. *Structure*, p. 3.
2. *Ibid.*, p. 4.

whose overthrow phenomenology is devoted. The way in which these positions are referred to in *The Structure of Behavior* can be confusing. While it is quite evident that intellectualism and empiricism differ seriously and in many ways, Merleau-Ponty (who is going to propose a third alternative) is prone to emphasize what they have in common. Each is a form of the *natural attitude*, which he also calls *la pensée objective*, or "objectivist thinking," the function of which, he says, is "to reduce all phenomena which bear witness to the union of subject and world, putting in their place the clear idea of the object as *in itself* and of the subject as pure consciousness. It therefore severs the links which unite the thing and the embodied subject."[3] With the exception of its final chapter *The Structure of Behavior* concentrates upon empiricism more than upon intellectualism. In speaking of this prevalent style of thinking in psychology he will use the terms *empiricism, causal thinking, mechanical thinking, naturalism,* and *materialism* interchangeably, and the reader of *The Structure of Behavior* must be attentive to this. The critique of these positions leads to the restoration of the links between the thing and the embodied subject, and to the substitution of phenomena for nature. It is, in short, a version of the *reduction* of the natural attitude.

This attitude can take several forms, and with each of these there corresponds a type of reduction designed to overthrow it. The most familiar version, the one most frequently given by phenomenologists when they are asked for examples, is carried out against a naive form of the natural attitude that operates in a simple visual experience. For example, I normally take the cube that I see before me on the table as a complete and independent entity. It seems to invite my interpretations as a set of juxtaposed and self-contained features—sides and angles of intersection—comprehensible when taken together and without reference to other objects. It may have superficial, causal relations with the things about it, but these relations are explained in terms of spatial position and temporal succession. When the visual situation is described in this way, its elements match in description the events in *nature* to which Merleau-Ponty referred in the remark with which he began this work. They have that type of completeness and independence peculiar to *things*, that parts-outside-of-parts character that fits them to

---

3. *Phenomenology*, p. 320.

the classic description of matter. The consciousness to which they manifest themselves must both penetrate them to grasp their intelligible relations and at the same time remain at the distance from them that their independence demands. In the first case one wonders about the integrity of the object and in the second, about its link with consciousness.

The "naive" reduction begins when I deliberately turn to the way in which the cube appears and carefully describe this appearing. I note that it never actually presents itself simply as a figure of six sides whose angles of intersection are equal. Rather, it presents itself in a series of profiles, each of which announces the cube in its entirety but without actually revealing it all. Furthermore, what the cube manifests concretely of itself *is* affected by the other things in its context—lighting, for example—and very markedly by the physical position that I take in relation to it. I see one profile or another depending on whether I stand left or right; if I am either too far or too near, the cube will not appear as a cube at all. Only to a completely disembodied and unlocated consciousness could a cube *actually* present itself as an independent six-sided figure. When I have recognized this and am willing to redefine the object and my consciousness of it on the basis of the experience in which they both appear, then I am prepared to operate in the phenomenological manner. I can pose again the classic questions concerning visual perception (problems of distance, perspective, depth, for example) in this manner and perhaps revitalize them.

The natural attitude permeates consciousness and extends beyond visual experience into areas where any attempt to overthrow that attitude encounters established scientific positions. Merleau-Ponty does not ignore the naive forms of the natural attitude; they are too useful to be ignored. However, one of the most significant features of his work as an exercise in phenomenology is that he gives the reduction the form of a critique of scientific positions—primarily in psychology—and of their philosophical presuppositions. In *The Structure of Behavior* this critique focuses on the notion of *behavior*. "This notion," he says, "is neutral with respect to classic distinctions between 'mental' and 'physiological' and thus can give us the opportunity of defining them anew." Although Merleau-Ponty knows that in the behaviorism of American psychologists like J. B. Watson the notion of behavior is anything but neutral with respect to these distinctions, he holds that the physiological—and atomist—interpretation that it received at their hands destroyed its value. In a note commenting on Watson's position Merleau-Ponty remarks:

> what is healthy and profound in this intuition of behavior—that is, the vision of man as perpetual debate and "explanation" with a physical and social world—found itself compromised by an impoverished philosophy. . . . In our opinion . . . when Watson spoke of behavior he had in mind what others have called *existence*; but the new notion could receive its philosophical status only if causal or mechanical thinking were abandoned for dialectical thinking.[4]

When one moves from the introduction of *The Structure of Behavior* to consider its argument proper, it becomes evident that the book can be considered from both scientific and philosophical points of view. From the former, it offers a three-part critique of psychology: the first (Chapters I and II) rejects physiological atomism in favor of gestalt thinking and of the priority that this gives to the notion of form; the second (Chapter III) criticizes gestalt thinkers for having compromised the most important implications of the notion of form whose priority they affirmed; and the third (Chapter IV) sets forth the phenomenological version of consciousness implied in the preceding critique. On the philosophical level *The Structure of Behavior* moves through two stages: in the first (Chapters I, II, and III) Merleau-Ponty attacks empiricism in defense of the priority of consciousness; and in the second (Chapter IV) he attacks intellectualism in order to advance the phenomenological notion of consciousness. These two points of view, the scientific and the philosophical, are really aspects of a single movement. The attack on physiological atomism and gestalt thinking in psychology constitutes an assault on the philosophical empiricism that they presuppose. To some extent, the unity of the argument is due to the single notion of behavior, the central reference point of his critique, and the reality that proves unmanageable in the available categories of either philosophy or psychology. To an even greater extent, however, the unity of his book is due to the emergence in the critique of a positive position in which science and philosophy enjoy the most direct mutual implication. In a later discussion of science and philosophy Merleau-Ponty will say, "There would doubtless be room to revise the classic

---

4. *Structure*, p. 226.

distinction of induction and reflection and to wonder if there are really two sorts of knowledge or if there is not, rather, one single knowledge at different degrees of naiveté or explicitness." This positive aspect is as important as the critique.

The documentation contained in *The Structure of Behavior* is drawn from the physiology and psychology of the period. Experimental data are introduced in substantial quantity and detail and are presented in so compressed a way that readers who are not specialists in these areas may have some difficulty in following. They would have even more difficulty were it not for a peculiarity of Merleau-Ponty's style. His position is developed not by linear addition but by a movement of expansion. In a sense he makes his entire case in every chapter, the advance in each being primarily a matter of shifting emphasis. Although the work is occasionally repetitious, this repetition, coupled with the author's rich and varied expression, helps reinforce the outline of his central ideas and makes them stand forth from the dense ground of supporting observations.

REFLEX BEHAVIOR

Merleau-Ponty begins his discussion of physiological atomism with a schematic description of its primary unit, the reflex. Proponents of this position hold it to be "scientific" in the sense that "the object of science is defined by the mutual exteriority of parts and processes." The reflex is "the action of a defined physical or chemical agent on a locally defined receptor which evokes a defined response by means of a defined pathway," and its parts certainly have that discreteness that the classic definition of the object of science prescribes. The physical or chemical agent—the stimulus—is conceived as a cause "in the empirical sense of a constant and unconditioned antecedent, and the organism is passive because it limits itself to executing what is prescribed for it by the place of the excitation and the nervous circuits which originate there. The consequence of this exteriority of parts and of the passivity of the organism can be seen in the scientific description of the visual response to the movement of a spot of light across a dark room. It might seem that I "follow" the light, but to "follow" is purposive behavior beyond the capacity of a passive entity like the organism. What "objectively" occurs is the successive stimulation of a series of distinct receptors, and these release the movement of the eyes. Understanding behavior "objectively" thus involves for the atomist appreciating the physical reality of light, of the parts of the receptive apparatus and their interrelationships. Merleau-Ponty rejects this position and maintains that behavior both in its rudimentary and higher forms is simply irreconcilable with the conception of the organism as passive and as the sum of its distinct parts. In explaining the activity and integrity of the organism he rejects the notion of reflex as an explanatory device and adopts instead the notion of behavior itself, conceived first as form and then as perception. Ultimately he inverts the relation between reflex and behavior so that the latter becomes the point of reference, and reflex is seen as a type of behavior.

In his treatment of rudimentary behavior Merleau-Ponty draws upon the results of work in physiology well known at the time.[5] He introduces the categories that contemporary researchers have already developed and that he will extend. The problem is posed in the following way:

> If the order in the reflex—that is, the adaptation of the response to the stimulus and the coordination of partial movements in the total gesture—is assured by pre-established connections from the sensible surface to the effector muscles, the classical conception puts considerations of topography in a position of primary importance; the place of the excitation should decide the reaction; the stimulus should act by those of its properties which can modify the anatomical elements taken one by one; the nerve circuit should be isolated since the reflex, if it were not guided in this manner, could not be adapted to the stimulus as it is in fact. But it has long been known that the reflex thus defined is very rarely observable.[6]

Merleau-Ponty reviews the classical conception of the reflex in brief sections devoted respectively to the stimulus, the place of excitation, the

---

5. Goldstein's *Der Aufbau des Organismus* (The Hague: Nijhoff, 1934) is the most important single source of physiological support both in this chapter and in the rest of *Structure*. Later, in *Phenomenology*, Goldstein's classic researches on brain damage are drawn upon heavily. Merleau-Ponty owes a great deal to this researcher, to whose work he has, in turn, drawn considerable attention in France. In this chapter Von Weizacker's article "Reflexgesetze" in A. Bethe (ed.), *Handbuch der normalen and pathologischen Physiologie*, Vol. X, also provides data, as do observations by the gestalt psychologist Koffka and the Dutch physiologist Buytendijk.

6. *Structure*, p. 10.

reflex circuit, and the reaction. From Goldstein and other physiologists he cites evidence that the *stimulus* does not act simply according to its elemental components, but often according to "its spatial arrangement, its rhythm and the rhythm of its intensities." Nor does the *place of excitation* decide the reaction: "excitation of one receptor can evoke different reflexes and the excitation of two distinct points can give rise to the same reflex." The *reflex circuit* is not isolated and seems "under the influence of a series of chemical, secretory and vegetative conditions powerful enough to cancel or even reverse the expected effect of a certain stimulus. To this must be added the cerebral and cerebellar influences which, at least in man, probably intervene in all reflexes." Finally, Merleau-Ponty concludes that the notion that the adaptation of stimulus to response could be assured by preestablished circuits in the nervous system would lead to the supposition of an absolutely dizzying number of such circuits in order to keep up with the variety and subtlety of human *reaction*.

In short, impressive evidence resists the tendency to explain by analysis into such components. Even the distinction of stimulus from response is unsatisfactory, and Merleau-Ponty recalls that physiologists have never been able to eliminate the response of the organism from the definition of the stimulus. The most familiar example of this is the "painful" stimulus. The inclusion of the organism in the definition of the stimulus offers an example of something that his discussion of rudimentary behavior has indicated generally: the organism imposes its own conditions as variable between the given stimulus and the expected response, and therefore it *cannot be taken as passive.* The introduction of these conditions constitutes some sort of regulation of response, and it is very difficult for those holding anatomical conceptions of behavior to introduce the notion of regulation or control into their scheme. If they insist on centers of inhibition or coordination, then one must wonder if these, like the rest of the stimulus-response scheme, consist of isolable anatomical parts. If they do, then the problem must be re-posed; and if they do not, then the anatomical conceptions must yield to the demands of regulation in a manner that compromises its physiological atomist assumptions.

Behavior does make such demands, and the gestalt school has arisen in response to them. A gestaltist like Koehler, for example, advances an alternative to the mechanist explanation of visual fixation (recall the example of following a spot of light). He considers his alternative the solution of a problem of tension in favor of the most advantageous equilibrium. Merleau-Ponty also notes that a person left by hemianopsia with the use of only two half retinas does not see only half of the visual scene. The organism reorganizes the function of vision so that the person, though he sees poorly, has access to the whole visual field. With this type of phenomena in mind, he remarks:

> the critique of reflex theory and the analysis of a few examples show that we should consider . . . the nervous system as a field of forces which express concurrently the intraorganic state and the influence of external agents; these forces tend to balance themselves according to certain modes of preferred distribution and to obtain movements from the mobile parts of the body which are proper to this effect.[7]

This view of the nervous system as a field of forces does not deny the constancy in behavior but makes that constancy the functional result of certain privileged equilibria. These, in turn, imply certain values in terms of which the organism acts. For Merleau-Ponty the anatomical structures lose their role as guarantors of constancy and can be considered either "topographical conditions of the original functional development" if they are innate, or "the result of the most habitual functioning" if they are acquired.

Merleau-Ponty does not deny the existence of the reflex. He simply insists that it is not the explanation of behavior and therefore not the principal object of physiology: "It is not by means of it that the remainder can be understood." Further, "the object of biology is to grasp that which makes a living being a living being, that is, not—according to the realist postulate common to mechanism and vitalism—the superposition of elementary reflexes or the intervention of a 'vital force,' but an indecomposable structure of behavior." An empiricist might quarrel with such a conception of the nature of life sciences, protesting this reading of essences as the introduction of phenomenological presuppositions. Merleau-Ponty can respond that it is the encounter with the very object of these sciences that demands such a reading and can cite the gestaltists in his support. He holds that the facts the latter have discovered or emphasized are decisive as a criticism of mechanism and sees in their category of *form* that "indecomposable structure of be-

---

7. *Ibid.*, p. 46.

havior" of which he has spoken. The nervous system, and behavior itself, should be understood as forms. And what are forms? They are:

> total processes whose properties are not the sum of those which the isolated parts would possess. . . . there is form whenever the properties of a system are modified by every change brought about in a single one of its parts and, on the contrary, are conserved when they all change while maintaining the same relationship among themselves.[8]

Form, however, is not a *thing* acting causally, and it must be clearly distinguished from such objectivist interpretations. Merleau-Ponty insists that form simply expresses "the descriptive properties of certain natural wholes" and that to introduce it is in no sense to introduce an additional entity into biology. Gestalt psychologists have not always recognized this themselves, and this issue is raised by Merleau-Ponty in his third chapter. Prior to this, however, he again criticizes physiological atomism, this time for its interpretation of higher behaviors.

HIGHER FORMS OF BEHAVIOR

Merleau-Ponty regards Pavlov's position as typical of the physiological atomist interpretation of the higher forms of behavior. Pavlov's objective was to explain the ability of the organism to enter into a relationship with an environment that is far richer and more complicated than the stimulus-response apparatus with which it (the organism) seems to have been endowed. His solution was the theory of conditioned reflexes: when a stimulus acts upon an organism together with a stimulus to which that organism is accustomed, the new stimulus takes on the reflexogenic power of the latter and in this way becomes part of the reflex behavior of the organism. The establishment of the new reflex is called conditioning, and the reflex itself is termed "conditioned." The reflex power of the organism is thus enriched, and a theory of learning, for example, becomes possible. But the conditioned reflex, Merleau-Ponty makes clear (citing Pavlov for emphasis), is still a reflex. Hence, "the essence of nerve activity remains the same: it is a process which can be broken down into real parts." Merleau-Ponty's case against Pavlov's position is essentially the same as the argument used previously but now adapted to accommodate the higher forms of behavior.

---

8. *Ibid.*, p. 47.

While he challenges Pavlov, Merleau-Ponty's own interpretation of behavior as form emerges more clearly and positively, and he begins the description of a theory of behavior that might replace the one he is criticizing.

Higher forms of behavior—learning, for example—quite obviously involve a greater degree of regulation than do those that are rudimentary forms. Therefore the higher forms raise an even greater threat to atomist postulates and tempt empiricist thinkers even more toward one of the most familiar vices of theoreticians—the proliferation of gratuitous auxiliary hypotheses to shore up original hypotheses. Merleau-Ponty complains that Pavlov has done this: irregularities in the behavior of the famous salivating dogs have been accounted for by postulating the presence of inhibitory and counterinhibitory forces, often highly selective in their effect and usually lacking experimental justification. This certainly violates the spirit of scientific inquiry that Pavlov's work is supposed to exemplify. The central criticism, however, bears not on the divergence of scientific practice from scientific spirit but on the impossibility of explaining either *brain function* (the physiological substratum of higher behavior) or *learning* (the crucial behavior itself) in terms of atomist postulates.

The theory of brain function fashioned according to these postulates and corresponding to the Pavlovian view of nervous behavior assumes that the brain is a mosaic of neurological entities in which behaviors are strictly localized. But this hypothesis of strict localization was early rejected. Drawing again from Goldstein[9] and also from the work of Pieron, Buytendijk, Fischel, and others, Merleau-Ponty indicates why it was rejected and what seems destined to replace it. The summaries of empirical observations bear chiefly on the effect of brain damage. The hypothesis of strict localization would lead one to expect that brain damage would simply eliminate the particular perceptions or activities whose apparatus was located in the damaged area.

But this is not what generally occurs. Localized damage in the optical "zone" does not cause the patient to cease to see this or that color, but rather it causes a general de-structuring of vision in which all the colors first lose their intensity, and then gradually the whole spectrum goes grey. Buytendijk and Fischel reach analogous conclusions on rats.

9. From *Der Aufbau des Organismus* and the article "Die Lokalisation in der Grosshirnrinde" in A. Bethe (ed.), *op. cit.*, Vol. X.

Lesions of the central cortex did not destroy any one movement but made all their movements rigid, awkward, and less effective.[10] What is lost, in short, is something global—the articulation and differentiation of perception and activity. What brain damage does is to cast a new and reduced meaning over the entire range of behavior. Merleau-Ponty remarks that this sort of conclusion was accessible to those who have formed it only because they brought to the problem non-atomist preconceptions—that is, they proceed "by concrete description and ideal analysis."

With them he maintains that what brain damage impairs (and therefore what brain function involves) is primarily a process of organization. With this in mind Merleau-Ponty insists upon the priority of that activity by which the following occurs:

> Local excitations distributed at the surface of the receptors undergo, from the moment of their entrance into the specialized sectors of the cortex, a series of structurations which disassociate them from the context of spatio-temporal events in which they were really engaged and which orders them according to the original dimensions of organic activity.[11]

However, if this activity of organization is not strictly located and thus is not simply a function of the physical reality of the brain, neither is it completely indifferent to location. For example, injuries to the posterior region of the brain next to the optic sector can be expected to produce deficiencies in perception, while disorders affecting speech result when lesions occur in the anterior region or in the auditive region. These are examples of "preferential localization." A given region is "not the seat of certain autonomous devices, but the terrain for the exercises of an activity of organization."

Of course, the preferentially localized function still involves the entire brain. Pieron indicates that every injury involves, in addition to circumscribed deficiencies, general disturbance of cerebral functioning—for example, the lowering of the level of effort and of attention or the creation of nervous tension. With Goldstein and the others Merleau-Ponty maintains that the relation of particular locality to brain in general is best understood under the category of form, since this category

---

10. Buytendijk and Fischel, "Strukturgemaszes Verhalten von Ratten," *Archives néerlandaises de physiologie*, 1931, Vol. XVI, pp. 55ff.
11. *Structure*, pp. 73–74.

emphasizes the priority of the whole over the parts, and determination by the whole of the particular properties of the parts. The brain's physiological reality, then, is no longer equivalent to its physical reality: function is not simply one anatomical part as opposed to another. The very notion of space or matter as applied to the brain loses its strict parts-outside-of-parts character. Function *is* deployed in space, and this deployment *is* accomplished by the brain. However, the laws by which the brain accomplishes its functions are not those governing the interaction of atomic elements but rather those of whole and part that one encounters in perception. For example, what one sees always appears as a figure against a background from which it seems to have emerged, a background that modifies the way in which we see it.

Pavlov's understanding of brain function is found wanting. Even his order of priority—physiology over psychology—must be reversed. One of the implications of the activity and originality of the organism—its structuring of what it receives—is that "it is not the real world which constitutes the perceived world"; the perceiver and his perceiving share in its constitution. In addition the figure-background scheme, which the description of brain function elicits, "has meaning only in the perceived world: it is here that we learn what it is to be a figure and what it is to be a background." Physiology shall come to depend on psychology for its intelligibility.

The failure of the attempt to understand brain function in terms of strict localization turns attention to behavior itself. For the physiological atomist the key behavior is learning. In the learning process the reflexogenic power of the organism is extended and with it his ability to deal with the rich and complex world. But the attempt to understand learning as the capacity to repeat certain gestures fixed as habits after a period of trial and error—the Pavlovian behaviorist attempt—fails, as did their view of brain function. Koffka, Koehler, Guillaume, and Buytendijk support the view that the theory of learning must establish the priority of the activity and structure of the organism—its originality, one might say—in his perceived world. They show that learning is not the fixation of a particular gesture as response to a particular situation but rather the establishment of a general aptitude with regard to the structure or essence of the situation. The cat that first succeeds in drawing food to itself by pulling a string with its paw does not simply repeat the gesture the next time but draws the food along with its teeth. The child who has learned to distinguish red and green is able more quickly to distinguish the next pair of colors and all colors. Each situation, then, is the analogue of many others, and what our experience with them generates are global aptitudes, not simply repeatable gestures.

Merleau-Ponty also increasingly emphasizes the fact that each situation is situated-perceived—that is, a situation *for* the organism—as he analyzes the learning process more closely and in light of his notion of structure. Rejecting any hypothesis about the physiology of the brain, he offers a classification of behavior according to its own structure. More precisely, he delineates three types of behavior—*syncretic, amovable,* and *symbolic*—distinguishing them according to the degree to which the behaving organism is "submerged" in its concrete situation or "emerges" from it. The implications of this for behavior are such that the more emergent the structure can be for a given animal, the more effectively can that animal dominate situations and learn. The more effectively the organism can withdraw from and dominate its immersion in the concrete, the more it triumphs over immediacy and the more fully the situation in question can articulate—can "be"—for that organism.

The first type of behavior (*syncretic*) is exemplified in the ant and the toad. For these, all situations are treated as direct analogues of vital situations, the prescriptions for which are built into the organism. As a result the unexpected situation elicits only prescribed responses. For example, when food is offered to a toad but separated from him by a glass, the toad repeatedly attempts to seize the food but repeatedly fails. His instinctual equipment allows him no improvisation, and he must adhere strictly to the concrete situation.

Higher animals, those whose behavior Merleau-Ponty calls *amovable,* are not so tightly bound. The distinctive feature of their behavior is that it is behavior according to a *signal*. The signal is not built into the animal's instinctual equipment, and it can be considered a conditioned reflex. In behavior according to a signal "the 'situation' to which the organism adapts is the simple temporal or spatial contiguity of a conditioned and an unconditioned stimulus"—that is, of the signal and what it signifies.

But the organism does not simply transport this contiguity into behavior. Rather, the animal finds in the situation a *structure* to which it responds and for which it develops an aptitude. For example, in an experiment by Koehler chickens were conditioned to choose the pile of grain marked by light grey rather than the one marked by a medium grey. When the medium grey was replaced by a grey lighter than the original light grey, the chickens responded to the replacement even though the original light grey should have become the conditioned stimulus. Koehler concludes that the response is to the lighter, and Merleau-Ponty agrees. It is the relations that are essential: the stimulus or signal is a structure, or gestalt. Furthermore, the response is to a structure *for the animal.* Chickens, for example, react to optical illusions as do humans, so that the one trained to choose according to the smaller sign chooses according to the one that looks smaller even if it is not.

Commenting on Koehler's classic, *The Mentality of Apes,* Merleau-Ponty attempts to outline more fully the world of the animal. He begins by noting that a branch or stick viewed by an ape has all the objective physico-geometric properties to qualify it as an instrument. It becomes an instrument, however, only when the *vital* situation creates pressures requiring it. Thus the stick will be used by the animal if placed in visual proximity to the food that it might serve to reach. The further away it is placed, the less likely it is to become an instrument. "Mechanical structures," Merleau-Ponty remarks, "become reflexogenic only if stronger structures which assign a useful value to objects are first recognized." Contrary to what empiricist and intellectualist psychologists maintain, it is not the length or rigidity of the stick that have the characteristics of *stimuli:* "What is not seen is that the field of animal activity is not *made up* of physico-geometric relations, as ours is." Our field of activity requires a special structuration to which we contribute but that is beyond the range of the animal's consciousness.

Koehler traces the seeming failure of animal aptitude here to visual deficiency, but Merleau-Ponty holds that the deficiency is of a more fundamental sort. There are no *things,* properly speaking, in the world of the animal. A *thing* is taken to be "a concrete unity capable of entering into a multiplicity of relations without losing itself." There are *things* only for a being whose behavior allows him to find in an object "an invariant under the diversity of its aspects." For example, for an ape a box by itself easily becomes an instrument for building a shaky tower, but a box serving as a seat for another ape does not. The ape that can quite easily avoid obstacles in his approach to food cannot push food around obstacles to draw it to himself. The first of these examples points to the inability to distinguish the *thing* amid the variety of its own relationships. The second suggests the nature of the demand that *things* impose upon the consciousness for which they exist. The ape can avoid obstacles with his own body in seeking a goal and can compensate (again, with his own body) for the most varied demands of equilibrium—say, when climbing an unsteady tower of crates. But he cannot find the invariant in the crates nor make *himself* the goal of the action of seeking food. *He seems unable to treat a thing like himself, to make of himself a truly effective symbol of things.*

There are *things* in man's perceived world. In his very brief treatment of this Merleau-Ponty refers to the human behavior that makes this possible as *symbolic*. Comparing the symbol to the signal to which the animal responds, he says that what characterizes the latter is its empirical relation to a particular event. What is distinctive of the symbol, however, is its relatedness, not simply with the thing or event for which it stands, but *with other symbols*. Adopting for the moment the more generic term "sign," Merleau-Ponty says of the symbol: "its relation to other signs is the same as the relation of the object signified to other objects." These lateral relations among symbols open up the "possibility of varied expressions of a same theme . . . which is lacking in animal behavior." They open the way to genuine human cognition by making it possible to grasp the "invariant under a diversity of perspectives," and not to lose the concrete unity of the object amid the multiplicity of its relationships. Thanks to symbolic behavior, in short, there are *things* for man.

In addition to noting that human expressive behavior measures up, so to speak, to the complexity of what is to be expressed, Merleau-Ponty also calls attention to its freedom and creativity. Here, as in most cases, his examples of human behavior are drawn from the non-conceptual order; he discusses not an act of knowledge but the performing of the typist or musician. Thus the piece of music and the instrument on one hand are integrated into a whole with the expressive gestures of the musician, a whole where all three communicate from within and to which every stimulus-response relationship is completely subordinated. Their relation is not mechanical but dialectical—that is, their relation is intrinsic; they are poles of behavior that "participate in the same structure." At the same time, each piece of music is the practical equivalent of every other piece of the same music, each piano or organ the equivalent of every other, and the talented musician is capable of playing any piece on any instrument. His behavior is not subordinated to music and instrument as response is to stimulus. It has a life of its own where it seeks out music and instrument for its own purposes. In this sense his expressive behavior is free and creative.

The stimulus as it is seen by the physiological atomist is an absolute property of some entity—in short, a *thing*. But in the light of the position that Merleau-Ponty is advancing, there are *things* only if there is human symbolic behavior. Hence the stimulus and with it all reflex behavior would have to be considered as something proper to man. In support of this Merleau-Ponty calls attention to the breakdown of animals in stimulus-response experiments and to the fact that reflexes tend to be more perfect in the species with the greatest cerebral development. The empiricist's error, then, has been that he substitutes sophisticated behavior for what is primitive when he gives the reflex interpretation for expressive behavior. This "higher" level of behavior, however, should not be identified with thought. There is always a tendency to see reality as *either* thought or thing, and the argument just developed against treating behavior as a thing might lead to this other classic alternative.

It is also true that making behavior a whole that dominates its parts, and an active rather than a passive response to stimuli, "idealizes" it somewhat—that is, endows it with certain of the characteristics conventionally attributed to ideas or thought. But Merleau-Ponty is insisting that in behavior we have a dimension of reality that is *neither* thought nor thing. One significance that the notion of form has for him is that it offers a means of avoiding certain classic difficulties in the psychological analysis of behavior. Another is that it "saves us from the alternative of a philosophy which juxtaposes externally associated terms and of another philosophy which discovers relations which are intrinsic to thought in all phenomena."

THE PHYSICAL ORDER, THE VITAL ORDER, AND THE HUMAN ORDER

Merleau-Ponty's analysis of behavior led him to the notion of form as an alternative to thought and thing. It might also be claimed that the arrival at the notion of form is also an arrival at the phenomena, for the description of form does coincide with that of phenomena as we saw it in the previous chapter. Merleau-Ponty notes, however, that historically the elaboration of the notion of form has not terminated in the priority of the phenomena but has tended to one of two forms of objectivism. The first and rarer of the two is a philosophy of form that demands that the distinctions among levels be secured by sharp structural differentiation. Such differentiation (Merleau-Ponty does not cite a proponent, but it is probably Cassirer) would restore the antinomies of materialism and mentalism that the notion of form should overcome.

The more common development of form theory, and that of the gestalt pioneers themselves, went in another direction. Perhaps because of heavy pressure to maintain respectability as scientists, men like Koehler, Wertheimer, and Koffka seem to have been willing that their advance be simply from atomist to non-atomist empiricism. In his *Principles of Gestalt Psychology* Koffka says, "I admit that in our ultimate explanations we can have to do only with one universe of discourse and that it must be the one about which physics has taught us so much."[12] His definition of consciousness as that property "which certain events in nature have of revealing themselves" is in that materialist tradition. This type of explanation misses the phenomenal dimension of reality and its peculiar constitution. It holds, for example, that perceptive consciousness is an imitation of things by the nervous system that in some way or other gives itself a double of what is seen, heard, felt, etc. This famous isomorphism is actually a representational theory of consciousness, in virtue of which consciousness is considered as a thing in the objectivist tradition.

Confronted by this, Merleau-Ponty argues both for the ability of the notion of form to integrate the varied levels of reality and at the same time for the originality of the orders that it integrates. He analyzes the notion of form in inanimate, living, and human beings, finding the originality on each level in the distinctive types of *relations* that are manifest there. At each level form is distended to accommodate these different types of relations, and as the descriptions advance toward the human level, form becomes more and more a structure *for* consciousness. Finally, intentionality appears as one of the dimensions of form that more and more is seen to belong to the realm of phenomena. Thus,

---

12. Cited in *Structure*, p. 133.

from his earlier description of form as a decisive category achieved by the detailed analysis of a large mass of biological and psychological material, Merleau-Ponty proceeds to a more synthetic and at times even visionary discussion designed to show the range and versatility of this conception by demonstrating its capacity to *integrate* one's view of reality.

THE PHYSICAL ORDER. If it is said of any form that it "constitutes a field of forces characterized by a law which has no meaning outside the limits of the dynamic structure considered, and which on the other hand assigns its properties to each internal point so much so that they will never be absolute properties, properties *of* this point," then it is not difficult to see the reality with which the physicist deals as form. Merleau-Ponty finds in an early work by Koehler,[13] in remarks by Brunschvicg as well as in his own experience, a series of examples that support his view. This view is that all physical laws express a *structure* and can only make sense when this structure is recognized. The law of falling bodies, for example, is valid and verifiable in the context of the present cosmological structure of the earth. Should this structure change, the law will change also. Such an overall context is a functional whole or system. There are many other systems within this, some as small and trivial as a soap bubble. Speaking of physical form in any or all of them, Merleau-Ponty calls it an individual—that is, an entity "possessing internal unity inscribed in a segment of space and resisting deformation from external influences."[14] The notion of form, which displaced the notion of the atom—itself an individual in an unoriginal way—is now called upon to restore an individuality. This it does on its own molar level. With it "a principle of discontinuity is introduced and the conditions for a development by leaps or crises, for an event or for a history, are given." When physical or inanimate reality leaves room for leaps, crises, and even a history, it is no longer "nature" as the mechanist understands it. Again, Merleau-Ponty insists that form is not a *thing*. The law that manifests physical structure does not imply physical structure as its *distinct* ontological foundation. Neither law nor structure is intelligible without the other, and each stands as a moment

---

13. W. Koehler, *Die Physischen Gestalten in Ruhe und im Stationaren Zustand* (Erlangen: Braunschweig, 1920).
14. *Structure*, p. 137.

in an exchange in which consciousness takes part, for it is the physicist who establishes the law. The law—the expression of the form, formulated to comprehend as much data as possible—appears as a limit toward which knowledge tends. Form, resisting division and localization but governing what goes on in several places, is more *idea* than thing—though not completely idea—and its unity is the phenomenal unity of the perceived object.

THE VITAL ORDER. What is distinctive about the relationships at this level is their orientation toward a set of tasks. In considering them Merleau-Ponty again takes most of his data from Goldstein's work, *Der Aufbau des Organismus*. The relations described are those of *aptitude* with *milieu*, and the examples are drawn primarily from the *human* organism. The organism is characterized by a certain style of "address"—an aptitude—to the world. This can and does vary from individual to individual, and it shows itself even in the way one walks or carries one's head. Aptitude determines the optimum conditions for activity and is the norm according to which environment is satisfying or not for the behaving organism. Its world, then, is literally a world-in-view-of-a-certain-set-of-tasks. As Merleau-Ponty puts it:

> equilibrium is obtained, not with respect to real and present conditions, but with respect to conditions which are only virtual and which the system itself brings into existence; when the structure, instead of procuring a release from the forces with which it is penetrated through the pressure of external ones, executes a work beyond its proper limits and constitutes a proper milieu for itself.[15]

The elements of behavior are integrated into this structure, which supplies them with an authentic intelligible framework. It is only when biology respects the peculiar intelligibility of the aptitude that the authentic organism will be available to it, and respecting this intelligibility means taking a point of view that allows it to appear. This point of view is not the mechanist version of objectivist thought, nor is it the vitalist point of view; for vitalism, if it recognizes the originality of behavior, also tries to explain it by appeal to another *thing*—soul, entelechy, or *élan vital*. But when it does, the problem of the integration of the two orders again becomes acute.

---

15. *Ibid.*, pp. 145–46.

By means of a phenomenological view the intelligibility of the organism emerges and can be recognized. Merleau-Ponty's critique of objectivist thought invites a shift to this view; and the positive description of the organism invites the attempt to try a notion, such as *meaning* (always *for* a consciousness), as a fundamental category, for this notion allows the organism to show itself as capacity for action. The instinctive aptitudes that structure such animal behaviors as building a nest or seizing a prey emerge and can be recognized when one is attentive to meaning or signification. To understand the biological entity, then, means "to unite the ensemble of known facts by means of their significations, to discover in all of them a characteristic rhythm, a general attitude toward certain categories of objects, perhaps even toward all things." It means dealing with the phenomena.

THE HUMAN ORDER. The originality of the human order is manifest in its symbolic behavior. When he described the performing of the musician, Merleau-Ponty exemplified very clearly the dialectical character of the relations existing among the factors in symbolic behavior: music, instrument, and musical talent formed a single structure dominated by the last, but within this structure each communicated with the others. His first description of perception in *The Structure of Behavior* follows the pattern of this example: "Perception is a moment of the living dialectic of a concrete subject; it participates in its total structure and, correlatively, it has its original object . . . , the actions of other human subjects." When he elaborates on this description, he develops primarily the *intentionality* dimension of this moment, making clear both that perception is lived experience, rather than objective knowledge, and then that it is dynamic and a source of meaning.

Turning to the description of perception as it begins and develops in infants, he is led to conclude that "nascent perception has the double character of being directed toward human intentions rather than toward the objects of nature or the pure qualities (hot, cold, white, black) of which they are the supports and of grasping them as experienced realities rather than as true objects." Thus the child's first experienced realities are the face and gestures of its mother. Her face is not an object or a collection of qualities but a center of expression. After this it is apparently objects of use that the child first knows, and, when natural things become significant for him, it is by the mediation of words, themselves objects of use. The notion of form can help formulate this perception by the child because form is itself a configuration prior to the distinction of parts, even of senses and qualities. But this notion of form must be completed by the notion of intentionality. If a child is able to grasp the human intention in things immediately, they must be "prefigured" in some fashion for him.

This prefiguring, however, cannot be a sort of Kantian a priori; the infantile consciousness is not an organizing principle operating on sensible multiplicity, for we have seen that he grasps meaning prior to qualities. For the child there is another a priori in the form of such "indecomposable structures" as the other person and speech. These structures are in no sense innate; Merleau-Ponty finds such an idea absurd. The child's consciousness of structures, in fact, cannot be conceived as primarily representative at all—cannot be inner pictures that would be *things*—because the child's materials for representation are so poor. If this is the case, then the representational life of consciousness cannot be the entire life of consciousness. Perhaps "desire could be related to the object desired, will to the object willed, fear to the object feared, without this reference—even if it always includes a cognitive nucleus—being reduced to the relation of representation to represented." By such "blind knowledge" the child would know his mother, would grasp human meanings prior to given qualities—as one knows that the décor of a room is "right" or "all wrong" prior to having noticed the color of this or that item of furniture. Beyond representation, then, there are several ways for consciousness to envision its object—several intentions that are direct relations to it. Consciousness is, in fact, "a network of signifying intentions, sometimes clear for themselves and at others lived rather than known."

Defined by its intentional object perceptual consciousness is essentially a lived involvement in a concrete situation. Merleau-Ponty makes it clear that this involvement is not only active but creative by linking perceptive intentionality to *work*. In fact he holds the human order to be characterized by the exchange between *perceived situation* and *work*, as the animal level is distinguished by the dialectic *vital situation* and *instinctive reaction*. Bergson's notion of *action*, often linked with consciousness as an alternative to work, does not do justice to the emergence of the human over the vital situation. Action is always taken as behavior in the interest of natural needs, and in this perspective instruments become the extensions of organs, clothing an artificial skin; and the theory of consciousness focuses on how natural objects are constituted for us. *Work,* however, is understood as "the ensemble of activities by which man transforms physical and living nature." It does not simply fit man into nature, but changes nature according to the human vision. The appropriateness of the connection between work and perception emerges even more clearly when one recognizes that, because it transforms physical and vital nature, work is fundamentally the negation of a given milieu in the interest of a new one. Work demands the possible, the future. The consciousness with which it is linked— human perception—is precisely what reveals objects as capable of supporting a future. This occurs when things show themselves capable of entering into indefinitely extended and ramified new relations, precisely those that can make up the new milieu. Thus in simply allowing objects to be objects-for-man perception opens up the possible and the future. The human dialectic, Merleau-Ponty says, is such that its acts "all reveal the same essence: the capacity of orienting oneself in relation to the possible." Again, he says that the human dialectic is *ambiguous*:

> it is first manifested by the social or cultural structures, the appearance of which it brings about and in which it imprisons itself. But its use-objects would not be what they are if the activity which brings about their appearance did not also have as its meaning to reject them and to surpass them.[16]

In his first application to man of the term *ambiguous* we can see the profile of that committed yet compulsively free being to which postwar existentialism is to give so much attention. By its commitment in various structures human consciousness brings about the appearance and the meaningfulness of these structures. They are structures for it —that is, phenomena. Yet consciousness refuses to be identical with them: it returns to itself and passes beyond. This consciousness, which is the condition for the phenomena, *this* is what Merleau-Ponty calls *perception.* It is the relation *perception-phenomena* that is primitive, and all others—the relation of consciousness to nature included—can be understood only if this is recognized.

This passage from a natural to a phenomenological attitude, however, is a passage from problem to problem. Although now near the

---

16. *Ibid.,* p. 176.

end of Merleau-Ponty's critique of objectivist thought, we do not yet have a series of solutions to crucial problems. Rather, we have a new and promising way of posing such problems. Once, we might have asked how perception and phenomena could occur among things and ideas. Now we must ask how things and ideas are to make sense as phenomena. He who overthrows the natural attitude must eventually explain the natural attitude; and while it may well be the case that consciousness is perception and world is phenomena, it does not ordinarily seem this way. How and why they are lost in favor of their products—that is, in favor of the meanings that spring from them—is a question that is not raised at this point.

Instead, Merleau-Ponty changes the perspective of his critique of objectivist psychology and tries to show how the latter's worthwhile discoveries can be preserved. Using Freud as an example, he suggests how what is valuable in this previous thinking can find a place in the phenomenological framework. His tone with Freud is gentle, though he notes that the latter's language when treating repression and complexes, for example, is objectivist and suggests a psychic content of unconscious forces and entities. Could this be translated into a non-objective language? Merleau-Ponty says that it could and that all that is basically required by the facts that Freud describes is "the possibility of a fragmented life of consciousness which does not possess a unique significance at all times." But the ambiguity of consciousness as well as the levels of meaning within human life offer just such a possibility of fragmentation. Thus various complexes or instances of repression can be taken as more primitive manners of organizing life in instances where an experience has neither been transformed or assumed into the general movement of existence. Some persons can synthesize, and these achieve the fullest humanity. Others cannot, and much of their behavior is in a lower dialectic or a simplistic form of the highest.

Higher levels of behavior, as we have seen before, assume and reorganize the lower levels. They are not "two *de facto* orders external to each other, but two types of relations, the second of which integrates the first." Mind "is not a new sort of being but a new form of unity, it cannot stand by itself" and is inseparable from the very orders that it integrates. Neither materialist nor mentalist realism in psychology can manage this "immanent structure and meaning of behavior which is the only psychic reality."

Objective description—that of the sciences—need not, then, be disdained, but it should be followed out in all its implications. Merleau-Ponty insists that he has done just that in his first three chapters. "There is an objective analysis and an objective definition of perception, intelligence and emotion as structures of behavior, and we have attempted a description of this kind in the preceding chapter." It has led him to the introduction of consciousness, and he explicitly says of this that in introducing it he is doing no more than "denominating the relations of the milieu and the organism as science itself defines them." The natural attitude, in short, cracks under the weight of the very results obtained from it. But the phenomenal dimension that then appears has its own typical structure in which one meaning integrates another while being founded on the latter. Its affinities with the classic soul-body issue are sufficient to make this issue the framework of the final chapter.

THE RELATIONS OF SOUL AND BODY AND THE PROBLEM OF PERCEPTUAL CONSCIOUSNESS

Merleau-Ponty measures his position against classic philosophies of subjectivity. As a result his work here is philosophical in a more familiar way. Descartes, for example, is the most frequent partner in dialogue. The positions challenged are Cartesian Intellectualism and critical philosophy in its Kantian and post-Kantian forms. The mind-matter relation is dealt with both as the body-soul problem and as the intimately related problem of perception. The development in *The Structure of Behavior* was destined to culminate in some such considerations. We have seen criticism of naturalism in psychology lead to a priority of the subject, to a transcendental attitude in which the fundamental structures of the world are structures *for* consciousness. But this position does not assume full significance until the question *what kind of consciousness* is answered. Merleau-Ponty's conception of subject must be compared with that of other philosophers who would agree with him that the world's structure is a structure *for* consciousness. He must, in short, distinguish the phenomenological version of the transcendental attitude from the versions offered by intellectualism and critical philosophy. Perception, of course, is the key to his view. He rejects the other positions for their inability to cope with it philosophically, an inability directly reflected in the soul-body conception that they maintain. The revised conception of soul-body relations that he proposes results from his accommodation of perception by insisting upon its philosophical primacy.

The chapter is not simply the philosophical culmination of prior critical reflections. Merleau-Ponty brings the criticism of relevant philosophical positions to a level comparable to the one that has been reached in the criticism of psychology, and he explicitly exercises the phenomenological description as a technique for dealing positively with the question at hand, indicating briefly how the fundamental structure of phenomena can underwrite a renewed comprehension of the relations of spirit and matter. The fundamental structures of phenomena are invoked not only to explain the things about which naturalism is in error but to indicate why there should be an error called naturalism in the first place.

Merleau-Ponty begins his criticism with a "naive" reduction. By means of it he accomplishes again the rupture of the natural attitude (as he had already done in the critique of psychology) and in addition is able to challenge the claim that naive consciousness is realistic. In the actual perceptive experience to which the reduction leads—as distinguished from the mechanical model of this experience that objectivist thought builds—the subject lives "in a milieu which is neutral with regard to the substantial distinctions between organism, thought and extension; in direct commerce with beings, things and his own body." In this direct commerce the object—the cube, for example—offers itself as " 'in itself,' that is, as gifted with an interior which I shall never have finished exploring; and as 'for me,' that is, as given 'in person' through its momentary aspects." So conceived, the phenomenal dimension is not only accessible, but richly structured and ontologically solid. Its decisive feature from the point of view of intelligibility is the *profile-object* structure: not everything about the cube actually appears, for I can see at most three sides at a time.

But the whole cube is present to me in these three sides that together form a profile of the object and are seen precisely as sides *of* the cube. The "momentary aspects" are such profiles and do not present themselves as "subjective deformations of the things" but as its "essential properties." The presence of the object in every profile, together with its transcendence of each profile, guarantees to naive consciousness a sort of empirical realism—this is, "the assurance of an external experience in which there is no doubt about escaping 'states of consciousness' and acceding to solid objects."

This, of course, is a far cry from objectivists or naturalists realism. In the same experience the body is not lived as a distinct material mass. Rather, "the body proper and its organs remain the bases or vehicles of my intentions [which find] their embodiment in movements, and are expressed in them as the object is expressed in its perspectual aspects." All in all, then, "the ego as center from which his intentions radiate, the body which carries them, the being or things to which they are addressed are . . . only three sectors of a unique field." A technical treatment of the rupture of this primitive unity would be equivalent to a theory of the generation of nature and idea in their objectivist senses. Here, however, in keeping with the type of reduction operated, Merleau-Ponty offers a "naive" version of the objectifying of the situation; the experience of being resisted by one's body at a time of sickness or fatigue. This resistance makes the body seem to be a *thing* standing between self and objects, and this in turn makes necessary some device to make it an *instrument* serving perception, rather than a screen preventing it. The devices offered range from the pineal gland (Descartes) to zones of association or the isomorphic structure preferred by gestaltists. But the instrument is still a thing or object; the various devices are all ways of allowing a physiological representation of the perceived object to be generated in the body; but a representation of a perceived object is itself an object perceived, and in its regard all the traditional Cartesian problems still remain.

Merleau-Ponty does not caricature Descartes; he avoids identifying the philosophy of Descartes with either that series of the latter's texts that emphasize the soul-body divorce or with the Cartesianism of the sciences (which he calls pseudo-Cartesianism). Indeed, as far as Merleau-Ponty is concerned, Descartes' most significant philosophical step was "to abandon the extra-mental things which philosophical realism had introduced in order to return to an inventory, to a description of human experience without presupposing anything at first which explains it from the outside." Such a priority of consciousness is quite similar to that of phenomenology. For both philosophers "the analysis of the act of knowledge leads to the idea of a constituting or naturizing thought which internally subtends the characteristic structure of objects," and as a result a description of phenomenology like the following is quite applicable to Merleau-Ponty's endeavor and yet prior to the distinction of types of subjectivity involved:

> In order to indicate both the intimacy of objects to the subject and the presence in them of solid structures which distinguish them from appearances, they will be called "phenomena" and philosophy to the extent that it adheres to this theme, becomes a phenomenology, that is, inventory of consciousness as milieu of the universe.[17]

But the consciousness that is milieu of the universe, whose thought is "naturizing" for the characteristic structure of objects cannot be consciousness as Descartes or Kant understand it. Descartes' intellectualism "accounts for the thought of seeing, but the fact of vision and the ensemble of existential knowledges remain outside it," consigned, in fact, to confused thought or infra-intelligible lived experience. The existential dimension of awareness remains out of Kant's reach also, for in his scheme intelligibility lies in a form that is a priori—that is, belonging to consciousness and maintaining no significant relations with matter, whose role is reduced to that of limiting consciousness and accounting for its contingency. For both Descartes and Kant the inability to deal with perception results in a separation of mind and matter, a withdrawal of soul from body. Merleau-Ponty's conception of the organization of mind and matter leads to an idealization of the body. This diminishes the likelihood of withdrawal: an idealized body seems quite susceptible to relations with consciousness. Such a conception has also been employed by post-Kantian critical philosophy of the sort that Merleau-Ponty identifies (casually) with Brunschvicg. In this view there is a comprehension of mind-matter organization as levels of dialectic quite similar at first view to Merleau-Ponty's. Thus, "the physical, the vital, and the mental individual are distinguished only as different degrees of integration." But post-Kantian critical philosophy gave a very heavy priority to the third of these degrees. To be a man is to be identified with the mental, and to the extent that this identification occurs, a man "no longer allows systems of isolated conduct to function in him, his body and soul are no longer distinct." Inferior levels are completely submerged and annulled. As a result "we never deal with a body in itself, but with a body for a con-

---

17. *Ibid.,* p. 199.

sciousness and . . . we never have to put consciousness in contact with an opaque and foreign reality."

To this post-Kantian, critical insistence on a total idealization of the body, Merleau-Ponty opposes the results of his appraisal of psychology. He reminds us, for example, that the delivery of brain function from strict localization is not a delivery from all localization and that the alteration of a given region of the cortex has effects on one type of thought process rather than others. In short the integration accomplished by the spirit does not annul the specificity of the inferior levels. Though they may at times be submerged, they can at any time emerge to disrupt the superior level or to serve as its indispensable means of expression. Merleau-Ponty's description showed behavior to be "a meaningful whole for a consciousness which considers it." But "it was at the same time and reciprocally to make manifest in 'expressive conduct' the view of a consciousness under our eyes, to show a mind which comes into the world." What has been called the idealization of the body is also the incarnation of the soul, then, for without the body as its means of expression the soul would simply cease to be *anything*. The dualism that remains is not, as he noted in a previous chapter, a dualism of substance:

> the notions of soul and body must be relativized. . . . there is the body as mass of chemical components in interaction, the body as dialectic of living being and its biological milieu, and the body as dialectic of social subject and his group; even all our habits are an impalpable body for the ego of each moment. Each of these degrees is soul with respect to the preceding one, body with respect to the following one. The body in general is an ensemble of paths already traced, of powers already constituted; the body is the acquired dialectical soil upon which a higher "formation" is accomplished, and the soul is the meaning which is then established.[18]

Such, then, is the relation of body and soul as seen in the contrast between the classic views of Descartes and Kant and the implications of Merleau-Ponty's criticism of the philosophical basis of modern psychology. The situated consciousness whose primacy is implied in the description of the soul as "mind which comes into the world" is identical with that to which both critical work and the naive reduction lead—perception. In describing perception Merleau-Ponty points to the

---

18. *Ibid.*, p. 210.

phenomenal underpinning of the soul-body structure, of objects, and even of naturalism.

Merleau-Ponty calls perception "the apprehension of an existence." "But it is when objects give me the unique impression of the 'sensed,' when they have that direct manner of taking hold of me, that I say they are existing." This apprehension of things "in person" is lived individually, mutely, and inarticulately as the "flux of individual events, of concrete and resistant structures." Let us note again that the structure that dominates the phenomena as they are lived is the profile-object structure: "For there to be perception, that is, apprehension of an existence, it is absolutely necessary that the object not be completely given to the look which rests on it, that aspects intended but not possessed in the present perception be kept in reserve." The lived consciousness that is perception is characterized by its *perspectivism*—that is, it is situated in a point of view from which the object can be seen only in its profiles. But this kind of consciousness must be distinguished from knowledge. What distinguishes the latter is that it overcomes perspectivism: for knowledge the cube *does* have six equal sides and does therefore imply as its knowing subject a general and unlocated consciousness.

In speaking further of the differences between consciousness as perception and consciousness as knowledge Merleau-Ponty freely introduces the most classic opposition: existence and essence, reality and concept or idea, phenomenon and logical signification, real existence and logical signification, actuality and virtuality, using all of these familiar philosophical contrasts to suggest a distinction that he does not work out in detail. Whatever the implied priority of perception one cannot *name* what he perceives without appealing to the level of knowledge. Yet the latter is bound to perception as soul is bound to body: "these acts of expression or of reflection intend an original text which cannot be deprived of meaning."

Perspectivism, as we said, dominates that text. Immanent in each of its profiles, the phenomenal object forever maintains features that I do not see, features that it offers to other observers. Perspectivism also characterizes the phenomenal body but not the perspectivism of the object: unlike the object my body is not susceptible to an unlimited inspection. But among its constituents there are some (the brain, the retina, for example) that I cannot see, though others can. Merleau-

Ponty calls this "a particular case of the perspectival character of perception" and proceeds to a generalization of the profile-object structure. The body is my point of view on things, and its being as point of view is known indirectly and in virtue of its correlation with the profiled revelation of the objects. A thing can reveal itself little by little only to a perceiver who is there now, and not everywhere always. This situation and its structure give Merleau-Ponty the opportunity to advance a non-causal formulation of the relation of body and soul: "Reduced to its positive meaning, the connection of soul and body signifies nothing other than the *ecceitas*—the here and now character— of knowledge by profiles."

The substitution of translation for text—of *things* for objects-in-profile and of organs for body—is the fundamental error of naturalism. But naturalism, Merleau-Ponty argues, is a motivated error. Like any other phenomenon it is comprehensible in terms of some authentic phenomenal structure. "The proper structure of perceptual experience, the reference of partial 'profiles' to the total signification which they 'present,' would be this phenomenon." The basic structure of phenomena must now supply an answer to why the structure itself is ignored. As we have seen, the body is my point of view on objects. "But to be situated within a certain point of view necessarily involves not seeing that point of view itself, not possessing it as a visual object except in a virtual signification." The very structure of body as point of view demands that it be unknown. Similarly, the profile—because it is a profile—effaces itself before the object, and the phenomena are lost to strictly logical meaning though not to concrete description. These structures are immediately evident, but their evidence has been lost. As a result Merleau-Ponty considers the tendency to detach these meanings and the attempt to reconstruct perception on their basis as quite *natural*. But it is just as natural that the attempt fail: "as we have seen, one cannot reconstitute the structure of perceptual experience by combining ideal significations (stimuli, receptors, associative circuits . . .)." What is natural, then, is in conflict with itself, and again the natural attitude seems to crack under its own weight. To point out the conflict is not to solve it, however. Rather, we must understand "the lived relation of the 'profiles' to the 'thing' which they present, of the perspectives to the ideal significations which are intended through them." The notion of intentionality will be useful here. Prior to his concluding remarks Merleau-Ponty extends the application of the notion of perspectivism, saying that there is a perspectivism of lived experience that dominates my awareness of myself as well as of others and that thwarts total expression. Thus my life is inhabited by a general immanent meaning that I may or may not grasp, and I live out a coexistence with others that is the foundation of social relationships but that also resists becoming totally explicit.

In the remarks with which he concludes *The Structure of Behavior* Merleau-Ponty summarizes his response to the question about the reason for the objectivist error and also his thinking about the kind of consciousness to which the structures of the world appear. The *intentional* character of consciousness is central in each case. "It is natural for consciousness to misunderstand itself precisely because it is consciousness of things." Things can so absorb consciousness—"the 'I think' can be as if hallucinated by its objects"—that it loses sight of itself and its involvement in them. *This* is the reason why objectivist thinking ignores consciousness: consciousness is in the habit of ignoring itself. Perhaps, in fact, it is even necessary for consciousness to lose sight of itself in order that there *be* objects for it. Whatever the case, however, the intentionality theme underscores the involvement of consciousness in the world, and with this the existential character of Merleau-Ponty's response to the question what kind of consciousness. Perceptual consciousness, to whose primacy his work seems to have led, is nothing if not situated, involved—a consciousness-in-a-world.

The Structure of Behavior very consciously leaves open certain questions about the philosophical implications of this position. Particularly do these concern the relation of thought with perception, the primacy of which has been proposed. At the end of the book he asks, "Can one conceptualize perceptual consciousness without eliminating it as an original mode; can one maintain its specificity without rendering inconceivable its relation with intellectual consciousness?" Perhaps *Phenomenology of Perception*, which extends the investigation of the relation of consciousness with nature begun in *The Structure of Behavior*, will answer this. We turn to the former work now.

Chapter 2

The Body
and Perception

The central problem of *Phenomenology of Perception* is the following:

> We must discover the origin of the object at the very center of our experience; we must describe the emergence of being and we must understand how, paradoxically, there is *for us an in-itself*.[1]

We must discover, in short, how things and meanings emerge from our general perceptual involvement in the world and take their place around us. This attention to the source of meaning is what makes *Phenomenology of Perception* an essay in *genetic phenomenology*. In its preface, which we discussed in our introductory chapter, Merleau-Ponty carefully situated this point of view in relation to the traditional themes of phenomenology. In its rather long introduction he relates this genetic phenomenology to science, carrying out the phenomenological reduction again in the form of a critique of the presuppositions of psychology. A critique of this sort was done in *The Structure of Behavior*, and a remark like this could be the conclusion of the earlier work: "consciousness must be faced with its own unreflective life in things and awakened to its own history which it was forgetting: such is the true part that philosophical reflection has to play." One would, of course, expect some overlapping in books that, like these, carry out a single project. But the introduction to *Phenomenology of Perception* does not simply restate previous results: its meaning is clearly de-

---

1. *Phenomenology*, p. 71.

terminated by the fact that the problem of the relations of consciousness and nature has become a problem of the *genesis of meanings* on the basis of perception. In this connection we are told that "the central phenomenon of perceptual life [is] the constitution without any ideal model, of a significant grouping." This constitution points, as we shall see, to the presence of a constituting consciousness—one which generates meaning. The attempt to understand this consciousness and the process by which it institutes meaning defines genetic phenomenology.

The title of the introduction is "Traditional Prejudices and the Return to Phenomena." It deals, in fact, with a single general prejudice that it calls the "prejudice in favor of the world" but that is actually the objectivist mentality habitual with the scientist. This mentality can no more deal with perception than it can with behavior in general. This is because perception as it is actually lived (and phenomenologically described) presents ambiguities, twilight zones, and, above all, *structure*: "the perceived, by its nature . . . is shaped by its context." Such structure simply cannot be reconstructed from empiricism's discrete elements. Even less can any form of objectivism account for the *becoming structured*—that is, "the constitution without an ideal model of a significant grouping."

The phenomenon of *attention* offers Merleau-Ponty the opportunity to make a decisive point in this connection. In a world of complete objects—the objectivist world—there would be nothing to solicit consciousness in one direction rather than another. But if we refer to our *experience* of attention, we find that it establishes figures on what had previously been background. Attention is "the active constitution of a new object which makes explicit and articulate what was until then presented as no more than indeterminate horizon." The affinity between this description of attention and the description of the central phenomenon of perceptual life is overwhelming, and it assures the phenomenon of attention a crucial place in the discussion of the constitution of meanings. Attention has, in fact, an importance in *Phenomenology of Perception* as a visual model quite comparable to the importance that the profile-object structure has in *The Structure of Behavior*. Each is a structure-for-consciousness, though the example of attention is more suggestive of constitutive or generating behavior on the part of consciousness than is the response to the profile-object structure. At this point Merleau-Ponty uses the notion of attention to transfer the unifying and determining function of consciousness from any distinct, intellectual level to the level of perception. Still referring to the act of attention, he says, "this passage from the indeterminate to the determinate, this recasting at every moment of its own history in the unity of a new meaning, is thought itself." A few pages later he will say that as a consequence of the return to phenomena, *understanding* must also be redefined: "the general connective function ultimately attributed to it by Kantianism is now spread over the whole intentional life."

After this diffusing of the function of thought Merleau-Ponty sharply curtails the role of judgment in perception. Judgment has sometimes been introduced into perception to supplement sensation—"to explain the excess of perception over the retinal images." At other times it has become the very reality of perception. Descartes, for example, takes perception for "inspection by the mind." In either case there is an attempt to supply from the mind what Merleau-Ponty insists emerges from the structure perceived. Merleau-Ponty's earlier criticism of atomism is applicable to the view that judgment is supplemental to punctual sensations. And, as we saw earlier, the purer intellectualism that Descartes exemplifies inevitably falls short of the constitutive dimension of perception, the *arising of the here and now perspective*, in which the full impact of existence is to be found. Intellectualism falls short of the phenomena. The return to phenomena is a return to a revised conception of what is initially and immediately given in consciousness. These data are not an impression of some sort, a Cartesian *cogito*, or an inexpressible Bergsonian intuition. Rather, they are "the meaning, the structure, the spontaneous arrangement of parts" that characterize perceptive life. When Merleau-Ponty speaks of what it is that is spontaneously arranged, we see the roots of his conception of rationality and communication:

> The tacit assumption of perception is that at every instant, experience can be coordinated with that of the previous instant and that of the following, and my perspective with that of other consciousness—that all contradictions can be removed, that monadic and intersubjective experience is one unbroken text—that what is now indeterminate for me could become determinate for a more complete knowledge, which is as it were realized in advance in the thing, or rather which is the thing itself.[2]

---

2. *Ibid.*, p. 54.

Science pretends to realize in advance the synthesis that perception only promises. But it is perception, "the prescientific life of consciousness which alone endows scientific operations with meaning and to which these latter always refer back." This reference of science to a life richer than its own is decisive in Merleau-Ponty's thinking about science. In *Structure of Behavior* he called forth from this prescientific life the categories requisite for an understanding of behavior. "By taking the Gestalt as theme of his reflection, the psychologist breaks with psychologism . . . the transcendental attitude is already implied in the descriptions of the psychologist." This reference also allows (and in some cases has even forced) scientific psychology to outrun itself by recognizing the originality of phenomena and thus becoming phenomenological psychology. And when we attempt to comprehend everything on the basis of phenomena, phenomenological psychology becomes phenomenological philosophy.

We should notice as we consider Merleau-Ponty's remarks about science that there are positions in the philosophy of science that simply deny that science is so related to any dimension of being (of which it is the explanation) that such being can make demands upon it. This attitude is particularly prevalent among those who emphasize formal method or who import the methods of physics into psychology. It is not easy to find the ground for a comparison between these positions and phenomenology as method. Nor is it easy to find room in these positions for the historic role played in scientific method by the observation of data and the alignment of conceptual framework according to these data. Still, it is quite evident that many who would at least tacitly admit that the method should measure up to the object are not led to the structures that the phenomenologist sees. There is a continuous reflection on method woven into *Phenomenology of Perception*, a reflection in which the phenomenological approach is held to be clearly preferable to empiricism and intellectualism in physiology. An "existential analysis" is also sketched out and presented as preferable to a conventional psychoanalysis in clinical matters, and an existentialist conception of history is offered that has advantages over conventional *Marxism*. This is in addition to the argument for phenomenological existentialism as philosophy.

Though he is sharply critical of what he considers scientific pretentions, Merleau-Ponty refuses to allow a complete opposition between science and phenomenology. He consistently distinguishes between the central meaning of scientific positions and the objectivist manner in which they are formulated. He did this with Watson, with the gestalt psychologists, with Freud (as we saw when we discussed *The Structure of Behavior*), and will do it again in *Phenomenology of Perception* with Freud and Marx, in each case espousing their central meaning when it is shorn of its "indigent philosophy." Psychoanalysis, behaviorism, and so forth, are not bound by the objectivist formulations that can be given to them; it is possible for them to be presented in another language.

But why should a phenomenological language be preferable to an objectivist language? Merleau-Ponty concedes that there is no decisive experiment that can prevent the empiricists or others from calling the phenomenological view an illusion and from continuing to construct and refine their own models. Only a shift of vision could do that. Two things might contribute to such a shift. The first is that although the objectivist style cannot be refuted, "it is discredited because it overlooks and does not permit of any understanding of phenomena." The second factor that might contribute to the shift is the fact that the psychologist *is* what he studies and must intrude, so to speak, on his own data. Yet one can be unaware of such intrusion as well as of the limited comprehension of facts that his position allows. However imposing such presence and such limitations are, "nothing is more difficult than to know precisely *what we see*." Merleau-Ponty closes his introduction by repeating the warning that philosophy, too—and phenomenological philosophy is no exception—runs the risk of not knowing what it sees. Its tendency to do this is something that it must not only resist but must also attempt to understand:

> A philosophy becomes transcendental, or radical, not by taking its place in absolute consciousness without mentioning the ways by which this is reached, but by considering itself as a problem; not by postulating a knowledge rendered totally explicit, but by recognizing as the fundamental philosophic problem this *presumption* on reason's part.[3]

The *body* and *the world as perceived*, the topics for discussion in the

3. *Ibid.*, p. 63.

first two sections of *Phenomenology of Perception*, lend themselves to the sort of concrete treatment that discourages philosophy from running away from its source.

THE BODY

The attempt to "discover the origin of the object at the very center of our experience . . ." begins with an extended reflection on the nature of the body. For Merleau-Ponty the body is "that by which there are objects." In the course of this reflection he justifies a conception of the body as *subject* rather than *object* by an appeal to the intentional theory of consciousness and the conception of phenomena that is integrated with it.

"What prevents its [the body's] . . . ever being an object, ever being 'completely constituted' is that it is that by which there are objects." Not only is the body held to be *not* an object (and therefore, as it turns out, a subject), but the reason for its *not* being an object lies in its being the *condition* for objects. The relation here is dialectical rather than causal: the terms are bound together because of their differences. The object that is essentially a structure *for* consciousness would simply cease to be in the absence of that consciousness, just as the consciousness that is essentially consciousness *of* something would cease to be in the absence of its object. They are joined in their opposition, opposed in their mutual dependence. Sartre emphasizes the opposition within this relationship to the point that its terms become the *being* and *nothingness* of his central work. Merleau-Ponty is much less extreme, but he does operate comfortably with the notion of the subject as non-object, which the opposition implies. This dialectical relation— the contrast between object as "completely constituted" and the status of the body—is not the simple juxtaposition of plenitude and lack, for what is identified as lack clearly contributes to constituting the plenitude. *That the body is not "completely constituted" is in some way a mark of its intimacy with the constituting function, which is consciousness.* If the body becomes subject, then it is because the subject has become body, transforming the latter in the movement by which it fulfills itself. This movement of existence is the process of generating meanings or significant groupings and is what Merleau-Ponty will ultimately call temporality.

MECHANIST PHYSIOLOGY AND THE BODY AS OBJECT

The failure of contemporary physiology to deal adequately with certain types of physical defects opens up the opportunity to introduce the "subjectivized" body. The body deficiencies in question are the "phantom limb," that phenomenon frequently experienced by amputees who "feel" the absent member and often quite painfully; and anosognosia, where a member that is present but paralyzed is not felt.[4] Prevailing explanations of the phantom limb tend to be either physiological or psychological. The former explanation maintains that the phantom limb is due to the persistence of stimulation in nerves that served the now absent member, and they note in support of this that the phenomena can be eliminated by severing these nerves. In this explanatory framework anosognosia would be a loss of stimulation. The psychological explanation, however, calls attention to the fact that the phenomenon can be induced by remembering the circumstances of the original loss. Such remembering and the accompanying emotional states cannot be regarded as physiological. Where the phantom limb is a remembering, anosognosia is a forgetting.

The claims of each position stand on evidence too strong to be simply dismissed, and the attempt to unify them leads to a very difficult spirit-matter problem. Merleau-Ponty, however, argues beyond these alternatives toward an existential category. He notes that a patient afflicted with anosognosia regards his paralyzed arm as "a long cold snake." This militates against believing that he does not feel his arm at all. There is, then, a remembering in his forgetting, which makes his habit of extending the "good" arm when asked for the other a *refusal* of his deficiency. The more obvious refusal of mutilation by the patient who relies on a phantom limb *now* also has its own remembering—a peculiar remembering without the distinct note of past. This *refusal* is the *existential* category that Merleau-Ponty considers preferable to the physiological or psychological schemes and to which his analysis of these body deficiencies leads. In each case his explanation involves consciousness, but not the clear and explicit consciousness proper to objectivist thinking. It is not a thinking over alternatives,

---

4. Merleau-Ponty's factual material is here drawn from the work of L'Hermitte, *L'Image de notre corps* (Paris: Nouvelle Revue Critique, 1939).

not a clear "I think that," but an inarticulate consciousness. This is, of course, the inarticulate consciousness woven into our inherence in the world, that fundamental attunement to things that is our existence as being-in-the-world. The refusal phenomena open the way for Merleau-Ponty to project the characters of this inherence:

> What it is in us which refuses mutilation and disablement is an I committed to a certain physical and inter-human world, who continues to tend towards his world despite handicaps and amputations and who, to this extent, does not recognize them *de facto*. . . . To have a phantom arm is to remain open to all the actions of which the arm alone is capable; it is to retain the practical field which one enjoyed before mutilation.[5]

In such a perspective the loss of a limb is not a corresponding loss of engagement. We must distinguish the actual body in which a limb is missing from a *habitual* body that maintains the "practical field" of this commitment. The concept of this habitual body resembles Merleau-Ponty's earlier notions of the idealized corporeal space and time. The distinction between actual body and habitual body can be read in the meanings of the objects with which consciousness is involved: for the actual body (possessing its limbs) these objects are *manipulatable for me* and reflect my concrete here and now being; for the amputee who cannot touch them they are manipulatable in themselves, reflecting for him a body that is general and impersonal. Merleau-Ponty refers to the habitual body as general and impersonal rather than as "idealized," and he treats this level of impersonal and generalized consciousness as the locus of our incarnation in the world.

The mute yet selective remembering that characterizes the phantom limb leads Merleau-Ponty to treat that phenomena as a kind of *repression* and then to use repression as a model for understanding the body in a non-objective way. The phantom limb is a repression because the distinctive refusal has a temporal dimension: it is a refusal of a *past* event. The repressed event is one that has refused to become fully integrated in the movement of existence. It becomes then an impersonal and quasi-autonomous style operating to structure that movement. One experience acquires some special value and threatens the value of all other experiences: one cannot "get over" an unfortunate

---

5. *Phenomenology*, pp. 81–82.

adolescent experience, for example. The non-reflective character of the repressed experience's influence is occasion to recognize the impersonal character of the time that unfolds in what is being considered our zone of incarnation in the world. Ordinarily, the movement of time allows us to focus our existence in each present, yet by its continuing onward allows us to move toward yet other presents. This is what the repressed event—loss of limb or whatever—distorts. Turning from this model to the body itself, Merleau-Ponty says that the latter is rather like an "inborn complex," crystallizing and stabilizing the movement of existence in a way comparable to that in which the repressed event does. The body, of course, is far more broadly focused: this non-objective or phenomenal body is the vehicle of the entire temporal movement.

Returning, then, to the emotional and memory dimensions of body deficiency Merleau-Ponty treats them as modalities of engagement in the world: memory is the direct opening of consciousness on the past itself, allowing us to retain the situation that occurred there; and emotion is the shattering of the objective world, the alteration of a given difficult situation in favor of another in which one can live symbolically. In this perspective the phantom limb is "quasi-present"— that is, present to a situation no longer actual, but that has become a style of existence influencing the actual present. But what place can be found for nerves and muscles—indeed, for the entire sensorimotor circuit, which is the basis of the physiological explanation—in this interpretation according to the movement of existence? According to Merleau-Ponty the stimulations in this circuit keep the absent limb in the movement, "establish and maintain its place." Why should existence be maintained by recourse to such physical apparatus? This apparatus allows us to dominate the various events of our lives, in the way in which habits allow us to manage routine demands: automatically and without having to greet each situation as new and taxing. "It is by giving up a part of his spontaneity, by becoming involved in the world by means of stable organs and pre-established circuits that man can acquire the mental and practical space which will theoretically free him from his environment and allow him to *see* it." Thus there is a freedom from milieu that results from what is stable and preestablished in the subject. This promises to balance out the conventional existentialist emphasis on spontaneity as the sole reality of freedom, an emphasis that sets freedom and stability in the most radical opposition. That relation between the physiological and psychological that at first seemed contradictory is now seen as necessary: "It is an inner necessity for the most integrated existence to provide itself with a habitual body" if it wishes both to be engaged in the world and to dominate its engagement.

CLASSICAL PSYCHOLOGY AND THE EXPERIENCE OF THE BODY

The classic psychologists recognized certain characteristics of the body that should have led them to distinguish it from objects. Merleau-Ponty says that his predecessors recognized, for example, that the body was *permanent* in a way quite different from the way in which objects in the perceptive field were permanent. The latter are *before me* and in principle are susceptible to indefinite exploration, while the body is *with me* and not accessible to such exploration. It is, we are reminded again, the point of view upon which I cannot take a point of view. The permanence of the object is reconcilable with the possibility of its disappearance from the perceptive field: it is a permanence in relation to its own profiles. But the permanence of the body is in relation to all objects. Its absence from the perceptive field and even radical variability in its perspective are unthinkable, because its invariability of perspective is the condition for things presenting themselves in perspective, and its presence is the condition for their presenting themselves at all. Thus, "if it [the body] is permanent, the permanence is absolute and is the ground for the relative permanence of disappearing objects, real objects. The presence and absence of external objects are only variations within a field of primordial presence, a perceptual domain over which my body exercises power."

Other long familiar characteristics might also have suggested, in one way or another, this body as subject. Double sensation—touching the hand that touches—indicates a rudimentary reflection in the body. The fact that the body was taken as an affective object, rather than simply a represented one like exterior objects, indicates a non-causal relation between such a sensation as pain, for example, and the body. Finally, the kinesthetic sensations that were acknowledged to give a global sense of the body manifest clearly the directness and immediacy of my relation with it.

Why, then, were all these data not exploited by classical psychology? Although present in its descriptions, why was it not included in its formulations and explanation? We saw the answer in the preceding chapter where Merleau-Ponty called the naturalism of the sciences a motivated and, in a sense, natural error: it is the nature of consciousness to lose sight of itself in favor of its objects. Classical psychology, desiring to be "scientific," moved from description to formulation by simply following this "natural" bent of consciousness. But there is an even *more* natural movement in consciousness that works to counteract this. The psychologist *is* his body and his experience, living out from within the characteristics that belong in his formulations. This doubtless accounts for the presence in his descriptions of the distinctive features of the body proper, despite their absence from his theory. Merleau-Ponty indicates that this also occasions the breakdown of objectivism among psychologists and their recognition of the fact that "to be a consciousness, or rather, to be an experience is to communicate interiorly with world, body and others, to be with them rather than beside them." He emphasizes this experience to justify in more detail his position that the body as impersonal consciousness is the source of objects.

MOTILITY AND THE SPATIALITY OF ONE'S OWN BODY

Merleau-Ponty's project of subjectivizing the body now must deal with the fact that the body has that most objective of all characteristics—deployment in space. He also needs to establish that the object's deployment in space is due to the body as subject. He argues his position here in the same pattern in which he previously discussed the relation of body with object-in-general. Just as I am not an object because I am the condition for there being objects, so also am I not *in* space because I am the source of space. We noticed in the preceding chapter that when he discussed the nature of brain function, Merleau-Ponty demonstrated that the parts of the body are not simply "outside of parts" as the traditional definition of objective space would have it but that they mutually imply each other because of their integration in a single form. Because of such a form, which Merleau-Ponty now refers to as *body image*, I have an undivided possession of the parts of my body, for this image envelops them. It is also the case, as we have seen, that the structure of the appearing object is a structure *for* consciousness. Hence the presence of this body is demanded by the objects experienced. Referring to this involvement of the body Merleau-Ponty calls it "the third term, always tacitly understood, of the figure-background structure." Thus the body enters the figure-background structure and forms a system with the world. In view of this system the spatial character of the body is called a "spatiality of situation" rather than of position:

> The word "here" applied to my body does not refer to a determinate position in relation to other positions or to external co-ordinates, but the laying down of the first co-ordinates, the anchoring of the active body in an object, the situation of the body in the face of its tasks.[6]

It is by its action and ultimately by the very movement of existence that the body enters the figure-background structure or addresses any of its tasks, and hence it is in action that its peculiar spatiality is accomplished.

Through a study of bodily action, which he calls "motility," Merleau-Ponty delineates the nature of human spatiality. In his discussion he draws heavily on data supplied by clinical psychology, particularly the classical studies of brain damage by Goldstein in association with others.[7] Schneider, Goldstein's patient, had deficiencies that made him almost completely incapable of abstract or imaginative behavior, although his ability to manage concrete situations was left intact. He could blow his nose, light a lamp, and assemble the objects that his vocational training and experience had fitted him to make. But he could not play, pretend to knock at a door, or even bend and straighten his fingers simply on request. Lying still he could not tell what part of his body was being touched by the doctor, nor could he describe the position of his limbs. He could find his nose to blow it but not to

---

6. *Ibid.,* p. 100.
7. K. Goldstein, "Über die Abhängigkeit der Bewegungen von Optischen Vorgängen," *Monatschrift für Psychiatrie und Neurologie Festschrift*, Liepmann, 1923; also "Zeigen und Greifen," *Nervenarzt*, 1931. Gelb and Goldstein, "Über den Einfluss der Vollständigen Verlustes des Optischen Vorstellungsvermögens auf das Taktile Erkennen," *Psychologische Analysen Hirnpathologischer Falle*, Gelb and Goldstein (eds.) (Leipzig: Barth, 1920). W. Benary, "Studien zur Untersuchung der Intelligenz bei einem Fall von Seelenblindheit," *Psychologische Forschung*, 1922. W. Hocheimer, "Analyse eines Seelenblinde von der Sprache aus," *Psychologische Forschung*, XVI, 1, 1932.

point to it; he could not point to his elbow, but he could slap at a mosquito as it bit him there. Apparently, then, the possession of the body and the very locatedness of its parts can vary with one's intention. The patient's body is at his disposal when his intention is direct and concrete but not when the intention is designatory or otherwise abstract. Knowledge of *place*, when it is knowledge of the location of a part of the body, is not necessarily, or even primarily, a distinct awareness of definite qualities.

> I can therefore take my place, through the medium of my body as the potential source of a certain number of familiar actions, in my environment conceived as a set of *manipulanda* and without, moreover, envisaging my body or my surroundings as objects in the Kantian sense, that is, as systems of qualities linked by some intelligible law.[8]

Again the phenomenal body, the habitual body, emerges and with it a phenomenal world. Concerning the phenomenal body Merleau-Ponty notes that "it is never our objective body that we move, but our phenomenal body." Schneider's phenomenal world, the milieu in which he operates habitually, is barren and shallow, indicating on his part a loss of the power of projecting an abstract or virtual world. While the normal person's body can be mobilized not only by the situation directly present but by the verbal, the fictitious, and even the fantastic (as when one dances or mimics), Schneider's body is shut up in the actual world of direct contact. Objects that present themselves to normal perception evoke a far greater range of reactions; they simply *say* more to the normal person than to Schneider, because the normal person overcomes the natural weight of the actual and projects a series of possibilities while Schneider cannot. His is a lack of vigor, of creativity or freedom.

> to be in possession of my body independently of any urgent task to be performed; in order to enjoy the use of it as the mood takes me, in order to describe in the air a movement formulated only verbally or in terms of moral requirements, I must reverse the natural relationship in which the body stands to its environment, and a human productive power must reveal itself through the density of being.[9]

To this phenomenological description of the Schneider case the em-

---

8. *Phenomenology*, p. 105.
9. *Ibid.*, p. 112.

piricists respond that it substitutes a description of *essence*, which is
of questionable value, for a discovery of the cause of the patient's
deficiencies. The empiricists call attention to the fact that Schneider
has substantial visual deficiencies and hold that the difference between
the abstract movement (pointing) and the concrete movement (grasping) is the difference between *vision* and *touch*: he cannot point at
a distant object simply because he cannot see it. Their case seems to
be reinforced by the fact that certain "abstract" movements become
possible to Schneider when he follows the member involved with his
eyes. In this empiricist interpretation the ability to project possibilities
for action is localized in sight, and the failure of abstract or imaginative
behavior is caused by visual deficiency. Merleau-Ponty's response to
the empiricist position is that no psychic fact is the *cause* of any other,
because psychic facts are not sufficiently isolable to be considered in
the antecedent-consequent way that causality demands. The normal
person can perform abstract movements with his eyes closed. It can
be justly said that in the normal person the response is of the entire
body, so that sight and touch are interwoven, and touch might serve
him when his eyes are shut. But if this is true, it cannot be maintained
that in Schneider's case *only* the vision has been damaged and that
touch is still normal. It would be very difficult to show this, and it
would be even more difficult to account for a case very similar to
Schneider's where the patient cannot pretend to knock on the door—
even when he sees it—if the door is out of reach. In this case one
might conclude that the deficiency is one of touch, rather than vision,
and that objects beyond the patient's immediate grasp are not tactile
for him. When he follows the member with his eyes, it is to compensate for a deficiency of touch. The decision as to which of these
explanations to choose—the phenomenological or the empiricist—has
something arbitrary about it. No experiment can locate the function
of projecting possibilities in any one sense operation because it inhabits
them all. We must therefore seek the element that is common to them.
As Merleau-Ponty describes it—and the description applies to tactile
as well as visual sensing—"It is not because [vision] is deficient that
designatory movements become impossible, but, on the contrary, because the attitude of [designation] is impossible that the visual stimuli
arouse only partial reactions."

Intellectualists would agree with Merleau-Ponty's criticism of the empiricist position but would also urge that we seek a reason for such deficiencies that would be consciousness itself—a single, symbolic consciousness, manifesting and realizing itself in various phenomena. Merleau-Ponty replies that where a single function dominates, what is common to various disturbances is effectively seen, but "the empirical variety of consciousness—morbid, primitive, childlike consciousness, consciousness of others—cannot be taken seriously." One cannot simply deal with the form that is the structure common to troubles without the content in which they are realized: "after all, Schneider's trouble was not initially metaphysical. . . . It would be . . . ridiculous to think that the shell splinter directly struck symbolic consciousness." Schneider has real difficulty seeing, and this is not simply the *consequence* of deficiencies on the level of thought any more than it is their *cause;* for these two "levels" are interwoven in the dialectical relation characteristic of the phenomenal realm, and they *can* be revealed in the description of the concrete essence of the malady. Revealing them is the task of genetic phenomenology, which finds consciousness animating a physiological order that, in turn, incarnates consciousness— that is, makes possible the latter's being-in-the-world.

Merleau-Ponty extends his description of this central process of incarnation by showing that it makes intelligible those of Schneider's disturbances that are of a more "intellectual" nature, those that interest intellectualism in particular. Schneider comprehends analogies (for example, the eye is to color as the ear is to ———— and identifies ordinary sensible objects (a fountain pen) by deliberate and laborious groping among words, strongly suggestive of the scientist's quest for a hypothesis that would unify varied data. The normal person, in contrast, seizes the analogy directly and later comprehends the terms explaining it, often only with difficulty. He grasps the meaning of the fountain pen in its appearances. For the patient, then, the sensible and the intelligible have come apart, and his move into meanings fixed in words is a detour made necessary by his failure at directly comprehending the data. If, however, one insists upon this direct involvement of consciousness and conceives its essence as spontaneity and projection into the world, how is one to account for the unity of consciousness and for those stable meanings that are at the disposal of not only intellectualist thinkers, but everyone?

Merleau-Ponty attributes the unity of consciousness to the fact that each of its modalities—sight, touch, thought, etc.—is access to the *same world*, a world that to the subject is self-evident prior to any assertion about it. As for the available significations, the stable meanings that are so much the joy of the intellectualist, these are the sedimentation of acts accomplished, a wake containing the remains of our acts of consciousness, which cling as memory and which consciousness bears with itself in its movement of existence. The stability of this acquisition by sedimentation cannot make it the equivalent of a world of fixed meanings, and it must be reconciled with the dynamic character of existence. The reconciliation lies in this: that what is acquired by sedimentation is only really acquired when it is taken up again in a new movement of consciousness, and this taking up depends upon the energy of consciousness. It is in its commitment to such a past as well as to the present and future, we should also notice, that consciousness is exposed to degeneration and illness. Merleau-Ponty has remarked that consciousness animates a habitual body, and we have seen that to have such a body is to be involved by action in a world. This places demands on consciousness to which it may not in some cases—Schneider's for example—be equal. Speaking of this patient he remarks that

> beneath the intelligence as an anonymous function or as a categorial process, a personal core has to be recognized which is the patient's being, his power of existing. It is here that the illness has its seat. . . . he is "tied" to actuality, he "lacks liberty," that concrete liberty which comprises the general power of putting oneself into a situation.[10]

Where that freedom—or power—of consciousness is available, it floods and animates the body and can even annex instruments, thereby distending the "subjective spatiality" of the body.

The body is subject, though spatial, because it is the vehicle of that concrete power and process that is consciousness. Its spatial character is itself transformed by its role: its parts are not outside of parts, but mutually imply each other; its parts are not firmly established qualities but may or may not be available, according to intention; its location is not one among many but the center in relation to every location. The body is the deployment of consciousness in time and space, its stabilization as habit, generally, and its presence to a world, or *incarnation*.

In an attempt to characterize the body more globally Merleau-Ponty

---

10. *Ibid.,* pp. 134–35.

seeks an expression that will signify it in its synthesis with consciousness. The unity of this synthesis is much too variable, subtle, and flexible to be conveyed by any classic or otherwise established formulation. Rather than offer such a formulation, Merleau-Ponty proposes an analogy with another reality whose unity is highly mysterious but nonetheless unquestionable: the work of art. His comparison emphasizes both the deploying character of the body ("In a picture or a piece of music, the idea is incommunicable by means other than the display of colors and sounds") and the nature of the entire synthesis deployed.

> A novel, picture or musical work are individuals, that is, beings in which the expression is indistinguishable from the thing expressed, their meaning, accessible only through direct contact, being radiated with no change of their temporal and spatial situation. It is in this sense that our body is comparable to a work of art. It is a focal point of living meanings, not the function of a certain number of mutually variable terms.[11]

The analogy draws, obviously, upon one's sensitivity to the unity in the work of art. This unit is no more explicitly formulable than that of the body's synthesis.

THE BODY IN ITS SEXUAL BEING

Merleau-Ponty's discussion of "The Body in its Sexual Being" begins with what its title promises: an existentialist picture of sexuality. Before this picture is completed, however, the discussion broadens to treat the general question of existence and to say more about the role of the body in relation to it. *Incarnation* is the term now constantly introduced to characterize this role. In the preceding discussion where the relation of man with nature was the issue, incarnation meant the body's being a vehicle of one's presence to things and the natural world. Where the question of sexuality brings into focus relations among persons, the body must be the vehicle of one's presence to other subjects and even the condition of their being for me. Once again, Schneider's case supplies most of the clinical data that introduces this discussion of intersubjectivity.[12]

---

11. *Ibid.*, p. 151.
12. J. Steinfelds, "Ein Beitrag zur Analyse der Sexualfunktion," *Zeitschrift für die Neurologie und Psychiatrie*, CVII, 72, 1927.

Schneider has no sexual initiative and is indifferent to normal, erotic stimulation. Describing this condition in situational terms Merleau-Ponty says that what has failed the patient is not in the order of reflex or representation but "his power of projecting before himself a sexual world, of putting himself in an erotic situation." He "no longer asks, of his environment, that mute and permanent question which constitutes normal sexuality." Normal sexuality, according to Merleau-Ponty, gives perception an erotic structure, an attunement that allows the other person to be present as sexually significant. The "presence" of the other person is established by a blind comprehension linking body with body in desire. It is evident that Schneider's sexual deficiencies are of the same intentional order as his other troubles: he is cut off from other persons just as he is from abstract or virtual being. Existential analysis comprehends this deficiency by viewing it as part of the general waning of Schneider's existence:

> We discover that sexual life is one more form of original intentionality, and also bring to view the vital origins of perception, motility and representation by basing all these "processes" on an "intentional arc" which gives way in the patient and which, in the normal subject, endows experience with its degree of vitality and fruitfulness.[13]

Once sexual problems are seen as problems of existence, Merleau-Ponty speaks again of Freud, emphasizing the affinities between their views. The real accomplishment of psychoanalysis, Merleau-Ponty maintains, is to "reintegrate sexuality into the human being." This reintegration had involved for Freud a generalizing of sexuality in view of which the sexual is no more to be identified with the genital than the sensible is to be identified with the sense organs, or the function of the brain with its topography. In this light Merleau-Ponty views the libido, for example, as "the general power, which the psychosomatic subject enjoys, of taking root in different settings, of establishing himself through different experiences, of gaining structures of conduct."

This generalizing of sexuality raises the problem of the relation between sex and existence. Will not sex cease to be sex by a sort of dissolution in the more general intentionality; and if sex does cease to be itself, how can we account for the distinctive and dramatic place it holds in our lives, its ability at times to dominate our personal

---

13. *Phenomenology*, p. 157.

existence? Or will not existence cease to be existence in order to become only sexuality, a much more explicit—and more narrow—intentionality? The pattern of the problem is familiar enough: how to maintain both the intimacy and integrity of a general function on one hand, and a particular current that it animates and that expresses on the other? Merleau-Ponty calls the relation between the terms "sex" and "existence" one of *sign* and *signification*, and also *expression* and *the expressed*.

Merleau-Ponty feels, however, that a frequent application of these terms to this problem tends to promote a false dichotomy between the aspects of man that they designate. In other words the expressed, or signification, quickly becomes *soul*, while expression or sign becomes *body* in a way that restores the classical spirit-matter conflict. Consequently, he does not simply define and apply the terms but offers an example of the kind of relation that they designate. It is, again, a clinical example: In a case described by Binswanger a young woman had lost her voice when she was forbidden to see the man she loved. Her "loss," according to Merleau-Ponty, was a refusal of intersubjectivity—that is, of existence with other persons or subjects. This refusal had become stabilized and generalized at the level of that most intersubjective dimension of her being, speech. He compares this "refusal" to the non-reflective consciousness of the amputee who "refuses" his mutilation. The refusal is not a deliberate and explicitly conscious act, although it is in some sense conscious, as is indicated by its selective focusing. The voice has been "lost" as a memory is lost (in the Freudian interpretation): it is held at a distance and must be considered refused. There is a self-deception here, of course, and one that has had its classical description in Sartre's *Being and Nothingness*[14]— not a deliberate lie in which one deceives another by concealing one's thoughts, but a "sincere" deception that profits from the impersonality that the body puts at the disposal of consciousness. This impersonality offers an escape into generality for anyone facing an intolerable situation, much as sleep is an escape from an exhausting day. The patient becomes mute in the way that one goes to sleep—not by willing it, but by slipping into a condition where the movement of existence is consigned to the physiological functioning seconded by the "anony-

---

14. We have in mind the description of bad faith, pp. 47–70.

mous alertness of the senses." As the refusal becomes a situation of fact—muteness—it points up the role of the body, which is "to ensure this metamorphosis. It transforms ideas into things, my mimicry of sleep into real sleep." It also makes it possible for me to awaken and for the patient to overcome her refusal of existence, because it continually proposes to me some intentionality that may be espoused.

> Bodily existence which runs through me, yet does so independently of me, is only the barest raw material of a genuine presence in the world. Yet at least it provides the possibility of such presence, and establishes our first consonance with the world. I may very well take myself away from the human world and set aside personal existence, but only to rediscover in my body the same power, this time unnamed, by which I am condemned to being.[15]

Serving in this way, the body at one time releases one to the human world and at another offers refuge from it. It allows for the actualization of existence, and it is this that Merleau-Ponty has in mind when he says that it *expresses* existence. What he insists upon primarily in the relation of the expression (the body) with the existence that it expresses (the sign with its signification) is the intimate union of the two: "the body is solidified or generalized existence and existence [is] a perpetual incarnation." Indeed, he defines each in terms of the other and maintains that the totality that is comprised of the two taken together is what is genuinely real, rather than either taken separately: "this incarnate significance is the central phenomenon of which body and mind, sign and significance are abstract moments."

Because it serves both one's *presence* and one's *absence* to the world the body is the sort of dimension for which the term *ambiguous* quickly suggests itself. Actually, *ambiguous* and its derivatives are important items in Merleau-Ponty's vocabulary, and one should take note of it.[16] The body is ambiguous, he says, "in the experience we have of it, and pre-eminently in sexual experience and through the fact of sexuality." In my relations with another person, for example, I may

---

15. *Phenomenology*, pp. 165–66.
16. Early works on Merleau-Ponty's work tended to seize upon this theme. Thus DeWaelhens' appraisal bears the title *Une Philosophie de l'ambiguité*. Earlier still, Fernand Alquié had commented on the same work in an article whose title was identical with DeWaelhens'. It was published in *Fontaine*, XI, 59. Eventually Merleau-Ponty grows tired of the association with ambiguity and leans away from it.

experience myself both as subject (who loves or desires) and object (ashamed before the gaze of the other). Or my value as a personal subject may be recognized by the other person in her desire, but now the other is fascinated and may not count as a subject for me. Notice that this ambiguity of the body, its simultaneously being quite different *for me* and *for another*, is a direct result of one's being among other persons. The ambiguity of the body is also a manifestation of the nature of human existence: "ambiguity is of the essence of human existence, and everything we live or think has always several meanings." It has several meanings—and this is the basic sense of the term *ambiguity* for Merleau-Ponty—because its many parts are not isolated from each other but rather permeate and interpenetrate each other. Thus sexuality surrounds one "like an atmosphere" and "diffuses" into existence so that it can be said to be "coextensive with life" where *life* obviously means existence.

It would be a mistake, then, to endow *ambiguity* with an excessively negative or irrational sense. What it conveys is not incoherence but the intimacy of the relation of one's existence with one's world and attributes. Merleau-Ponty directly associates ambiguity with dialectic and with metaphysics:

> The dialectic is not a relationship between contradictory and insepa-
> rable thoughts; it is the tending of an existence towards another
> existence which denies it, and yet without which it is not sustained.
> Metaphysics—the coming to light of something beyond nature—is not
> localized at the level of knowledge: it begins with the opening out
> upon "another," and is to be found everywhere, and already, in the
> specific development of sexuality.[17]

His definition of metaphysics is etymologically precise as well as historically relevant: the metaphysical is what is *beyond the physical*. The physical must be understood as the mechanical—nature in the objectivist sense—where parts are outside of parts. What is beyond the physical is that dimension of reality where parts diffuse among each other and where they are defined dialectically. This is not spirit but existence, human and intersubjective.

In addition to the intimacy of part with part there is a dynamism about existence that the term *ambiguity* allows for and that appears

---

17. *Phenomenology*, p. 168.

when Merleau-Ponty speaks of the indeterminateness of existence, which the notion of ambiguity implies:

> Existence is indeterminate in itself, by reason of its fundamental structure, and in so far as it is the very process whereby the hitherto meaningless takes on meaning, whereby what had merely sexual significance assumes a more general one, chance is transformed into reason; in so far as it is the taking up of a *de facto* situation. We shall give the name transcendence to this act in which existence takes up, for its own purposes, and transforms such a situation.[18]

Ambiguity is reconcilable with coherence in existence. This means that man is *not* to become fixed in a single value and that he does not have a necessary essence determining his development. But if it allows full play to the dynamic and transcendent in him, it does not deny that there are certain bases of coherence, such as involvement in a single world or the sedimentation of experience. It invites the shift in emphasis that is apparent in the remark: "Man is a historical idea, not a natural species," but the convergence of traditional themes is still quite evident in the new emphasis.

In a lengthy note on Marxism that closes the chapter he associates the economic order with the total movement of history in a manner strictly analogous with his relating of sex to existence. History itself is ambiguous—always having many meanings but never free in any of its dimensions from the presence of economic concern. The "existential conception of history" allows for the projection of ambiguity on this broad human scale and with this, the human drama and the economic drama are thinkable together and always mutually implicate each other but neither one is reducible to the other.

SPEECH AND
THE BODY AS EXPRESSION

If the description of sexuality opened up the dimension of *intersubjectivity*, the discussion of speech leads to the area of communication where intersubjectivity is most explicitly and most clearly recognized. One might expect that the "subjectifying" of the body would reach a new level of refinement here because of the refinement of the relations

---

18. *Ibid.*, p. 169.

into which it enters. However, this is not what actually occurs: there is much more incarnating of thought than idealizing of the body in these pages. This is because the formal structure of language, the seeming independence of its forms, pose a threat to the notion of existence as involvement in a world. Merleau-Ponty will again use body action—specifically, the gesture—as the model for understanding language. This will allow him not only to maintain the primacy of the incarnation, even in the case of thought, but also to propose an existential interpretation of speech difficulties. Once again it is with Schneider's problems that the discussion begins.[19]

Schneider cannot speak gratuitously any more than he can play, but he can find the words for action in a concrete situation. What he has lost is not a stock of verbal images (the empiricist interpretation) but something more general—namely, a way of using them. He has difficulty in classifying: he begins sorting ribbons according to color and then inexplicably begins to associate according to shade. Merleau-Ponty maintains, as he did in the case of Schneider's handling of analogies, that the difficulty is not the loss of certain thought categories (the intellectualist interpretation) any more than it is the loss of verbal images. Schneider's inability to classify is yet another example of the world's refusing to take shape for him. The conception of verbal behavior as a use of acquisitions of either the "image" or "thought" type overlooks the fact that there is a concrete subject speaking, that expression is essentially activity, and that, most of all, the *word* itself has *meaning.*

Merleau-Ponty turns to this concrete subject to make clear what he means when he says that the word itself has meaning. *Word* for him is a phenomenon with two primary dimensions. There is the word as institution, established both as the accumulated past in an individual's experience and as a cultural deposit. The established word is a linguistic world available to everyone. The linguistic world figures in expression in the same way that the natural world serves as background for natural perception. Second, and more important, is the *activity of expression*—i.e., speech. Here, Merleau-Ponty specifically means the expressing that formulates meaning for the first time: "that

---

19. Gelb and Goldstein, "Über Farbenamnesie," *Psychologische Forschung*, 1925; and Goldstein, "L'Analyse de l'aphasie et l'essence du langage," *Journal de Psychologie*, 1933, are the most frequently cited works.

of the child uttering its first word, of the lover revealing his feelings . . . of the writer and philosopher who re-awaken primordial experience." By comprehending the verbal behavior in terms of these structures Merleau-Ponty both institutes the genetic perspective and situates the accomplishment of verbal meaning outside the person in his relations with things and other persons.

Verbal behavior is described in relation to the one who speaks, to the things about which the word is uttered, and to the other subjects to whom it is addressed. If speech were merely the outward sign of thought already possessed, it would be very difficult to account for that quite familiar effort of a person who is trying to find the right word for his thought, a word in the absence of which the thought is neither accomplished nor possessed by the thinker. By means of the word the subject's thinking is delivered to him. The verbalizing that accomplishes thought is not superficially related to the object either. Rather, it calls the object forth from its context: "The denomination of objects does not follow upon recognition, it is itself recognition. . . . for the child, the thing is not known until it is named, the name is the essence of the thing and resides in it on the same footing as color and form." The word, then, is part of the perceiving, and the accomplishment of thinking enters into that generation of an object against its background for which the act of attention is the model.

Communication with others calls into play both dimensions of the word. Established or instituted words are available to speaker and listener, but were these the sum total of meaning, there would be no communication and nothing to communicate, for each person already *has* the words. That there is communication testifies to the fact that established words are not the sum total of meaning and also invites attention to the manner in which these words are *had* by each. Such words must be established in a way that does not interfere with the institution of further meaning among them. Merleau-Ponty avoids any version of the preservation of images or concepts and uses the notion of established linguistic world as background for verbal behavior. He says that words persist in the subject in a manner that

> is much less the representation of a former perception than a highly specific emotional essence, which is yet generalized and detached from its empirical origins. What remains to me of the word once learnt is its style as constituted by its formation and sound.[20]

20. *Phenomenology*, p. 180.

Such sedimented experience is available without representation and accessible to me like the parts of my body. Communication occurs when I play upon this verbal institution which I share with the one with whom I am speaking by means of my expressive intentions. This intention is empty in the sense that it is not committed to specific words, but organizes around itself—polarizes—available meanings, both incarnating itself in them and at the same time modifying them. The signifying intention is as close as Merleau-Ponty comes to formulating a "pure thought." Like Kantian pure form, Merleau-Ponty's "pure thought" demands incarnation but, radically unlike the Kantian version, its being is activity:

> "Pure thought" reduces itself to a certain void of consciousness, to a momentary desire. The new sense-giving intention knows itself only by donning already available meanings, the outcome of previous acts of expression. The available meanings suddenly link up in accordance with an unknown law, and once and for all a fresh cultural entity has taken on an existence. Thought and expression, then, are simultaneously constituted when our cultural store is put at the service of this unknown law, as our body suddenly lends itself to some new gesture in the formation of habits.[21]

The analogy between this description and the earlier one, which made perception the generation "without model" of meanings, is a striking indication of their belonging to the same central family of phenomena. My partner's understanding intention—his commitment to think according to me—is likewise empty, but my manipulation of the verbal deposit that we share can be taken up by him in a move that crystallizes his intention.

All of this, Merleau-Ponty feels, should be much clearer if we learn to take the word as *gesture*: "The communication or comprehension of gestures comes about through the reciprocity of my intentions and the gestures of others, of my gestures and intentions discernible in the conduct of other people. It is as if the other person's intention inhabited my body and mine his." Again the body serves as the model: just as a gesture requires physiological equipment, so does the word require a substructure of linguistic acquisitons. Just as the gesture transcends this substructure (my gesture of anger is not reducible to the position of my limbs but transforms these), so my genuine expressions transcend the

---

21. *Ibid.*, p. 183.

verbal accumulation of which they make use, referring to it as a physical gesture does to the world. Thus speech is "the surplus of our existence over natural being." Just as the gesture communicates itself directly and is read without representation or deciphering, so my spoken intention communicates itself and is read by the other person who "catches" it or takes it up. Thus the transcendence of nature is accomplished at the level of intersubjectivity and the reciprocity of consciousness, but it demands the support of nature as its condition.

If we consider the word as a gesture, we do encounter a basic and familiar difficulty. It is easy to accept the fact that emotion is directly readable in the gestures that manifest it—for example, we smile when we are happy, scowl and clench our fist when angry. But while these gestures are natural signs of emotion, the word is usually regarded as a conventional and somewhat arbitrary sign of thought. The existence of a number of languages supports this. Merleau-Ponty, however, rejects such a distinction between natural and conventional because of his conception of the interpenetration of the natural and the human. Approaching this problem also from the genetic perspective "we need, then, seek the first attempts at language in the emotional gesticulation whereby man superimposes on the given world the world according to man." Such a seeking, he feels, would take one behind conventions, mechanical laws for phonetics, and the like, to an original—if reduced—system of expression that would, for example, "make it not entirely arbitrary if we designate night by the word 'nuit,' to use 'lumière' for light." If the seeming arbitrary character of language is not really arbitrary, the "natural" character of emotion is not necessarily consistent either. We are reminded that, for example, Japanese smile in anger. Thus in this "emotional gesturing" there lies the basis for a variety of linguistic styles, a diversity of languages. This leads him to say that "behavior creates meanings . . . speech is merely one particular case of it."

Still, the word *is* an exceptional case. Unlike any other gesture it can become an established deposit shared by many through a process of sedimentation. Furthermore, in some manner or other "speech implants the idea of truth in us as the presumptive limit of its effort. It loses sight of itself as a contingent fact, and takes to resting upon itself; this is . . . what provides us with the ideal of thought without words." There is, then, a "privileged position accorded to reason." It is manifest in the fact that speech can be indefinitely reiterated, that one can speak about the word and even hope, as a philosopher, to say the word that terminates the need for future words. Reacting very briefly to this, Merleau-Ponty simply points toward a position that will restrain the privilege of the word: our ability to verbalize about verbalizing does not indicate a self-possession of consciousness by itself but a capacity for reiteration that prepares the way for the association of speech with time and an eventual explanation of its privilege by the process of accumulation through sedimentation. Whatever the privileged position of reason may be, he insists that understanding it begins with placing it among the phenomena of expression with their demand for time and space incarnation.

Psychology has been moving, Merleau-Ponty feels, in the direction of an "existential theory of aphasia . . . which treats thought and objective language as two manifestations of the fundamental activity whereby man projects himself toward a 'world.' " Cases like Schneider's elicit such interpretation and hence converge in their implied understanding of verbal expression. As we noticed earlier, the patient cannot classify effectively; he suffers from a disability due to neither the loss of verbal images nor the loss of ideas. While for the normal person, the person who can maintain a world, the ribbons of the problems show themselves to be similar—to organize themselves, so to speak—Schneider cannot animate such an organizing. Now that we have seen the role of the word in establishing figure on background ("the word *is* recognition"), we can understand Schneider's situation by noting that the word has lost for him its crystallizing power. The word is "the subject's taking up of a position in the world of his meanings." Schneider cannot take up such a position, and what is comprehensible as the "emptiness" of words for him (a reference to their content) can be associated with his inabilities in the behavioral order and especially with his general inability to project meaning. Merleau-Ponty here emphasizes again the priority of word as activity and as basically the same activity of creating meanings that he noted when describing the body.

> We must therefore recognize as an ultimate fact this open and in-
> definite power of giving significance—that is, both of apprehending
> and conveying a meaning—by which man transcends himself towards
> a new form of behavior, or towards other people, or towards his own
> thought, through his body and his speech.[22]

22. *Ibid.*, p. 194.

At the climax of his description of this operation of signification he turns to the work of the artist—of Cézanne—to exemplify the generating of meaning. In *Peau de chagrin* Balzac described a "white tablecloth, like a covering of newly fallen snow, from which rose symmetrically the plates and napkins crowned with light-coloured rolls." Of painting this, Cézanne said, "I know now that one must try to paint only 'the plates and napkins rose symmetrically,' and 'the light-coloured rolls.' If I paint 'crowned,' I am finished." But "crowned" is there; it is a meaning emerging from the operation that did not fashion it but called it forth. Searching for a word that fits this "final fact," the power of signification from which the word and all meanings emerge, Merleau-Ponty calls it a "miracle." This dramatic term underscores his determination not to attribute this power to any soul, mind, or otherwise traditionally specified entity. Usually he expresses this power in a more negative way, a way reminiscent of Sartre's style and making use of the ambiguity theme that we recently discussed. Thus we see him speak of the human transcendence of nature as accomplished by "a sort of leakage and through a genius for ambiguity which might serve to define man." At another moment he speaks of the authentic act of expression as rooted in "this ever recreated opening in the plenitude of being." Contrasting with this type of allusion we also find a rare, direct assertion of the power of signification: "productivity which is man's deepest essence and which is perhaps revealed nowhere so clearly among civilization's creations as in the creation of language itself." We are reminded again by this that the ambiguity of the body as well as that of existence itself is something positive: the variety and versatility of its being.

Chapter 3

The World as Perceived

"The cube with six equal sides is the limiting idea whereby I express the material presence of the cube which is there before my eyes, under my hands, in its perceptual self-evidence." The pursuit of the in-itself-for-me continues. Having recovered the sense of the body as incarnate presence by awakening the experience of it beneath the expressions that science has given that experience, Merleau-Ponty turns to the material presence[1] of the object and the experience of the world. This is the subject of Part II of *Phenomenology of Perception*. Near its beginning we read that "the thing, and the world, are given to me along with the parts of my body . . . in a living connection comparable, or rather identical, with that existing between the parts of my body itself. . . . The synthesis of the object is here effected, then, through the synthesis of one's own body." The body is the condition for objects, then, but what is the nature of its conditioning and of the objects that owe their meaning to it? We would expect that the phenomenal object might differ from the objectivist thing just as the phenomenal subject does from its objectivist counterpart, and this turns out to be the case. The phenomenal object is, as we shall see, less solid and blocklike. As a result it seems easier to conceive it as owing its meaning to the action of the subject. The attempt to characterize the action itself leads Merleau-Ponty to use several terms without, apparently, being quite

1. Merleau-Ponty's expression is *la présence charnelle*, which recalls Husserl's references to the "flesh and blood presence" of the thing.

satisfied with any of them. Thus in the remark quoted above he speaks of *synthesis*. At other times, when the issue is the relation with other persons, he will use the term *coexistence*, which by itself is not very suggestive of action. At still other times (and in fact most often) he will use the term *constitution* to designate the originating activity of the phenomenal subject, despite the intellectualist history of that term.

SENSE EXPERIENCE

The investigation of the perceived world and its objects begins with a discussion of sensation. This is the second explicit treatment of sensation in *Phenomenology of Perception*. The first, in the introduction, was highly schematic and primarily critical, insisting that sensation could not be comprehended in "objectivist" terms. The present discussion conducts its own criticism of these positions, but its primary purpose is positive: to fashion an intentional conception of sensation. The central theme is commitment or, more technically, intentionality. It must be made to account for—or at the very least be reconciled with—both the overall unity of sensation and the diversity of the particular senses. This one-and-many problem more than anything else helps to structure the working out of this analysis of perception. Its solution lies in seeing the synthesis of sensation as *corporeal* rather than *intellectual*. The clinical data to which he appeals are again drawn primarily from German sources with work by Goldstein and Rosenthal,[2] Werner's study of perception,[3] and Von Senden's observations of patients who were born blind but whose vision was restored.[4]

Sensation resists being resolved into the isolated sense qualities of the empiricists, not simply because its features are integrated in a gestalt, but also because each "is inserted into a certain form of behavior." The fact that color, for example, elicits a motor response is clearly observable in patients where damage to cerebellum or frontal cortex has disturbed the integration of stimuli in view of particular tasks. Habitual positions of limbs are modified, movements are smooth or jerky accord-

---

2. K. Goldstein and E. Rosenthal, "Zum Problem der Wirkung auf den Organismus," *Schweizer Archiv für Neurologie und Psychiatrie*, 1930.
3. H. Werner, "Untersuchungen über Empfindung und Empfinden," *Zeitschrift für Psychologie*, 1930.
4. M. Von Senden, *Raum und Gestaltauffassung bei Operierten Blindgeborenen vor und nach der Operation* (Leipzig: Barth, 1932).

ing to whether surroundings are either blue or green on one hand, or red or yellow on the other. The former two colors favor accuracy in pointing and, generally, adduction or movements toward the world; the latter promote inaccuracies and movements of abduction or withdrawal. This testimony of the injured is paralleled in remarks by artists like Kandinsky ("green . . . makes no demands on us and does not enjoin us to do anything") and Goethe the poet (blue seems to "yield to our gaze"). Experiments with very faint or very brief stimuli indicate that the body anticipates and amplifies stimuli in ways that vary with the "qualities." Color, like corporeal space, then, has a behavioral or motor significance. This prompts us to see it as intentional and to conceive the subject who senses as involved in color rather than simply facing it as an object. Generalizing, Merleau-Ponty speaks of the subject of sensation as "a power born into, and simultaneously with, a certain existential environment, or . . . synchronized with it . . ." and also refers to the relation between subject and object in sensation as *communion*.

This is as much a challenge to the tendency to conceive the sensing subject as self-contained mind as it is to treating the object as isolated quality. Experience supports it nonetheless. When I dwell on the blue of the sky, "I do not possess it in thought . . . . I abandon myself to it . . . . 'it thinks itself in me.'" Not only does the intentional nature of sensation stand out in this familiar example of the immersion of the subject in what he experiences, its anonymous and impersonal character also appears: "if I wanted to render precisely the perceptual experience, I ought to say that *one* perceives in me, and not that I perceive."[5] In the interest of contrast Merleau-Ponty speaks of the personal self as the subject that chooses deliberately.[6] This subject emerges from the "impersonal self" or *moi naturel*, which is my "primordial contract" with the world, to find itself already in a given situation, its powers already at work. It is, then, not the permanently established *cogito* of traditional metaphysics. The perceptual consciousness from which it emerges is both *anonymous*, as the experience just described suggests, and *partial*: the object that I perceive is *never* all

---

5. *On perçoit en moi*, which Smith translates as "one perceives in me," might also profitably be rendered "perception takes place in me."
6. "I can see because I am *sensitive* to colors, whereas personal acts create a situation: I am a mathematician because I have decided to be one." (*Phenomenology*, p. 215.)

that there is to perceive, nor is the sense by means of which I perceive it, all of myself, the perceiver. Each particular sense is a sort of specialized self, an explicit involvement in a particular object standing out against the background of my general perceptual involvement in the world that animates the particular object's general context. Speaking comprehensively of the conceptions that he is introducing here, Merleau-Ponty remarks:

> Vision is *a thought subordinated to a certain field,* and this is what is called a *sense.* When I say that I have senses and that they give me access to the world . . . , I merely express this truth which forces itself upon reflection taken as a whole: that I am able, being connatural with the world, to discover a sense in certain aspects of being without having myself endowed them with it through any constituting operation.[7]

The "constituting operation" that he rejects is quite evidently the intellectualist type, rooted in creative spirit. But his discussion of the matter takes the form of a dialogue with intellectualism because the positions have certain crucial themes in common. Each argues for the unity of the senses partly because it holds all senses to be spatial in character. Merleau-Ponty's previous association of the spatial character of the body with its motility—that is, its very act of acceding to a world, justifies this on his part. The Kantian style of intellectualism, on the other hand, takes all sensation to be spatial because space is an a priori form of sensibility, a structure of consciousness. But this view is vulnerable because it separates the unity of the senses as an a priori structure from their diversity, which would be factual or a posteriori. Merleau-Ponty asks what is the source of such notions as a pure and independent consciousness (the a priori structure) and of an integral system of truth possessed by it. Such notions must themselves be justified by a review of their genealogy, and this is the task of a phenomenological reflection that would grasp them as they take shape from the "primordial layer at which both ideas and things come into being": experience conceived as actual engagement. But to take this experience as the source of knowledge is to make of it a new and more basic a priori. Both the unity of sensation and its diversity are to be discovered there, where they are likely to stand on a more equal footing and therefore be more easily reconciled with each other than are the distinct Kantian levels.

---

7. *Ibid.,* p. 217.

A certain fundamental unity emerges immediately: the primordial involvement of consciousness is "constitutive of a setting for co-existence, in other words, of a space." The very presence of consciousness, then, has a spatial character that is not existence *in* space but the institution of the fact of coexistence. Description must now make the diversity of senses and their interrelation in this unity comprehensible.

"The senses are distinct from each other and distinct from intellection insofar as each one of them brings with it a structure of being which can never be exactly transposed." The blind person who knows by touch the configuration of a tree and of a man is astounded, after his cataracts are removed, at the difference between them. This suggests that touch and vision embrace areas of space that are different not simply in detail but in structure. Advancing this view, Merleau-Ponty notes that there are only a few vague analogies in touch for the illumination-illuminated structure of sight, for example. And the far more narrow range of touch means that time enters its structure differently from the way it enters vision. Because of the scope of the latter, the parts of the object seen are simultaneous—that is, each is present to the others, but the parts of what is touched are not. This diversity of structures is, in turn, quite different from the multiplicity of sense qualities that appears when I cease to actually perceive and take up an analytic attitude toward what offers itself to consciousness. This is intellection, and the rupture of the perceptual field into qualities that it causes has an irrevocable character about it, since these qualities cannot be synthesized to restore the original unity of perception.

But experience, which leads to the distinction of the senses, also leads again to their unity by revealing that they interpenetrate. It has been known for some time that subjects under the drug *mescaline* hear colors and feel sounds, but one need not appeal to the narcotic experience to find the intercommunication of the senses. It is present in ordinary experience where we *see* the rigidity and fragility of glass when we look at it and *hear* it when it breaks; when we feel the elasticity of steel and see the fluidity of water and the weight of the brass half sunk into the sand. The sensible features of the thing find in it a dimension of intercommunication and in return deliver its inner structure directly: "each one in its particular essence being a manner of modulating the thing, they all communicate through their significant core." Thus the unity of sensing is accomplished in the particular perceived object   a particular unity that diversifies the unity of the world in which I am generally engaged, as a figure perceived diversifies the unity of the background against which it is seen, transforming its homogeneity into structure.

Understanding this, like understanding the activity of attention of which he spoke in the introduction, is a matter of taking the perceptual synthesis as something accomplished by the body rather than by thought. The model of corporeal synthesis that he offers now is that of the converging of the eyes in the vision of a particular object. More explicitly, he speaks of the movement from double vision to focused vision in the fixing of an object by sight. The unity accomplished when the eyes converge is not a matter of thinking the similarity of the two images, because their merging can lag behind one's recognizing them as identical. But permanent neurological apparatus cannot account for it either because the unity is sometimes lacking. Merleau-Ponty says the double vision that precedes focusing is sensed as disequilibrium and that this disequilibrium is, in turn, anticipation of the act that will restore equilibrium: that move that is at the same time the focusing of the eyes and the emergence of the object perceived against its background. Thus the phenomenal body's gathering itself together in a unified intentionality and the establishment of the concrete (in this case visual) presence of the object are a single action.

The intersensory object—that is, the object of several senses—is to be understood by analogy with the visual object just considered,[8] and Merleau-Ponty leads the discussion back to the sensing body as a whole. When I see or hear, I operate with my entire body (as the discussion of motility indicated) but primarily with the particular sense called upon. The figure-background scheme comes to mind with sense as figure and body as background. As for the unity and diversity of the senses, "The senses translate each other without any need of an interpreter, and are mutually comprehensible without the intervention of any idea." This points to the body as a system of intersensorial equivalences.[9] Its unity has the same kind of relation to the perceived world as a whole that

---

8. "The intersensory object is to the visual object what the visual object is to the monocular images of double vision." (*Ibid.*, pp. 233–34.)

9. Equivalence is, of course, never perfect, nor is translation complete. The senses remain distinct.

the unity of visual intentionality has with the object seen, so that the concept *body image* translates not only the unity of the body but also that of object and world. "My body is the fabric into which all objects are woven." It is that point in reality where they accomplish their meaning, where they utter themselves. The body, Merleau-Ponty says, "is that strange object which uses its own parts as a general system of symbols for the world."

It is easy enough to admit a descriptive value in taking sensation in this way, but is there any real philosophical understanding in it? Is there not a serious challenge to be faced in the charge that if one abandons pure object and pure subject he must also abandon the possibility of really *knowing* what it is that he experiences? The issue has a classic statement in Descartes' position that the *union* of body and soul (as opposed to their realities taken separately) cannot be *thought* at all but only *experienced*. Does not reflection and the transcendental attitude require that I be able to withdraw from experience into a subject that surveys experience from a position independent of it? Merleau-Ponty denies this and reiterates his confidence in the subject conceived as perceptual involvement. The synthesis described in the preceding pages is on the perceptual level. This is to say that it occurs habitually, rather than by deliberate act, and is to be attributed to the phenomenal body. The possibility of a withdrawal on the part of the reflecting consciousness can be conceived on the model of perception if one gives the temporal dimension its due recognition. When I simply fix upon an object in a perceptive field, I place in the *past* the undetermined character of the field that I sensed as disequilibrium. Since this sense of disequilibrium is also an anticipation of the equilibrium that is established when the figure emerges, my perceptual fixing also reveals a prospective or *future* dimension of consciousness. Thus the act of perception creates the distances necessary for recognition of objects *in a horizontal or temporal dimension*. For its part thought, or the act of reflection, places what it thinks about in the past and in this way sets up a distance between itself and its object in this same temporal dimension. The perceiving subject incessantly renews the focusing—that is to say, deploys the dimensions of time, from which the subject itself never completely emerges. Merleau-Ponty returns constantly to the relation of thinking and time, one of his most serious problems.

SPACE

In the previous chapter we saw that Merleau-Ponty conceived the spatial character of the body to be fundamentally intentional in nature. He saw it as a capacity to possess the world and to deploy certain relations in it. Now he examines a series of specific spatial characteristics in things—horizontal and vertical, depth, lived space—to indicate their basically intentional character. He shows them to be modulations of corporeal presence.

The treatment of horizontal and vertical takes the form of comment on G. M. Stratton's venerable experiments on vision without inversion of the retinal image[10] and also on parts of Wertheimer's experiments with the perception of movement.[11] Stratton put glasses on his subject that rectified the normal inversion of retinal images, thus inverting the surroundings as they were seen by the subject. On the first day things appeared inverted and unreal. On the second day they no longer seemed inverted, but the body did not feel "normal." During the succeeding days the body gradually came to feel "normal" in its inverted world. In Wertheimer's experiment the subject lives in surroundings that are tilted at a 45-degree angle from what is normally vertical. Here the "adjustment" takes place sooner—abruptly, in fact—and without actual motor exploration.

In an empiricist view the body as a mass of tactile sensation gradually rejoins the high-low coordinates first accomplished by vision. High and low are dictated by the positions of head and feet, respectively, and when body sensation adjusts to the reversed positions of these, then confusion disappears. But head and feet are part of the image in question; and if the variation in perception in the experiment shows anything, it indicates that no part of the content is oriented in itself and thence that no item of content can dictate the orientation of the rest. If the position of the head dictated what was "up," then the initial inversion would not be comprehensible. Of course, if empiricism is in difficulty here, intellectualism is in even more difficulty, because high and low cannot mean anything to an unlocated spirit.

But they do mean something to man in his experience. An appeal to

10. G. M. Stratton, "Some Preliminary Experiments on Vision without Inversion of the Retinal Image," *Psychological Review*, Vol. III, 1896.
11. M. Wertheimer, "Experimentelle Studien über das Sehen von Bewegung," *Zeitschrift für Psychologie*, Vol. XIII, 1912.

the phenomenal body makes this coherent. According to Merleau-Ponty the new surroundings evoke from the subject that virtual body that he requires in order to inhabit them and to perceive a given spectacle. This corporeal possession of the scene is accomplished when "between my body as the potentiality for certain movements . . . and the spectacle perceived as an invitation to the same movements . . . a pact is concluded which gives me the enjoyment of space and gives to things their direct power over my body." This pact is concluded when a maximum level of clarity in perception and effectiveness in action is attained. It is in reference to such a behavioral optimum that orientation in space—horizontal and vertical—must be understood. Why such clarity in perception and assurance in action require an oriented space is not a question that one can solve by stepping beyond space and orientation, because there is no beyond. Orientation is a feature of every perception. If we cannot go *beyond* space to understand this, then we must say that it is essential to space to have always been "already constituted." It is to be acknowledged as a feature of my pre-personal history wherein a more ancient pact was concluded between an anonymous consciousness and a world-in-general. We are led once more to "another subject beneath me, for whom a world exists before I am here, and who marks my place in it. This captive or natural spirit is my body . . . the system of anonymous 'functions' which draw every particular focus into a general project." Once again an argument that might have led to a fundamental extratemporal form (the argument that every change in orientation indicates a more basic orientation and must ultimately reach *the* most basic orientation) is led back to the temporal dimension of being and the impersonal subject identified with it.

DEPTH

Depth no less than horizontal and vertical is to be defined by "the best hold our body can take upon the world." Both empiricism and intellectualism miss its originality by reducing depth to "breadth seen from the side." This is a particularly flagrant example of the objectivist tendency to turn a dimension of existence into a relation among things, for, according to Merleau-Ponty, depth is "the most 'existential' of all dimensions because . . . it is not impressed upon the object itself, [and thus] it quite clearly belongs to the perspective and not to things."

The classic explanation of the experience of depth makes it a matter of deciphering such facts as apparent size of the object at a distance and the convergence of the eyes. But since we are not explicitly conscious of these, the deciphering notion presents difficulties. When we rethink depth as phenomena, we allow these elements to recede into their appropriately implicit state, integrated as elements in a situation to be described. When this happens—that is, when we describe this experience as it is lived—we recognize that it does not pass through a deciphering stage but goes directly to the distant object. The man at two hundred paces is not seen as smaller than he is when perceived at five paces; he is simply the same man at a greater distance, less completely articulated and occupying less space in my visual field, perhaps, but not smaller. In this experience

> Convergence, apparent size and distance are read off from each other, naturally symbolize and signify each other, are the abstract elements of a situation and are, within it, mutually synonymous, not because the subject of perception posits objective relations between them, but on the contrary because he does not posit them separately and therefore has no need to unify them expressly.[12]

Taking apparent size as example Merleau-Ponty reminds us that it has long been recognized as depending on context: the moon, for example, seems much larger near the horizon because of the proximity of other objects in its visual field. I can make "apparent size" disappear if I isolate the moon from its visual context by looking at it through a tube.

Turning to the kind of relations that exist among the elements in this visual situation, he describes them as *motives*, and in explaining what he means by motive he makes it the *situational* version of (or substitute for) causality. A motive is an antecedent to an act that operates by offering a meaning but that is effective only when taken up by the act. In an example where the act in question is a decision, "motive and decision are two elements of a situation: the former is the situation as a fact, the second the situation as undertaken." The convergence of the eyes—offered above as a model of corporeal synthesis—provides an example in which the act in question is not a decision: the convergence is a motive of my focusing on an object at a distance, while the focusing is this motive assumed and made effective.

---

12. *Phenomenology*, p. 261.

The visual situation itself must be considered as motive soliciting from the body the act that is to assume or undertake it. Those who might have been led to feel that Merleau-Ponty takes the power of the body as arbitrary and uncontrolled will be surprised at the power of solicitation that he attributes to the situation and reminded that existence is the constant taking up of a situation of fact. The demands of this orientation may be quite faint, as it is in the case of optical illusions where the figure can be taken in a variety of ways. But it can also be imperious and in fact *is* imperious in the normal visual situation: one is simply not able to take the interval between the trees along the street as figure and the trees themselves as background. Taking the example of the vision of the cube again, he becomes more precise about these demands and at the same time about the nature of depth: "the six faces and twelve lines can both co-exist and remain equal for me only if they are arranged in depth." What my glance does under this solicitation is takes as right, angles that appear as acute or obtuse. In doing so it establishes the copresence of parts in another dimension—depth—"the dimension in which things or elements of things envelop each other, whereas breadth and height are dimensions in which they are juxtaposed."

As for the relation of the experience of depth with *time*, its various elements are not atemporal, but rather simultaneous—that is, belonging to the same wave of time. Merleau-Ponty holds it to be as futile to attempt to comprehend depth in terms of two dimensions—width and height—as it is to attempt to understand the past or memory in terms of cerebral traces that exist now. We are directly present at a distance both to what we remember and to what we see from afar: in no other way can we honor their originality. This futility is compounded in the case of death with the realization that length and breadth are themselves—as we said in the preceding section—the grasp of the body upon the world.

MOVEMENT

The most familiar analysis makes movement the passage of an object through a series of positions to which it is completely indifferent. But—as Zeno accurately saw—such analysis destroys what it is supposed to understand. The object in question is not altered, and the positions are simply positions: motion evaporates before this ensemble of static factors. And yet there is motion. Experience not only demands that we acknowledge this, but it offers us the terms for a genuine comprehension of motion if we attend to it carefully. The experience of motion does not, for example, give us an identical object and a series of positions. Wertheimer's experiments with the stroboscopic effect,[13] wherein alternating lights are taken as moving, challenges the necessity of perceiving an object moved in order to perceive motion. In the more simple experiment of moving a pencil rapidly before a point of reference, the experience of motion is not an explicit acknowledgment of object or position. It is only when motion ceases that object and position emerge. This prompts some to maintain that there can be motion without anything that is moved. Merleau-Ponty rejects this, but the argument he offers seems to be simply a blunt statement of the opposite position— the one occasion that we can think of where he does this. He says in various ways that movement, whether perceived or thought, is always taken as involving something moved and simply continues, then, to hold that what is moved is not necessarily an *object* in the objectivist sense. The flying bird itself unifies its motion not as an object underlying its properties but as a style or behavior whose features mutually imply each other as do the elements in the experience of the past or of objects at a distance.

> We know of movement and a moving entity without being in any way aware of objective positions, as we know of an object at a distance and of its true size without any interpretations, and as we know every moment the place of an event in the thinkness of our past without any express recollection.[14]

Movement, in short, is pre-objective and another instance where our body is motivated to take up and complete an event. As surely as movement demands something that moves, it demands a field, and our bodies are also indispensable in the constitution of this. The familiar case wherein one fixes his gaze on the cloud and sets the steeple in motion or on the steeple and sets the cloud in motion is relevant here. We determine this relation as we did the level of orientation in horizontal and vertical, entering deeply into the organization of the "fact."

---

13. M. Wertheimer, *op. cit.*
14. *Phenomenology*, p. 275.

As was the case there, too, any given change of level is in the interest of a prior and more basic set of reference points. These are to be found in our basic power to change our field within the world as a whole, something given as impersonal subject from the beginning.

LIVED SPACE

Reflection on the experience of the spatial dimensions of perceived objects leads back to the fundamental spatial character of human existence. Spatial deployment, we have seen, is an aspect of our original fixation in the world. As such, it is subject to fluctuation according to the energy with which the total subjectivity tends toward the world. It also permeates all features of that basic fixation, as do all the fundamental dimensions of existence. This mutual intimacy now allows an enlargement of the discussion: since spatiality is characteristic of our being-in-the-world, there should be a variety of types of space according to the various modes of that commitment. Merleau-Ponty turns to a description of the space proper to night, dreams, myth, and schizophrenia—each a distinctive mode of existence—to point out the variety. He must, then, justify the originality of such modes and the nature of their synthesis in the intentional subject. He makes use of the work of Fischer, Binswanger, and Minkowski in the process.[15]

At night I live in a space without objects or distinct contours. I live it directly, without intervening distance. It presses down on me, smothering my senses. I can, however, profit somewhat from the habits of daytime behavior, which I carry with me into the night. These allow me to orient myself and thus promote my security. Such is not the case in dreams, however. Here emotions, desires, and even respiratory rhythm receive a non-objective spatializing and are deployed in an arena where rising and falling, for example, take their meanings from the sexual or biological in our existence (the mounting of desire, rise and fall in respiration, etc.). In dreams the body, relieved of the objective world that consumes its energies during waking hours, shows itself

---

15. F. Fischer, "Zeitstruktur und Schizophrenie," *Zeitschrift für Neurologie und Psychiatrie*, 1929; "Raum Zeitstruktur und Denkstorung in der Schizophrenie," *ibid.*, 1930; "Zur Klinik und Psychologie des Raumerlebens," *Schweizer Archiv für Neurologie und Psychiatrie*, 1932–33. L. Binswanger, "Traum und Existenz," *Neue Schweizer Rundschau*, 1930. E. Minkowski, *Le temps vécu* (Paris: d'Artray, 1933).

yet more distinctly as the general power of transposition by realizing the one set of behaviors or tendencies in the coordinates of another. In the case of the mythical space of the primitive, dominated by some great entity—god or domicile, for example—we have an affective space where desire clearly dominates geometry. Such, then, is *lived space*, to use Minkowski's term, and Merleau-Ponty joins Minkowski to interpret schizophrenia according to that perspective. The schizophrenic lacks that energy with which the normal person projects a world in which things are consistent. As a result, things no longer touch him "with respect" but from a distance. Some invade and obsess him while others retreat and are lost completely. His world, then—his total lived space—is shrunken and private.

The significance of this anthropological space is sometimes challenged by citing its inability to stand up before a scrutiny that demands real evidence. The dreamer, one is told, is after all dreaming. When he awakens, his fantasies are recognized as, for example, some irritation in respiratory apparatus. The mental patient may well sense a dark space (the location of threatening powers) along with the space of things, but when we attempt to learn *where* it is, it disappears. The anthropological space of our various examples is at best the residue of geometrical space and of the objective world and makes sense only in reference to the latter. Merleau-Ponty's rejoinder is to challenge the type of scrutiny involved and its conception of evidence. Such reflection is, of course, thematic—it posits an explicit object—and since the consciousness of these other spaces is non-thematic, they are simply destroyed in the attempt to convert them into objectivist terms. The objectivist approach may completely ignore experience and its facts, in which case the basis for its own evidence is banished along with myth and dream. Or it may simply level the differences among experiences (reducing all space to geometrical space, for example) in the name of the experience of some general and homogeneous fact that would be taken as *reality*, while dream and myth are taken as *appearance*. But if there is anything that phenomenological description and theorizing emphasize, it is that things as they present themselves—experience—offer no justification for such a distinction. There may well be a general fact that I experience—the world is just such a fact—but it is not a thing itself behind appearances any more than reflection can be a complete desertion of the pre-reflective consciousness that is committed to the world and that often shows itself as non-thematic (in dreams, myth, and perception).

There is variety in space—or better, a variety in conscious spatializing. But Merleau-Ponty's option is not for a totally diversified spatial consciousness—a scattering of incommunicable *cogitos*—any more than it was in the case of variety in sensation. As was the case with senses and sensation, the problem here is to establish both the unity and the diversity of experience upon our engagement in the world. The incompletely determined character of the world and the ambiguity of the subject are essential here also. The experience that gives the distinctive character of, say, myth or dream also gives us its communication with the other modes of existence. The myth hangs together and has its own meaning (otherwise it would never even raise a problem), but it is in quite evident interaction with the more "objective" realities of the life of the primitive: hunting, fishing, etc. And when the dreamer awakens, he recognizes his dream: the realms of sleep and waking communicate. All of the modalities of space communicate, because my engagement in the natural world penetrates them all. "I never wholly live in varieties of human space, but am always ultimately rooted in natural and non-human space."

This dream, this myth, even schizophrenia use the structures of being-in-the-world to form the distinct meanings that constitute their worlds. One never completely withdraws from these: however exalted and intricate one's experience of a city is, for example, it is never completely free of his perception of its stones. Love and hate may each have their own peculiar perception, but it is always organized around something seen or otherwise sensed. "My body which through my habits ensures my insertion into the human world, does so only by projecting me in the first place into a natural world which can always be discerned underlying the other, as the canvas underlies the picture." Existence, then, is spatial—that is, it attaches me to a single, natural world on which all others are raised. It is in virtue of this general attachment that I can free myself from any particular milieu to pursue another engagement.

It is quite apparent that consciousness must be understood as ambiguous, as a *cogito* living a multidimensional existence, if one is to understand the facts of myth and dream. Hence the discussion of lived space leads to the same point as the previous discussion of "objective" space.

Now Merleau-Ponty argues that philosophy, which is the very endeavor that is appraising consciousness and world, also requires that consciousness be conceived in this way. Truth, error, evidence: these are philosophical essentials. But any truth or error is an explicit assertion that, because it is explicit, must leave unsaid an indefinite number of things that condition it and that can never emerge in full evidence before a finite consciousness. Only when I refuse to make any assertion and stand mute before the world can I attain absolute evidence. If there is an assertion that would express the effective life of this consciousness of world in general, it is that "there is significance . . . , there is consciousness of something, something shows itself, there is such a thing as a phenomenon. . . . such is the true cogito." The consciousness in question is "neither the positing of oneself, nor ignorance of oneself, it is *not concealed* from itself, which means that there is nothing in it which does not in some way announce itself to it, although it does not need to know this explicitly."

But truth and error are fashioned of the meanings that emerge in this involvement (as dreams and myths are fashioned of materials from the natural world). I am capable of each, and of passing from one to another, because the life of consciousness extends beyond any of its explicit assertions, making possible the correction of error by future experience but holding every truth gained open to possible revision. The phenomenal world and this life of consciousness are rigorously contemporary. "There is a world for me because I am not unaware of myself; I am not concealed from myself because I have a world."

THE THING AND THE NATURAL WORLD

Having viewed the various spatial dimensions of the world from the position of genetic phenomenology, Merleau-Ponty now turns to the features of things that are most stable and that, consequently, pose the greatest challenge to the idea that the subject contributes to generating them. He considers, respectively, the perceptual constants in the individual object (shape, size, color), the object itself, the natural world in which the perceptual object is found, and finally hallucination, which offers the possibility of counterproof in the degeneration of the world-for-me. Experimental data on perceptual constants are drawn from the

work of Katz and Gelb.[16] With the gathering density of the object
perceived we have a further expanding in the conception of the perceiving subject.

Beginning with geometrical properties Merleau-Ponty quickly rejects
what seems to be an intellectualist version of the gestalt position. This
would make the "real" size and shape of the object perceived some
sort of constant law according to which the phenomena and the conditions of its presentation (appearance of object and distance from the
viewer, for example) vary. This view has objectivist presuppositions in
virtue of which it simply misses what should be considered the crucial
problem: it assumes the constancy of shape and size, while the real
issue for a genetic phenomenology is how a particular size or shape
takes precedence over all other apparent sizes and shapes as *the* size
and shape of the object. His response is in terms of the body's modula-
tion of the world: Again, the size and shape of the object are those
at which my experience is best articulated. At this "culminating point"
of my experience

> The thing is big if my gaze cannot fully take it in, small if it does
> so easily . . . circular if, all its sides being equally near to me, it im-
> poses no deviation upon the regular curvature of my gaze, or if those
> deviations which are imposed are attributable to the oblique presenta-
> tion, according to the knowledge of the world which is given to me
> with my body.[17]

To advance this notion of constancy as function, Merleau-Ponty
analyzes the relation of the colored object both with its illumination
and with its field. In one of Katz's experiments the light from a
source is allowed to fall on a black disk in such a manner that the
circle of its focused rays covers the surface of the disk precisely. What
appears is a whitish cone whose base is the disk. If one introduces a
piece of white paper between source and light, the scene is abruptly
transformed the disk emerges as black, the paper as white, and the
illumination as illumination. The condition for the disk's receiving or
recovering its "own" color is the sufficient articulation of the field.

16. D. Katz, "Der Aufbau der Farbwelt," *Zeitschrift für Psychologie*, 1925;
"Der Aufbau der Tastwelt," *ibid.*, 1930. A. Gelb, "Die Farbenkonstanz der
Sehdinge," *Handbuch der Normalen und Pathologischen Physiologie* (Berlin:
Springer, 1927).
17. *Phenomenology*, p. 303.

Also, if we isolate an object from the influence of the visual field—by viewing it through a screen, or as a painter does when he squints—then color changes noticeably. Here the relation of objects to illumination is made to stand out and bear unusual weight in the visual experience.[18]

Pursuing this further, Merleau-Ponty takes these three features—articulation of the field, constancy of the color of the object, and illumination—as elements of a single phenomenon whose essence is accessible to a phenomenological reading. The tendency of illumination to become lost in the interest of the objects illuminated is quite familiar: when one first enters a lighted room after having been in daylight, the illumination seems yellow or blue according to the tint of the bulb in use. But this quickly disappears and the illumination tends toward neutral. As it does, the objects in the room take on their own colors.

Illumination, then, is not an object. It is situated in the intentional dimension of the visual structure: we do not see it, but rather we see *according to it*, just as in a dialogue we think according to the words of our partner. Just as our role in the dialogue calls into play (and requires) our linguistic establishment, so does our taking up of illumination as access to the visual situation call into play our body as visual power. Color, considered as a quality of the object, is mediated by illumination. Illumination, though it may begin as colored, tends to lose its own color and as it does so to become identical with its *function* of mediating color considered as quality. In each case it sets the level or norm according to which the color of objects will be distributed; but it does so insofar as it is appreciated by my visual body, which enters into the establishing of this level as it did into the establishment of the horizontal and vertical dimensions and the phenomenon of movement. The field itself solicits my visual effort, proposing an exigent "logic" to be espoused. The perception of the light in Katz's experiment as a solid cone and the presence in it of the piece of paper are simply not visually compossible. The interplay of color, mass, and line in a painting offers another example of visual logic demanding to be seen in a certain way and even imposing on the optimum distance from which it must be

---

18. Merleau-Ponty says in passing that the understanding of constancy in terms of organization of the visual field gives a single key quite adequate for the comprehension of all of Katz's empirical laws bearing on the constancy of size. (Cf. *Phenomenology*, p. 308.)

regarded. Again, the case for interpenetration of features is made, and it is rounded out by a gesture toward its ultimate reference points: "the constancy of color is only an abstract component of the constancy of things, which in turn is grounded in primordial consciousness of the world as horizon of our experience."[19]

The tactile situation presents surprising analogies to the one just described. For one thing, there is tactile constancy: A given weight is judged the same whether lifted by hand, head, foot, or teeth. This allows the body to appear again as fundamental power of transfer and equivalence in which the unity demanded by this constancy is somehow accomplished. Actually, body movement serves touch as illumination serves vision.[20] It enters as a component into the sensation of smooth and rough, for example, characteristically modulating the exploratory touch in order to take on its identity. This is so for the richer and more complex tactile phenomena: those of two dimensions where the smooth surface of the table resists penetration; those of three dimensions, like the current of water in which we dip our hand. Like the constancy of color, size, and shape, tactile constancy is "a constancy-for-my-body, an invariant of its total behavior."

THE THING OR THE REAL

The constancy of the thing perceived is one of its more "objective" characteristics, announcing its independence of any idiosyncrasies on the subject's part, and in this way asserting a kind of self-consistency. Once it is recognized that this can be understood in terms of behavior, the stage is set for the direct attack on the issue toward which *Phenomenology* has been aiming: that of understanding the *in-itself-for-me*. Turning to this now, Merleau-Ponty gathers together the previous descriptions and many of their implications to locate the issue as clearly as possible in its final framework. The path he follows—now well worn—leads again from object-in-itself to subject-in-world to time.

His previous descriptions have shown the thing perceived to be

19. Smith's translation repeats the term *constancy* where we have used *consciousness*. Since Merleau-Ponty's term is *conscience*, the error in Smith's translation is doubtless simply a misprint.
20. This seems to conflict with his earlier remarks about the light-object illuminated structure having little in it that is analogous to touch. (Cf. *Phenomenology*, p. 224.)

"correlative to my body and, in more general terms, to my existence, of which my body is simply the stabilized structure." Its properties should be seen as its complex appeal to us and, reciprocally, our taking up of this appeal. By their mutual implication they reveal the thing's meaning as a symbolic function that links each characteristic with every other and that inhabits the object as directly as the soul does the body. The body grasps this meaning in a perceptual move that is accomplished when it reaches that point of maximum articulation toward which the tensions in the perceptual field motivate it. This grasp is a culminating point in the "primary faith which binds us to a world . . ." and that is now referred to as "natural perception."

The adjective "natural" may be surprising as a modifier for perception conceived as *originating faith,* because at the outset of Merleau-Ponty's project no term had a more uncompromisingly objectivist ring than the term *nature.* When he proposed the question that he intended to investigate—the relation of consciousness to nature—it meant "a multiplicity of events external to each other and bound together by relations of causality." This change in usage is another mark of the shift in perspective that has been in progress throughout the investigation and that has been quietly revising the use of this term, which seems to defy banishment.[21] But how is one to find in this new perspective the ground for the relief and the independence that objects seem to have? With this crucial question genetic phenomenology reaches one of its climaxes. The object itself poses it: by giving itself as *more* than the simple correlate of our body and our life, it forces the issue of the *in-itself-for-us.* Merleau-Ponty points to the object's richness and at the same time to its indifference to us that is so striking when we take up a deliberately detached attitude toward it. Indeed, it is primarily because of this indifference—"the thing holds itself aloof from us and remains self-sufficient"—that it poses the question of the in-itself-for-us. What is the all-important behavioral correlate for this? *Our loss of consciousness, or better, that self-forgetting that we saw in* The Structure of Behavior *and to which he now returns: "We lose ourselves*

---

21. In the discussion of sensation the subject at which Merleau-Ponty arrived was said to accomplish a "natural perception" with his entire body, to be involved in "natural transactions" between sight and world. There is even a "natural attitude of vision," where the expression "natural attitude," one of the classic phenomenological epithets for the objectivist approach, is applied to a lived and antepredicative grasp of meaning.

(nous nous ignorons) *in the thing, and this is precisely what makes it a thing."*[22] The self-sufficiency of the object is traced to the *finitude* of the constituting consciousness. The thing in question is described as "perfect fulness": "The thing is an entity of a kind such that the complete definition of one of its attributes demands that of the *subject* in its entirety: an entity, consequently, the significance of which is indistinguishable from its total appearance."[23] The *total appearance* would lie at the end of an infinite exploration, so that the fullness here seems quite different from the massive and blocklike resistance of the Sartrian *en soi*, which is frequently characterized as fullness in *Being and Nothingness*. What we lose ourselves in is a plenitude of meaning, always yielding to our knowledge but never exhausted. Stating this all now as a problem of demands upon the phenomenal subject, he says that

> The perceiving subject must, without relinquishing his place and his point of view, and in the opacity of sensation, reach out towards things to which he has, in advance, no key, and for which he nevertheless carries within himself the project, and open himself to an absolute Other which he is making ready in the depths of his being.[24]

We shall understand the perceiving subject's doing this only when we attach his behavior to the paradox of time three chapters hence. Meanwhile, we must remember that the object *is* object experienced, given to the subject not as a block but as a perspectival—"porous"—reality that takes shape from the world as it is experienced. In view of what has been said about the soliciting of consciousness by structure perceived, the thing must be conceived as taken up by consciousness and not thrust upon it, and its description must honor this fact. The

---

22. Curiously, this sentence, which appears on page 374 of the eighth French edition, is missing in Smith's translation, where it would have appeared on page 324.

23. Smith translates the italicized word as "subject," which Merleau-Ponty's term *sujet* certainly invites. We have the impression, however, that the term is casually used here by the latter. The context is one in which, for many lines both before and after, he has been consistently discussing the structure of the appearing object without pointed reference to the subject. The immediate context is one of a description of the reference of parts of the phenomenal object to other parts of itself. In this case we speculate that the word *sujet* really indicates subject of the attributes of the phenomenal object and might more appropriately be translated as "bearer (of those attributes)."

24. *Phenomenology*, p. 326.

thing, according to Merleau-Ponty, is "bound up with a world, the basic structures of which we carry with us, and of which it is only one of the many possible concrete forms." With this, the problem of the in-itself-for-us reaches the level of our general engagement in a natural world.

THE NATURAL WORLD

> The natural world is the horizon of all horizons, the style of all possible styles, which guarantees for my experiences a given, not a willed, unity underlying all the disruptions of my personal and historical life. Its counterpart within me is the given, general and pre-personal existence of my sensory functions in which we have discovered the definition of the body.[25]

This world is ever present, and within it unfold all the events of my life. It guarantees the compossibility and ultimate interrelatedness of my experience, for each is simply a realization of its unlimited possibilities. It has this unity to offer because it is "one being, and one only, a vast individual from which my own experiences are taken."

One can wonder, then, at the status of the particular individual in relation to the vast individual. The genetic perspective will suggest in this case that an *incompleteness* in the world is necessary if we are to conceive of the emergence of particular meanings and things within it. This *incompleteness* poses a problem in relation to our comprehension of the world quite parallel with the problem of the particular object for us, a parallel that our taking the world as *individual* allows: Must we not choose between a world that is real and complete and one that opens to indefinite development, incomplete and unreal? Not if we appeal again to consciousness conceived as ambiguous, with that ambiguity that is comprehensible when we take consciousness as temporality. "The contradiction which we find between the reality of the world and its incompleteness is the contradiction between the omnipresence of consciousness and its involvement in a field of *presence*." Thus, nothing lies beyond the "range" of my total consciousness: it is coextensive with the world (Merleau-Ponty calls it the order of coexistences as well as the order of successions) and the condition for the world's presenting itself as world.

25. *Ibid.*, p. 330.

But in its omnipresence, consciousness is not "effective" but only "intentional." A description of this consciousness converges with that of time and its dimensions: past, present, and future are such that I am directly present to each but only effectively and actually present in the *present*. My past is accessible, but primarily as habit and style that anticipate the future and according to which the future will take shape. It is in the present, apparently, where that presumption of completion that is demanded of consciousness by the object is to be found. In any event it is thanks to time that they articulate and here, if at all, that the relation *thing-world* will be comprehended.

> Things and instants can link up with each other to form a world only through the medium of that ambiguous being known as a subjectivity, and can become present to each other only from a certain point of view and in intention. . . . The alleged plenitude of the object and of the instant springs forth only in face of the imperfection of the intentional being.[26]

We have returned to the incompleteness of the subject as condition for the object.

Merleau-Ponty will discuss time directly later. Now, by way of counterproof, he offers a reading of hallucination as disintegration of time and world.

HALLUCINATION

The discussion of hallucination stands as "counterproof" because the disintegration of the world that characterizes the hallucination lays bare as its presuppositions the same perceptive foundation that emerges from the description of naive experience in the preceding sections. Merleau-Ponty also uses the discussion to give the *cogito* the kind of attention that he has just given thing and world—to give it, that is, its ultimate characterization as an element in a perceptive situation.

The "all-important point" about hallucination, he says, is that the patient himself usually distinguishes between it and perception. This happens when "real" objects, voices, and tactile impressions are arranged to the specifications of the hallucination, and it indicates that the event cannot be grasped in the empiricist terms of *content*. On the other

---

26. *Ibid.,* p. 333.

hand the hallucination does pass for fact with the patient, and so it is impossible to conceive of the consciousness involved as in full possession of itself, as the intellectualist conception might have it. "If hallucinations are to be possible, it is necessary that consciousness should, at some moment, cease to know what it is doing, otherwise it would be conscious of constituting an illusion, and would not stand by it, so there would no longer be any illusion." The return from the objective world of empiricism and intellectualism to the hallucinatory phenomena, then, is a return to the consciousness that knows without exhausting its object: to phenomenal consciousness.

Approach to the phenomena of hallucination is possible because the patient and his hallucinations appear within my own situation. My own perceived world is grasped as public—accessible to many others—and as rich in meaning, but what is striking about the world of the hallucinated patient is that it is private (he knows, for example, that others don't hear his voices) and shallow: "it lacks the fullness, the inner articulation which made the real thing reside 'in itself,' and act and exist by itself." Thus most hallucinations are of the order of waves of heat or cold, pricking sensations, sparks, lights, silhouettes, voices, etc., and even where there is more "substance" than this, what appears does so more by style than by "normal" behavior—as in a dream where persons speak without opening their mouths. Broken off from the world, then, the patient evokes a pseudo-world for which his perceptual structure serves as vehicle. Sense data and sensory fields are called into play simply to bear his intention and are diminished to the specifications of this role and his reduced energy.

If the hallucination is not something perceived, it nonetheless stands as real for the patient. In fact, it comes to occupy a place more important than the real. This in particular leads one back to existence as being-in-the-world: "this fiction can have the value of reality only because in the normal subject reality itself suffers through an analogous process." His senses and body expose him to the threat of illusion. Both hallucination and perception, then, "are modalities of one single primordial function, through which we arrange around us a setting of definite structure, through which we are enabled to place ourselves at one time fairly and squarely in the world, and at another marginally to it." For the normal person there is a basic function thanks to which perceived objects have their index of reality—the movement of existence itself. The hallucination is possible solely because the connection of appearance with total experience is only presumptive. This means that the self-possession of the *cogito*, which animates this experience—its coincidence with self—is only presumptive, a non-actual intentional presence.

THE OTHER PERSON AND THE HUMAN WORLD

Merleau-Ponty treats the question of the other person quite briefly here, and this reminds us that although the world is *social* as well as *natural*, *Phenomenology of Perception* (as well as *The Structure of Behavior*) is chiefly interested in the latter. Previous discussions of intersubjectivity—in the treatments of sexuality and communication—served primarily to point out the presence of the body in these behaviors, indicating, so to speak, the suitability of nature for its role in incarnating them. In the face of the question of the reality of the other subject, there is the attempt to show that he too is reconcilable with the primacy of perception and the declaration that the social, like the natural, need be rediscovered.

Experience raises the problem of the other person. Cultural objects, for example, testify to the humanity that has given rise to them, testify to it in its generalized form of "one." But "one" has its roots somewhere in an *I* that can be directly encountered as a *thou*. For objectivist thought this other subject would be impossible: whatever is must either be in itself and before me or for itself and consciousness. But the other subject would be before me *and* consciousness. If we put the question here in language appropriate to idealism, we would ask: how can one constitute a reality whose chief characteristic is that it constitutes reality and that would therefore have to be seen as constituting my own? But the experience that raises this problem has never endorsed the categories of objectivist thought or its posing of problems. What it offers is openness to a world, not its creative constitution, and the problem that Merleau-Ponty poses is that of coexisting with the other person rather than giving rise to him. As for its solution, perceptive presence in the world is such, he feels, that "if I experience this inhering of my conscience in its body and its world, the perception of other people and the plurality of consciousness no longer present any difficulties." What this inhering contributes is, first of all, an *impersonal* consciousness, the possibility of common ground among personal consciousnesses. Secondly, it offers perspectives that are distinct from each other but that are nonetheless not exclusive of each other and can blend. It also offers the phenomenon of *incarnation*, which invites me to hold that if the consciousness that I know in myself permeates a body that is its deployment in space and time, then the body that I perceive can be the space-time deployment of a consciousness present in it.

For me, the body of the other person is primarily his behavior. When I perceive him, I enter into a system with him and take his actions as the accomplishment of intentions with which I am intimately familiar. This is particularly the case when we dialogue "at which time there is constituted between the other person and myself a common ground; my thought and his are interwoven into a single fabric." But does this "single fabric" conception really accommodate the *thou*? Is it not more likely to simply *level* the differences between self and the other person? And doesn't the experience to which we are supposed to be appealing tend rather to restore solipsism on the lived level? What the other lives, we are reminded, I shall only appreciate. Even when I love another and am committed to great sacrifice to him, still his good has become *mine* and is pursued out of *my* spontaneity. For all the blending of perspectives, they are *mine*; for all the impersonality of prereflective consciousness, it is I who live it. The *I* still threatens the grounds of the coexistence of the other person.

We could, of course, be equal in density by regarding ourselves as constituted by God, but here our reality would be lost in favor of the one true Being, which projects us. Merleau-Ponty turns down this alternative, as well as the lived solipsism just described, with a further appeal to the experience of other persons and a gesture in the direction of understanding it: "in fact other people do exist for me." If they did not exist in some way or other, the problem of their existence would not arise, and solipsism like every other reaction to this problem would be meaningless. He likens this question to that of reflection. It too exists in some way; otherwise, there would be no problem in connection with it, and it too raises the question of the relation of consciousness with consciousness. "Solitude and communication cannot be the two horns of a dilemma, but two 'moments' of one phenomenon." This central phenomenon is that "I am given to myself" by which is meant that the subject is aware of himself as a freedom engaged in a world. It is my freedom—my transcending of every particular event—which is the condition for the other person's coexistence with me: since no experience terminates my ability for further experience, my perspectives are limitless, and the other can enter without being reduced. This possibility of the other person's presence is further protected from the objectifying power that seems so determining in Sartre's conception of interpersonal relations by carrying the description of interpersonal relations to instances that the latter does not touch. The other person is object for me and I for him only when we either are strangers or take a deliberately detached view of each other. When he speaks to me and I listen, our behaviors are woven together. We are mutually accessible, then, and our consciousnesses of each other are not simply the gazes that turn their objects to stone. When I know the other person, I am caught up in the unfolding of his freedom across an indefinitely extended future. He is not only possible, however, but inevitable in the sense that one can never completely rupture with others the bonds that are set in our pre-reflective consciousness. Even the philosopher, attempting a withdrawal into a transcendental attitude, remains committed to others: "Transcendental subjectivity is a revealed subjectivity, revealed to itself and to others, and for that reason is an intersubjectivity."

Merleau-Ponty maintains, then, that the social dimension of the world, like nature, is a fact that we live: it is already *there* when we discover it explicitly. Thus nation and class, for example, have their original reality as modes of coexistence. They solicit consciousness that normally "takes hold" in times of crisis and revolution, when the sense of social situation becomes acute. This accomplishment of class consciousness is something that characterizes quite distinctively Merleau-Ponty's thinking on the social dimension of existence. It distinguishes his Marxism, for example, from others, including official communism.

What do we find now if we summarize the discussion of the thing and the perceived world? In its "flesh and blood presence" the object is a porous figure against the background of an incomplete world. We have learned again as we first did in *The Structure of Behavior* that things belong in a context that is the world and that world is phenomenal—that is, it appears to me. Its appearing has my incarnate consciousness as its condition, and the particular thing's presence is mediated by my senses. But this does not vacate the world of its consistency. The object has its profile-object structure, and the world is always background for a thing. Each structure—profile-object and figure-background—has a power of motivation that is at times irresistible. In the capacity of these structures to solicit consciousness ever beyond itself lies the secret of their being-in-themselves for us, for this loss of consciousness in the object is an essential and key feature in the latter's phenomenal independence.

But if the conventional boundaries between thing and thing, between subject and subject, are shown to be no boundaries at all, still the consistency of each term is not obliterated. They are not dissolved into each other but rather comprehended in another way. The manner of their comprehension—in the final section of *Phenomenology of Perception*—is in their being integrated with the central paradox of a transcendental subjectivity, itself understood as time.

Chapter 4

The Cogito,
Time,
and Freedom

Merleau-Ponty promises confidently that when the themes of the final
section of *Phenomenology of Perception* have been displayed, "we shall
understand that beyond these there is nothing to understand." Earlier
he referred to this ultimate stage of phenomenology as a "second-order
reflection" (that is, a reflection on reflection), reminding us with this
expression of Marcel's—that a philosophy of subjectivity makes its most
radical step when the subject turns upon himself. He also calls this
stage the "phenomenology of phenomenology," which means that in
it philosophy is to take itself as a problem. That philosophy's taking
itself as a problem should occur as the subject turns upon himself is
certainly to be expected: a comprehensive genetic phenomenology must
include the genetic phenomenology of philosophy, which in turn requires that philosophy be pursued to its source in the philosopher.

Comparison with Descartes' classic turn toward the subject is inevitable. Descartes made his way to the *cogito* by eliminating great blocks
of reality in systematic fashion when they failed to withstand the attempt to deny their existence. He arrived quickly at that isolated *I think*,
which was both subject and object of his basic certitude, directly accessible to itself and access to all other truth. *Immanence* is its salient
feature; the *I think* implied an *I am* that was in full, clear, and distinct
possession of itself and of the ideas of everything else. It intended to
deal with the rest of reality by deduction from, or at least clarification
of, these ideas. The second-order reflection occurs much later in the

philosophizing of phenomenologists. This is because it is preceded, not by a doubt that isolates the *cogito*, but by the reduction, an extended description that sees the *cogito* necessarily implied in the appearing of everything—that is to say, in all phenomena. The reduction is a gradual sharpening of vision, an often laborious and repetitive discovery of structure. Abrupt and dramatic breakthroughs are not typical. Rather can one say that the reduction is *always* to some extent accomplished but never *completely* accomplished. The *cogito* at which it arrives is also accessible to itself and access to everything else: its awareness is intuition. But *transcendence* (reaching out to a world), rather than immanence, is the mark of this *I think*. It is not in full, clear, and distinct possession of itself, much less of the ideas of all else. It is aware of itself mutely, as it reaches out to realize itself in the world, and if it comes to know itself explicitly, it is by reading its features reflected from the world that it animates as it fulfills itself. Such is the *I think*, and if we are to understand its being—the *I am* that it implies—we face a problem whose outlines we have already seen: "Whether we are concerned with the body, the natural world, the past, birth or death, the question is always to know how I can be open to phenomena which transcend me and which nevertheless exist only to the extent that I take them up and live them." At what point do we "strike bottom" with this issue as it seems we have been assured that we shall do? "If we rediscover time beneath the subject and if we relate to the paradox of time those of the body, the world, the thing and other people, we shall understand that beyond these there is nothing to understand."

THE COGITO

The discussion begins: "I am thinking of the Cartesian *cogito*." The "I" that is thinking is not the Cartesian *cogito*. It is—according to its own account at least—the phenomenological subject, for which the Cartesian *cogito* is "a cultural being of which it is true to say that my thought strains toward it, rather than that it embraces it . . ." and that consequently poses the problems posed by any object. But the same could be said of the phenomenological *cogito* when it reflects upon itself, as it does here. The problem of consciousness as object for itself is a serious one for Merleau-Ponty, and he touches upon it in what follows. We gain a better perspective from which to anticipate these extremely important pages, however, if we recall that the Cartesian *cogito* is a philosophical alternative to phenomenological consciousness and even more if we realize that Merleau-Ponty is taking up the dialogue with Descartes again, just as he did in the final chapter of *The Structure of Behavior*. Now, as then, this dialogue perspective is of the greatest importance. If every serious discussion of subjectivity must settle accounts with the author of the *Meditations*, the task is particularly serious for a philosopher who maintains the primacy of subjectivity but in a style different from that of Descartes.

Merleau-Ponty is quite obviously preoccupied with the *Meditations* as he works to establish the transcendent *I think* in place of the immanent one and to indicate the kind of *I am* to which this move leads. As a first step in establishing this *I think*, he examines several basic types of experience, which he shows to have transcendence as their essential structure, even though certain of their features might at first be taken to indicate immanence. Some of the material in this examination (that on perception and most of that on language) is simply a restatement of what has already been said. Some is not: the remarks on love and on mathematical thinking are brief sketches of positions that we are seeing for the first time. What is really striking, however, is that these experiences—exterior perception, interior perception, mathematical thinking, and abstract thought in general—*are treated in an order that clearly parallels the progressive stages in the exercise of Descartes' methodic doubt.* It terminates in an *I think* that is involvement in a world given to it as a task of clarification and fulfillment. The questions of certitude, evidence, and truth are then raised (as they are in the *Meditations*) in order to show that the self-transcending *cogito* can support a position on each of these philosophical issues superior to that founded on immanence. This particular discussion leads again to the distinguishing of the two types of intentionality: the particular, or explicit, intentionality involved in the experience of a particular truth and the general, or operating, intentionality that is our total involvement in the world. The latter, as one would expect, dominates the *I am*. This revised *I think* reveals its being to be thus: "I am a field, an experience . . . , [a] possibility of situations."

What would have suggested immanence to Descartes or others in the first place as the defining characteristic of consciousness? Their error too must have been motivated. The oriented character of perception would suggest it and so would the "interior" character of emotion and affection. On the level of understanding, the unity of thought, manifest across a mathematical demonstration, and the seemingly eternal nature of ideas also suggest it. Even when we take *perceptual* consciousness as transcendent (to return to the first of these), it affirms the reality of an object that it does not fully grasp. But since there could scarcely be an affirmation of what is completely unknown—a movement of transcendence completely without direction—perceptual consciousness must in some fashion be oriented toward its object: "my vision of the tree as a mute *ek-stase* in an individual thing already envelops a certain thought about seeing and a certain thought about the tree." In Descartes' hands the "thought about seeing" becomes the definition of seeing, and one can be certain of the thought but not of what was seen. All of Merleau-Ponty's previous descriptive work on the experience of seeing operates against this separation of the subject of perception from its object. Now, in addition, he insists that any feasible understanding of "thought about seeing" resists it as well. If we give this expression an empirical tone, it could be taken to mean "impression of seeing." But this would point to an effective experience of the object at *some* time (if not in the present, then in the past) at which the latter would have played as important a role in seeing as the self-possession of consciousness. An idealist "thought about seeing" might really mean the constituting of what is seen, but such an act would be incomprehensible if it did not include a reference to what is constituted, and the certitude of the former would extend to the latter. In either case, then, consciousness and things hang together: "Sight is achieved and fulfills itself in the thing seen" and the *cogito* need be taken as "the deep-seated momentum of transcendence which is my very being, the simultaneous contact with my own being and with the world's being."

The careful description of "interior perception"—the experience of our psychic states—offers the opportunity to challenge the transparency of this experience and in doing so to score again against consciousness conceived as immanence. My emotional and affective states—love is the example used—are not clearly evident to me. I can *discover* that the love I have lived is false—that is, that it did not embrace the unique existence of the other in its entirety or that it did not engage me completely. I can also discover a genuine love that was "at work" in me prior to my explicit acknowledgment of it. Not that it lay buried in an unconsciousness. It was accessible to me in the way my past is at a moment when I am not remembering or like the background in a situation where I am concerned with the figure. Love, like my other conscious acts, is a movement of transcendence, a movement toward another person in which he becomes "the vehicle of my relations with the world." Like the other acts it is lived as situation prior to being conceived and is never completely conceived and fully possessed: "our contact with ourselves is necessarily achieved only in the sphere of ambiguity."

Pausing for a moment to generalize upon these examples, Merleau-Ponty asks if such a *cogito* can really play the roles demanded of it. The full accomplishment of the "I" is *presumptive*, lying at an infinite distance. My existence is an *act*, and "an act is a violent transition . . . from what I am to what I intend to be." But can I really *be* anything *now*? And must I not stand in doubt as regards my every undertaking? When he responds to his own question he situates the issue more emphatically than ever in the dimension of transcendence: "I can effect the *cogito* and be assured of genuinely willing, loving or believing provided that in the first place I actually do will, love, or believe and thus fulfill my own existence." Even doubt is referred to effective experience rather than self-possession; it must first be effective doubt, and this makes it certitude of doubting and blocks any universal corrosion. When one adopts the perspective of transcendence, doubt leads beyond itself to certitude no less than it did in Descartes' perspective of immanence.

One of the classic examples of "pure thought"—and consequently one of the preferred focal points for intellectualist thinking—is the work of the mathematician. It clearly demands and exemplifies the overcoming of the dispersion of consciousness: when I demonstrate that the angles of a triangle equal two right angles, do I not necessarily exercise a grasp of triangle that persists from the discovery of the angles to the comparison of their sum with that of two right angles? Undoubtedly I do, and the dispersion is overcome, *but,* according to Merleau-Ponty, not by a pure idea of triangle, because every such idea lives on the intuition of a concrete triangle. The clearly retrospective character of its formulation testifies to this. Rather, the unity in such a mathematical experience is intentional, lying in the gesture that projects the triangle. I generate the triangle on paper, for example, and its dimensions, like all spatial dimensions, are modulations of my corporeal presence to the world. Its sides and angles are oriented components that solicit consciousness from an initial situation (discovery of the angles) to its implication (their equivalence with two right angles). The unity through the steps of the demonstration is that of productive imagination, which makes triangle and properties appear. Like the movement of perception the movement of productive imagination is never complete, and like the latter it operates in view of a presumption of such completeness, that "presumption of a completed synthesis in terms of which we have defined the thing." This presumption plays its role in the producing of the triangle by being the consciousness of the triangle to be produced.

The unity of the *cogito* peculiar to mathematical behavior is the result of expression, then, and does not precede expression as a permanent idea finding concrete instances here and there. Merleau-Ponty sees an analogous situation in linguistic or verbal behavior, and as he discusses it he also finds the opportunity to situate more clearly the claims of ideas to an eternal existence. In the course of this discussion he also comments on the status of *clarity* in the phenomenological perceptual scheme.

"Speech is precisely that act through which [thought] immortalizes itself in truth." We have already seen him distinguish speech as *activity* from language as *cultural fact* and place the priority squarely on the first of these. It is the expressive intention that gives rise to the established vocabulary in the first place and that then uses it in the way that a painter uses colors: as a vehicle. New meanings are set by expressive intentions that transcend those already established. In actual speaking such meanings crystallize, and we understand ourselves just as in the dialogue we understand others. Self-possession and intersubjectivity— that is, unity *within* consciousness and *among* consciousnesses—are accomplished and effectively experienced, but the clarity that is part of the experience involved owes nothing to immanence—to completely accomplished meanings, that is—or to total self-possession. Thus when I say "George is dead," I know what I mean and so do those to whom I say it. The presumptions, of course, are massive, and I can lose the clarity that has been obtained if I set about analyzing what it means to be George, to be dead, and to be. But it would simply be untrue to insist on the grounds of this openness to indefinite analysis that we did not clearly know what was said in the first place. Far better to take these presumptions (as Merleau-Ponty does) to be like the background of a figure perceived—the generalized obscurity inevitable in our being exceeded by our situation—and to recognize further that this obscurity not only can be reconciled with the clarity of the particular experience, but actually is so reconciled wherever we experience something.

If the clarity in our experience does not demand that we cease to be situated, neither in fact does the seeming non-temporality of the thoughts that rise from expression. It can be taken as an aspect of time rather than as the negation of time:

> To give expression is . . . to open a whole temporal cycle in which the "acquired" thought will remain present as a dimension, without our needing henceforth to summon it up or reproduce it. What is known as the non-temporal in thought is what, having thus carried forward the past and committed the future, is presumptively of all time and is therefore anything but transcendent in relation to time. The non-temporal is the acquired.[1]

Time, then, that fleeting menace to all permanence, in fact establishes what permanence there is by giving each event an inalienable position. Once something occurs it will forever be true that it occurred, not because it becomes lodged in an eternal thought, but because my existence assumes its past and because each present opens out upon the future with due acknowledgment of its prior acquisitions. Such a comprehension of the permanence of ideas—making this permanence ultimately a function of consciousness as presence, or even better, as *present*—leads to a distinctive view of the nature of factual truths and truths of reason. Just as clarity in experience rests comfortably with obscurity, the eternal is at peace with time. It is, in fact, steeped in time, in the event that gave it its status. Hence every truth is both a truth of reason and a truth of fact. It should be clearly understood that Merleau-Ponty does not reduce either of these to the other. He is simply maintaining their *inseparability* along with their *irreducibility*. This is quite apparent as he describes the relationship along with the relation of reflection to the unreflective consciousness and that of thought to language or to perception as reciprocal on the model of Husserl's conception of *Fundierung:*

---

1. *Phenomenology*, p. 392.

the founding term, or originator—time, the unreflective, the fact, language, perception—is primary in the sense that the originated is presented as a determinate or explicit form of the originator, which prevents the latter from reabsorbing the former, and yet the originator is not primary in the empiricist sense and the originated is not simply derived, since it is through the originated that the originator is made manifest.[2]

Such is the transcendent *I think*, where "all consciousness is, to some measure, perceptual consciousness." There are particular truths just as there are other persons and just as there is a world: this is a matter of effective experience. It also means that there is evidence and certitude, but never *absolute* certitude or the absolute evidence that the latter would demand. The preceding descriptions of expression show that great areas of past and present remain obscure and implicit in every experience. This is the case when thought reflects upon itself as well as in other experiences: thought has its own history, and in turning upon it consciousness does not disperse all obscurity but simply raises it to another level.[3] The existence of truths effectively for me, then, does not require the rendering explicit of these areas. Rather, there is truth for me when my consciousness comes to rest in this or that event, when it ceases to plunge questioningly into the ramifications of each. When this happens, other features of the world withdraw into a generalized background, while the truth—the event that is the "figure" against the background—emerges and allows me to begin the development of its consequences. But what dominates this conception of truth is that dimension of consciousness that assumes and bears with it the great generalized presence of the world. Merleau-Ponty speaks of it again as a primitive knowing—a primordial *I think*. "This is what calls up before us *something in general*, to which positing thought —doubt or demonstration—can subsequently relate in affirmation or denial."

Such is the transcendent "I think," and it has as its dialectical correlate "something appears to me," which is, according to Merleau-Ponty, "the only proposition which is absolutely certain."[4] Such a

2. *Ibid.*, p. 394.
3. "To think of thought is to adopt in relation to it an attitude that we have initially learned in relation to 'things'; it is never to eliminate but merely to push further back the opacity that thought presents to itself." (*Ibid.*, p. 396.)
4. Speaking of this *cogito* with philosophical method in mind, he remarks that

thinking, if it excludes exhaustive truth, also excludes total falsity. It is the ultimate framework for every truth and falsity. Of course, the fact that our definitive engagement is this *general* presence to the world leaves open the question of our transcendence toward the particular things around which our individual experience is organized. Each of these things opens up the possibility for consciousness to develop explicitly the themes that it proposes, but the point is never reached where further elucidation might not overturn the particular truth as known up to then. There always remains the possibility of doubt, then, but is it not supremely difficult in any philosophical perspective to shut out the possibility of subsequently doubting any particular experience? Playing the opportunist, Merleau-Ponty reads this openness to doubt as an indication of the freedom of the *cogito*: "there is no act, no particular experience which exactly fills my consciousness and imprisons my freedom: there is no thought which abolishes the power to think."

With this attention to the freedom of the *cogito* the emphasis of the discussion shifts from the *I think* to its implied *I am*. There is nothing abrupt about the shift: a conception of the *I am* as commitment has been developing throughout the discussion of *I think* as transcendence. Now another and, so to speak, more distinctively subjective dimension of consciousness emerges: not so much its general involvement in the world but its transcendence of any particular involvements—that is, of its own particular acts or *cogitos*. There must be such a *cogito* amid the multiplicity of particular *cogitos,* for otherwise they would in no sense cohere as *mine.* In a somewhat Sartrian tone he describes this transcendence as negative: "If there must be consciousness, if something must appear to someone, it is necessary that behind all our particular thoughts there should lie a retreat of non-being, a Self [*soi*]." To extend his description of this self he turns to the relation of expression with what is expressed as it is found in language. (It is with the phenomena of language, incidentally, that he later prolongs his researches in the interest of solving the problem of reflection in a phenomenological way.) Here we have an extension of his meditation on the *Fundierung* relation. The Cartesian *cogito* that I encounter in the writings of Descartes is an expressed or verbalized *cogito*. The verbalizing process that fixes it in words tends to lose sight of itself in favor of the words that it produces. This self-effacement seems to be a consistent feature of intentional consciousness. We saw it in perception. One result of it is that the product of this verbalizing fails to acknowledge its roots in a particular subject: this is the indifference and generality of the established term. A complementary result is that the *cogito* that acts to fix itself verbally inevitably escapes in part its own conceptualizing, because it, like every action, is distinguishable from its products. Furthermore—and now from the point of view of the listener—in order to make sense out of expressions like *I think* and *I am*, I must be in contact with my own thought and being, a contact in virtue of which these terms can strike in me their familiar echo. Thus, whether we view the situation from the point of view of speaker or hearer, we necessarily discover a pre-verbal consciousness that expresses itself in words and discovers itself only in its expressions. Because it contrasts with what is actually spoken (it transcends both expression and discovery) Merleau-Ponty calls this consciousness the silent, or tacit, *cogito*. Prior to all philosophy,

> silent consciousness grasps itself only as a generalized "I think" in face of a confused world "to be thought about." Any particular seizure, even the recovery of this generalized power by philosophy, demands that the subject bring into action powers which are a closed book to him and, in particular, that he should become a speaking subject. The tacit *cogito* is a *cogito* only when it has found expression for itself.[5]

Just as silence can be considered the absence or even the negation of sound and yet is aurally of great significance, so the *cogito* that is described negatively here emerges as of central significance for all being. "What remains, on the higher side of my particular thoughts, to constitute the tacit *cogito* and the original project towards the world, and what, ultimately, am I insofar as I can catch a glimpse of myself independent of any particular act? I am a field of experience." In this *I think*, then, whose being is in a sense non-being, lies the center from which meaning is generated and comprehended. And how is its being to be comprehended? How is this particular unity and diversity to be grasped? Through a meditation on *temporality*.

---

5. *Phenomenology*, p. 404.

TEMPORALITY

"We need, therefore, to consider time in itself, and it is by following through its internal dialectic that we shall be led to revise our idea of the subject." Merleau-Ponty has previously called the self *time*. This was because it is neither idea nor thing but that peculiar balance of being and non-being whose description converges with the description of our experience of present, past, and future. Now we are to approach this convergence from the side of time, discovering that it is conceivable only in that very domain between idea and thing that is subjectivity. Subjectivity is temporality, then, and temporality is subjectivity. The first thing that this suggests, of course, is that curious multiple identity that has regularly been called *ambiguity*. The opening page of this decisive chapter seems to reiterate this theme:

> existence . . . cannot be anything—spatial, sexual, temporal—without
> being so in its entirety, without taking up and carrying forth its
> "attributes" and making them into so many dimensions of its being,
> with the result that an analysis of any one of them that is at all search-
> ing really touches upon subjectivity itself.[6]

We must ask, of course, do they concern it equivalently? Is nothing more, or at least different, *philosophically* to be expected from the analysis of time than from the analysis of space or sex? Merleau-Ponty seems to say not when he follows the remarks above with: "there are no principal and subordinate problems: all problems are concentric." But if there are no principal or subordinate problems, might we not just as effectively carry on the phenomenology of phenomenology by an analysis of spatiality? Or might we not come to understand that there is nothing further to understand when we come to attach the paradox of time to that of sexuality?[7] There has been far more reluctance to establish hierarchical structures in *Phenomenology of Perception* than there was in *The Structure of Behavior*, and this reluctance can be taken as an attempt to avoid allowing a single key

---

6. *Ibid.*, p. 410.
7. The notion of problems as concentric allows for a set (and perhaps several sets) of priorities. Thus some might be considered closer to the common center of meaning than others. It is our impression that some sense of this kind of priority must be operating, though the explicit contrast that is drawn above between *concentric* on one hand and *principal and subordinate* problems on the other seems to deny this.

function to absorb or level the rich diversity in phenomena. But it is quite impossible to accept the notion that the selection of temporality was arbitrary and that any other dimension of subjectivity would have done as well. Indeed, there seems to be a convertibility between *time* and *subject* that bears a rough analogy to the convertibility among transcendentals that allowed certain philosophical traditions to hold that one could discuss being, unity, truth, etc., adequately in terms of each other. Time will illuminate subjectivity, then, and with a special adequacy that makes it a preferred vehicle of philosophical reflection: it will not reduce the subject to anything other than itself. This is the way it should be, for the subject is expected to be self-comprehending.

The being of consciousness, which we have recently seen described as the possibility of situations, will now be treated as the present (temporal perspective) and at the same time as *presence*, the perspective of subjectivity with which it is convertible. If in the previous chapter the problems of truth and certitude were uppermost, here where the concern is over the *being* of the subject—the *I am*—the problem of unity and diversity dominates. It is because it reveals in the being-non-being of the subject a central pattern according to which the singleness and variety of consciousness is intelligible that the meditation on time is effective. Once this pattern has been revealed, the investigation of the relation of consciousness and nature is declared to be concluded.

The development of the discussion in these pages no longer owes much to the *Meditations*. It occurs according to the familiar order that we have seen in so many previous key chapters: time is not in things or in ideas, and since it is not to be found among these objects, we must return to it as phenomenon and describe it. Its description reinforces the primacy of the phenomenal. There is no time in things themselves because they are complete, while time requires incompleteness or non-being. The subject must supply this: "Past and future withdraw of their own accord from being and move over into subjectivity in search . . . of a possibility of non-being which accords with their nature." But if we should simply transport time into the subject to which it owes so much, the differentiation of past and future would be threatened from another quarter. Merleau-Ponty feels that this occurred with both Bergson and Kant. The former's conception of memory had as an essential feature the "psychological conservation" of the past. In establishing it Bergson used that argument against the physiological conservation of the past in the form of physical traces that we saw used in the introduction to *Phenomenology of Perception*: how can a trace that is *now* be the index of a past that is no longer (to say nothing of a future that is not yet)? But this argument is valid against psychological as well as physiological traces, and as a result it undermines Bergson's position too. Time, then, cannot be derived from its parts, and so must be prior to them. Merleau-Ponty speaks of this as the "ideal nature of time" in virtue of which "it ceases to be imprisoned in the present." There is a transcending of these parts, then, that is at the same time responsible for the unity among them. But the transcendent feature cannot be non-temporal or eternal. It cannot unite moments as does Kant's form of sensibility, for example, because in this case each *now* would be the equivalent of every other—something that past, present, and future certainly are not. "There can be time only if it is not completely deployed, only provided that past, present and future do not all three have their being in the same sense." The genetic description of time will verify this conception that the critique of objectivism has suggested. Merleau-Ponty bases his descriptions of time on Husserl's[8] and also alludes frequently to Heidegger's as he proceeds.[9]

His description of time, which is, incidentally, extremely dense and compact, draws particular attention to the priority of the present, to the non reflective character of time and to the directly accessible character of past and future. It is in our "field of presence" that I contact time and come to know it. Notice that even when we evoke the past we situate ourselves in it as in a present with its own dimensions of past and future. My primary experience of past and future, however, is not of these insofar as they are explicitly evoked. I can pose them as discrete entities if I wish, and I do so when I deliberately remember; but when I do this, I draw them forth from a generalized and implicit presence. My primary experience of the past is in its weighing down upon the *now*, entering and qualifying it. The future is also available in experience but not as an event. It is a *style* with its own extension in my present. I do not represent past and future, then, but rather sense

---

8. E. Husserl, *Vorlesungen zur Phänomenologie des Innern Zeitbewusztseins* and *Formale und Transcendentale Logik* supply general descriptions of structure and movement of time, which he incorporates as valid. (Cf. *Phenomenology*, pp. 416–29.)
9. Heidegger's *Sein und Zeit* provides a number of succinct characterizations of the experience of time that Merleau Ponty finds useful.

them, divine them as I do when in the present I "count on" the objects in my surroundings without explicitly acknowledging them one by one. This non-reflective presence is nonetheless *direct* accessibility. Each event enters my present to take up its unalienable position. It then recedes into the past, where it is viewed through the accumulating thickness of subsequently experienced events. These may qualify but can never sever my relation to it. This relation is maintained by the operating intentionality that has been made the primary dimension of our being-in-the-world. There is, we see again, a singleness in time despite the diversity of its parts, and this is manifested by the presence of a bit of each in every other. The synthesis accomplished is not intellectual—that much we would expect. It is a "passive synthesis" or "transitional synthesis," to use two synonymous Husserlian terms that are clarified only at the end of the discussion.

Reflecting on this description, Merleau-Ponty places time beyond the domain of objectivist being: "since in time being and passing are synonymous, by becoming past, the event does not cease." One cannot then say that the various moments *are* successively nor simply that each is and then is not. Rather, they are differentiated within a single flow that both maintains and banishes them. Considered in terms of its relation present-past, this movement can be regarded as negative, a disintegration of each present by which it becomes past. Merleau-Ponty also calls it (again in Sartrian style) "a general flight out of itself" and (in a Heideggerian mode) an "ek-stase." But this disintegration is the reverse of a maturation of the present as approaching future, and the flight is a flight *toward* as well as a flight *out of*. There is growth as well as loss in time. Gathering all this together in a more austere way and borrowing the expression from Heidegger, Merleau-Ponty says that "temporality temporalizes itself as future-which-lapses-into-the-past-by-coming-into-the-present." Time is to be self-comprehending, then, because of its convertibility with subjectivity. The synthesis so far described demands nothing beyond time: no eternal subject, for example. Indeed, the mutual implication of parts is such that the finite subject can be responsible for it. Speaking of this responsibility—and making evident as he does that the move from being to time is identical with that move from being to subject that we have seen throughout the work—Merleau-Ponty says again that past and future only exist "when a subjectivity is there to disrupt the plenitude of being in itself, to adumbrate a perspective, and introduce non-being into it." I do not observe time, then; I effectuate its passage: "Time *is* someone, . . . temporal dimensions, in so far as they perpetually overlap, bear each other out and ever confine themselves to making explicit what was implied in each, being collectively expressive of that one single explosion or thrust which is subjectivity itself."

What is the ultimate in time, then, is ultimate in subjectivity. But what is ultimate in time is the present where every event takes on a status against which nothing can later completely prevail. This is "a constituting time," always flourishing, constant without being eternal. It is, precisely, my field of actual *presence*. The ultimate in subjectivity —the being of consciousness, that point where my being and my consciousness are one—would have to be a consciousness that has no other consciousness "behind it," to which it owes its reality. In the temporal scheme this must be my presence, that present in which every event takes on its meaning, that consciousness that is the root of every other consciousness, because each of these acts of consciousness begins in my present as an event. In the past and future the transcendent *cogito* is engaged in its object directly but at a distance. In the present it *is* consciousness of its object without distance, direct engagement in which its *to be* and *to be conscious* are one.

Given this unity and the peculiar diversity previously noted, how shall we comprehensively describe the subject? Merleau-Ponty states that "we must avoid conceiving as real and distinct entities either the indivisible power, or its distinct manifestations; consciousness is neither, it is both; it is the very action of time-creation . . . a self-anticipatory movement, a flow which never leaves itself." The relation of this "indivisible power" to its manifestations is highly dynamic. It is a genuine "self-positing" of consciousness, and time in its movement toward the future is the "archetype" of this relation of consciousness to itself. In this way an interiority is opened up, a plenitude shattered, and thus does conscious subjectivity fulfill its essential role, which is "to make visible." As for the "passive synthesis" (or "transitional synthesis") Merleau-Ponty holds that it means that on one hand I do not decide the existence or flow of time: it goes on no matter what I do. On the other hand I do have some recourse in the face of it and can turn it to the realization of myself. Gathering together these perspectives of unity and spontaneity, Merleau-Ponty declares "a spontaneity 'acquired' once and for all, and which 'perpetuates itself in being in virtue of its being acquired' is nothing other than time and subjectivity."

When he has offered this description of the subject, he turns to glance back across the endeavor that has led him to it. It was, he reminds us, a matter of "gaining an understanding of the relationships between consciousness and nature." These were the words with which *The Structure of Behavior* began. Now he says of the entire project that "the whole question is ultimately one of understanding what, in ourselves and in the world, is the relation between *significance* [*sens*] and *absence of significance* [*non-sens*]." The phenomenology of perception has become a philosophy of *signification*. As for signification itself, it must be comprehended in the most active way:

> In all uses of the word *sens*, we find the same fundamental notion of a being orientated or polarized in the direction of what he is not, and thus we are always brought back to a conception of the subject as *ek-stase*, and to a relationship of active transcendence between the subject and the world.[10]

Paul Ricoeur manifests some uneasiness over this development when he says that "the existentialism of 1945 could not include the more 'objective' notions of form, structure, order (physical, vital, human) despite the efforts of the philosopher to assume the entire theory of structure in a philosophy of signification."[11] His concern is worth taking seriously. Let us consider just what the philosophy of signification has been asked to assume in *Phenomenology of Perception*. When Merleau-Ponty opened *The Structure of Behavior* by declaring his intention to explore consciousness and nature, the latter term applied to the "organic, psychological and even *social*" (italicizing ours); and when by the middle of the third chapter he had drawn attention to the importance of perceptual behavior, he asserted that the proper object of perception was "the actions of other human subjects." But *Phenomenology of Perception* has a primary focus in relation to which the actions (especially the *personal* actions) of other human subjects are quite peripheral. It seeks "the origin of the object at the very centre of our experience . . . ," the *in-itself-for-us*. That the object takes its origin

---

10. *Phenomenology*, p. 430.
11. Paul Ricoeur, "Le Philosophe foudroyé," *Christianisme Sociale* (May–June, 1961), p. 394.

at a level of experience distinguishable from the human level is evident in the distinction between "a given world" and a "world according to man," which is superimposed on the former; and also in the polarity of nature and personal life: "just as nature finds its way to the core of my personal life . . . so behavior patterns settle into that nature, being deposited in the form of a cultural world." As for the world of man, "we must re-discover, after the natural world, the social world . . . as a permanent field or dimension of existence."[12]

It does seem legitimate, then, to speak of *Phenomenology of Perception* as limiting in some ways the perspectives opened in *The Structure of Behavior*. It might be said that there are moments when he treats perception in an all-embracing fashion. When he says, "that is perceived which is part of my environment, and my environment includes 'everything of which the existence or non-existence, the nature or modification counts in practice for me,' "[13] he seems to mean that perception must be taken to include what is human as well as nature in the traditional sense. But it is noticeable that the discussions of the human in *Phenomenology of Perception*—for example, the discussions of sex, of speech, and of the other person—are *not* really full-blown phenomenologies of personal encounter but tend rather to show that the personal and otherwise human dimensions of our experience are reconcilable with the conception of incarnation developed *apropos* of the relations of body and nature or, at most, that they profit from the analogy developed in reflecting on incarnation in a natural world by means of a body. When he says in conclusion that "what is true, taking one thing with another, is that there is a nature, not that of the sciences, but that which perception reveals to me . . . ," *nature* must be taken primarily as the matrix of *things*, and perception seen in relation to the in-itself-for-me and not primarily to for-itself-for-me—that is, not to the *social* that was mentioned in *The Structure of Behavior*.

This narrowing of perspective makes for a sharpening of focus that produces a philosophical order in which the more manageable problem is taken first. We say this in the conviction that the problem of the

---

12. We shall, in fact, soon hear the work in *Phenomenology of Perception* termed "preliminary" in view of this further need. (Cf. "Le Primat de la perception et ses conséquences philosophiques," p. 133.)

13. Merleau-Ponty is quoting Scheler with approval at this moment. We have departed from Smith's translation of this remark.

origin of the object is less demanding on a philosophy of signification than, say, the problem of the origin of another consciousness. It should also be noted that the perspective of *Phenomenology of Perception* brings the axis of Merleau-Ponty's major work into a position where it is more comparable with classical conceptions of perception than one might have thought. However different their resolutions of the issue, the attention to the problem of the relation of consciousness and thing characterizes the first post-critical move of both Descartes and Merleau-Ponty. Finally, we should acknowledge that this emphasis, with its attendant delay of the question of the nature of the human world, does not of itself cast a shadow over the claim at the beginning of the final section that with the encounter with time and the paradoxes associated with it, we shall "understand that beyond these there is nothing to understand." This was certainly never intended to suggest that there were no more problems to solve, nor even that there would be no further dimensions of time, itself subject to discovery. It means that no other dimension of time will be *more* primary than that which is the particular subject as *Phenomenology of Perception* has described it. We should hold this in mind when reading that

> The solution of all problems of transcendence is to be sought in the thickness of the pre-objective present, in which we find our bodily being, our social being, and the pre-existence of the world, that is, the starting point of "explanations," in so far as they are legitimate—and at the same time the basis of our freedom.[14]

We must not in our concern over the fate of the human world forget that the problem of nature is also a problem of transcendence. In fact if we look back upon Ricoeur's reservations, we will notice that the structures whose fate in *Phenomenology of Perception* disturbed him were not simply those of the human world but also those of *nature*. Does not the attempt to assume the latter into a philosophy of signification soften and blur these structures to a point where they lose the consistency that the reduction originally discovered them to have? Need we not say that Merleau-Ponty has completed his discussion of nature leaving quite unresolved the most familiar problem in any philosophy of process—that of doing justice to the stability of structures at the time that one is rooting them in movement? But for one thing it would

---

14. *Phenomenology,* p. 433.

not be wise to overstate the flux character of temporality in his position. Not only do phenomenal objects stabilize by sedimentation, but the present has an enduring central position—an omni-temporality—which, if it is not outside of time, nonetheless endures through time and gives rise to it. But whatever one decides on this, it would still be inappropriate to call the discussion complete. *What we have seen of the role of speech in crystallizing perceptive structures suggests that the problem of nature will not get its final solution prior to the comprehension of the world to which the word belongs.* The discussion of *Fundierung,* and particularly its refusal to reduce the founded to its perceptual foundation or even derive it from the latter, suggests the same thing. But let us not underestimate *Phenomenology of Perception* nor the priority of incarnate existence that it establishes. This is ground that Merleau-Ponty never deserts, nor does he ever abandon its priority. This fact marks most decisively every further move and gives each of them their characteristic features. As we turn to the final chapter of *Phenomenology of Perception,* we are reminded that the *liberty* to be discussed finds its foundation there along with everything else.

FREEDOM

This final chapter is what one might expect in view of its following the one in which the investigation to which *Phenomenology of Perception* was devoted (and *The Structure of Behavior* as well) was summarized and drawn to a conclusion. It extends the conclusions somewhat and situates the position in relation to the others competing for attention at the time. The extension involves viewing freedom as presence, situation, and transcendence. We should be careful not to limit the importance of this: if one takes consciousness as transcendent —that is, as essentially movement beyond any established position toward the future, then *freedom* becomes as appropriate a way to conceive of subjectivity as was *temporality,* which answers the same description. Thus we still remain at grips with the fundamental dimensions of subjectivity and profit from a series of illuminating remarks, which the author makes possible by approaching the question from the freedom angle. Furthermore, to assert the "convertibility" of the notions of temporality and freedom is to assert in a sense that phenomenology (preoccupied with the first) and existentialism (preoccupied with the second) are convertible with each other. This does not mean that every phenomenological existentialism is convertible with every other, however. The partner in dialogue in this chapter is Sartre, whose *Being and Nothingness*, published two years earlier, promoted and made popular a conception of absolute freedom. Merleau-Ponty challenges this and its assertion of an unmediated opposition between consciousness (for-itself) and thing (in-itself). He sees this as a rationalist or Kantian strain in the thinking of the most famous of the existentialists. The tone, incidentally, is completely non-polemical. Sartre is rarely mentioned by name as his position—which everyone recognizes—is delineated. Merleau-Ponty's own option is for a conditioned (therefore not absolute) freedom as the only one that is genuinely efficacious, and he insists upon the mediation of the opposition of for-itself and in-itself by the generalized and pre-personal engagement in the world. He pursues the question of an efficacious freedom into its historical dimension, too, and uses the occasion to situate himself again briefly and roughly in relation to Marxism.

Each of us experiences himself as irreducible to any one, or combination, of his acts or qualities: I am never simply my seeing of this object, my memory of that event. Sartre takes this transcending of each and every object and event as radical indetermination on the part of consciousness: neither world nor consciousness itself can "weigh" upon it in any manner whatsoever. He even rules out susceptibility to motivation as something that would attenuate the transcendence—the freedom —which defines consciousness. As a consequence the intentional relation between consciousness and anything other than itself and also the relation between consciousness and its own dimensions of past and future must be seen as the *refusal of relation*. This is the active negating that is so much the essence of Sartrian consciousness, and it is this that divides being into two opposing realms. But if consciousness can receive no meaning from the world or itself, it is according to Sartre nonetheless the reason for whatever meaning there is in the world and in the subject. Thus, to use the frequently quoted examples from *Being and Nothingness*, the stone in my path is unclimbable only in relation to my project of climbing it; the role of waiter that I play is sustained by my playing it. This refusal by consciousness of any relation with the world to which it gives meaning and with itself is at the same time pure spontaneity forever renewing itself, and it would contradict its nature as consciousness to become in any way crystallized as acquisition. It must negate or tear itself away from the world and from its own past to which it originally gave rise. Incidentally, Sartre refers to this spontaneity as *choice*, using that term to designate a level of consciousness more fundamental than that involved in the deliberate dealings with explicit alternatives to which it is usually applied.

Merleau-Ponty sees the Sartrian giving of meaning as purely centrifugal quite as is the giving of meaning in a rationalist view. He also maintains that such freedom would be impotent and meaningless. The transcending *cogito* must have *some* foothold in the world if the meanings that it is to establish are to take hold there. In particular it must be able to *acquire* some distinctive style of operation:

> The very notion of freedom demands that our decision should plunge into the future, that something should have been *done* by it, that the subsequent instant should benefit from its predecessor and, though not necessitated, should be at least required by it . . . a decision once taken and action once begun, I must have something acquired at my disposal, I must benefit from my impetus.[15]

Freedom, in short, must be power and power must be something more than the refusal of relation, something more than the ability to slip from behind any concrete act. Choice must also be choice of *something*, and this means that there must be some preliminary acquisition in view of which it operates even if its basic operation is not deliberate.

Once he has indicated in this general way the sense of his critique of Sartrian liberty, Merleau-Ponty describes the giving of meaning in a way that reveals it to be centripetal as well as centrifugal. This description plays successively across our relations with the "outside" world, with ourselves and other persons. It accords the inevitable priority to consciousness, conceived not as explicit choice giving explicit meanings, but as non-reflective spontaneity generating general meanings. Thus, given the project of climbing, one rock is an obstacle and another a passage. What the project has done is to promote a general structure *obstacle* and *passage* in which the particular stages of the climb are organized. The *corporeal* existent, operating as a generalized and anonymous power of signification, is the source from which is established this structure: whether I intend to climb those mountains

---

15. *Ibid.,* p. 137.

or not, they are, as he said previously, large if they tend to exceed the scope of my bodily presence, small if easily contained within it. These intentions are general—both in that they outline a system for the entire world applicable to all objects and also in that they are not peculiar to me but are found in other selves. In connection with the presence of these intentions in other subjects gestalt psychology has shown that there are certain common privileged behaviors. (Recall the example of the general inability to take trees along the boulevard as background and the space between them as figure.) It is in view of this spontaneous and non-reflective projection of value that we have a world as "a collection of things which emerge from a background of formlessness by presenting themselves to our body as 'to be touched,' 'to be taken,' 'to be climbed over.' " It is this incarnate existence and giving of meaning that is the basis for all explicit and deliberate giving of meaning.

Because of the sedimentation of experiences there is also a generalizing that extends to our personal lives and takes the form there of a habitual style. Thus the way in which I have led my life will strongly influence my dealing with pain, fatigue, etc. It is not that this influence will inevitably determine me: the inferiority complex that I have nourished since childhood is subject to my freedom in that I could upset it. But it *is* a privileged attitude, and its influence is probable: I am not likely to upset it. Sartre seems to wish to deny the significance of the probable, but Merleau-Ponty takes it as a phenomenal datum that marks the privilege of a certain style of behavior.

If one approaches history according to a "genuinely existential method"—genetic phenomenology, of course—he is again led to the priority of the generalized and inarticulate project. Here Merleau-Ponty finds that the objectivist approach to class consciousness either derives it from what it conceives to be "objective" social conditions among, say, the proletariat; or, if it is idealist objectivism, makes being a proletarian the result of explicit knowledge and a decision. But objective conditions are not enough: it has often been observed that the most profound misery does not always generate a revolutionary class. Nor do the revolutions that have actually occurred seem to indicate any clear sense on the part of the revolutionaries that they are conforming to a Marxist description of proletarian, much less a deliberate decision on the part of individual revolutionaries to embrace this condition. Rather, the sociopolitical situation matures gradually as an inarticulate project moving toward a goal not clearly seen nor actually recognized. The proletariat lives its condition and its aims inarticulately before it reaches that consciousness of these that makes the class a class. Nor is this necessary consciousness itself the clear representation of its goals: that does not occur until the goals are accomplished. But the class exists as a class, and the situation can be taken as revolutionary when it is lived by many in the form of the urgent feeling that their condition must change. For the individual involved any decision to be proletarian—or bourgeois—"draws together a spontaneous meaning of my life which it may confirm or repudiate, but not annul." "My life": the situation penetrates me and the others. That it is lived by many— coexisted—implies intersubjectivity. Sartre's conception of consciousness seems to make intersubjectivity impossible, leaving each person entirely alone: the negating by consciousness of everything other than itself inevitably makes the other person an object for me and I an object for him. Consciousness *for itself* is in this case radically opposed to consciousness *for others*.

But Merleau-Ponty reminds us that the other person is a fact for me and that this means that his being for me must imply—and to some extent deliver—his being for himself. That Sartre should take the other person as object is, he feels, the result of an idealist[16] tendency to treat all consciousness on the model of intellectual knowledge, where consciousness and object always tend to separate into thought in a relation of confrontation with thing. But love and sympathies are realities: the other is never necessarily or completely object for me. That he is not as fully subject for me as I am for myself does not condemn him to complete otherness and me to complete isolation. Hence I bear the other in me on the level of primordial faith, and we never lose complete contact with it: "I must . . . in the most radical reflection, apprehend around my absolute individuality a kind of halo of generality or a kind of atmosphere of 'sociality.' " Without this the very words *bourgeois* and *proletariat* would fail to echo in me and take on their meaning.

Thus does my life have a social sense that I do not constitute. In this "halo of generality" where our existences intersect and overlap, we

---

16. Merleau-Ponty introduces his description of this part of Sartre's position with the remark: "It will perhaps be objected from the idealist side." (*Ibid.*, p. 448.)

have the spawning ground for meanings that I do not establish but that count for me: the giving of meaning that is centripetal as well as centrifugal. History, as a result, is not totally amorphous any more than was the natural world. Nor is every intervention in it arbitrary: while history does not determine my action, it offers at least one set of possibilities rather than others and solicits the individual in certain recognizable directions. The France of 1799 at the time of the ebbing of the revolution offered as one of its most definite possibilities the role of military dictator. Napoleon assumed the role and accomplished the possibility. This was a decision freely taken by an individual but supported by the structure of the situation. In Merleau-Ponty's words: "The generality of the 'role' and of the situation come to the aid of decision, and in this exchange between the situation and the person who takes it up, it is impossible to delimit the 'share contributed by the situation' and the 'share contributed by freedom.'" Involvement always, then: if I can always interrupt one particular commitment and in fact always do slip out from behind particular projects, it is in favor of yet another particular commitment arising out of a general engagement in the world. Thus we do not have Sartre's for-itself and in-itself facing each other across an abyss and the dream of a contradictory synthesis between them at an infinitely distant future. They are instead mediated at the heart of time, which is the present where "I am all that I see, I am an intersubjective field, not despite my body and historical situation, but, on the contrary, by being this body and this situation, and through them, all the rest.

This synthesis of the for-itself and the in-itself in the present is in fact the very reality of phenomena and is understandable as *temporality*, as *presence* forever renewed, rather than heroic *choice* constantly sustained. But time is a center of relationships. If the ultimate meaning of subjectivity is temporality rather than unmotivated choice, then man can be seen again as essentially relationship, rather than the denial of relationship. This is the note on which *Phenomenology of Perception* concludes. Quoting St.-Exupéry, Merleau-Ponty says that "man is but a network of relations, and these alone count for him."

Part **II**

*THE
RELATIONSHIP
OF
CONSCIOUSNESS
WITH
CONSCIOUSNESS*

THE

Chapter 5

The Primacy of
Perception and the
Problem of Truth

INTERSUBJECTIVITY AND TRUTH

An examination of the professional reaction to Merleau-Ponty's work
in the years immediately following the publication of *Phénoménologie
de la perception* leads to disappointment. Not that comment was lacking: reviews exist in fair number and are often done by persons of real
competence.[1] They tend, however, to be simply expositions of the
position, coupled with cautious attempts to situate it in relation to
familiar landmarks. At times there are suggestions, sometimes negative
though more often affirmative, about its apparent value in dealing with
a series of established philosophical problems. These are usually quite
general, however. Prior to DeWaelhens' book in 1951, itself still devoted primarily to exposition, there seems to have been very little
comment that rested on a confident grasp of the position.

Disappointment over this, however, is unjustified and quite naive.
No philosophical community, not even one as illustrious as the French,
instantly comprehends the major work thrust upon it. Rather, it divines

---

1. We have in mind such persons as Paul Guillaume, who reviewed both *The
Structure of Behavior* and *Phenomenology of Perception* together for the
Journal de Psychologie Normale et Pathologique, Volume XXXIX, 1946, pages
489–94; Simone de Beauvoir, who reviewed *Phenomenology of Perception*
briefly in *Les Temps Modernes*, Volume I, 1945, pages 363–67; Roland Caillois,
who reviewed it in *Deucalion*, Volume I, 1946, pages 125–39; and Alphonse
deWaelhens, who appraised it in *Revue Philosophique de Louvain*, Volume
XLVII, 1949, pages 366–76.

the importance of such work and then sets about a ritual of assimilation in which the repeated exposition of the position plays an essential part. It is as if one had to speak it aloud or hear it spoken to seize upon it adequately—that is, to grasp its style and its content—and it is to this that the early reviews testify more than anything else. For his part the philosopher who is suddenly taken seriously by his peers may be surprised at the apparent slowness with which they comprehend the themes he has lived with for the preceding years and surprised too at the frequency with which he is asked simply to explain himself. Yet the invitation to explain is an invitation to preside over one's own assimilation into the philosophical community. For Merleau-Ponty this is a demanding task, because his position is unusual and because *Phenomenology of Perception* is such a dense and complicated work. Explain he does, however, to some extent in every work, but especially, as we mentioned in our introduction, in his "La Metaphysique dans l'homme" published in 1947[2] and in his earlier lecture to La Société Française de la Philosophie, "Le Primat de la perception et ses conséquences philosophiques."[3] He also explains in a brief report that he gave to Martial Gueroult for incorporation into Gueroult's presentation of his (Merleau-Ponty's) candidacy for the chair of philosophy in the Collège de France. The report was published by Gueroult after Merleau-Ponty's death.[4]

Naturally, these writings are more than the simple rephrasing of what he has already said. The dialogue with his peers demanded more than this: the latter may have been groping about in his position, but their groping contained a critical dimension so that their gradual appreciation of its possibilities was accompanied by a developing sense of its problems. One problem in particular that bore upon the very legitimacy of his work as *philosophy* was raised regularly. Has not the "ek-static" conception of the relation of consciousness with itself, that conception that leads to the identification of consciousness and time, made impossible the self-possession on the part of the philosopher's consciousness that is essential if he is to generate an explicit

---

2. Compare our Chapter I, page 33. We shall cite this from the collection *Sens,* in which it is included on pages 165–96.
3. Compare our Chapter I, page 33. We shall refer to this as "Le Primat."
4. Martial Gueroult, "Un Inédit de Maurice Merleau-Ponty," *Revue de Métaphysique et Morale,* No. 4, 1962, pp. 401–09. We shall cite this simply as "Inédit."

truth fated to endure? More generally, did Merleau-Ponty not form
a conception of consciousness as he treated it in its relation with nature
that will make it difficult for him to form a tenable position on its
relation to consciousness—that is, to itself and to the consciousness of
other persons? In responding to this, he rectifies, first of all, any mis-
conception of his own estimation of what he has already accomplished.
Phenomenology of Perception, he tells the Société Française de la
Philosophie, is "preliminary, because it scarcely mentions culture and
history," and he authorizes Gueroult to tell those judging his candidacy
for the Collège de France that "we are obliged to respond to these
questions with a theory of truth, first of all, and then by a theory of
intersubjectivity."

He had linked these two issues—truth, or reflection, and intersubjectivity—in *Phenomenology of Perception* as problems that were similar
in that they involved the relation of consciousness to consciousness
and also insofar as they were integrated in the expression with which
perception culminates. Recall, in connection with the latter, that the
perceptive act was said to be complete only with the *denomination*
of what is perceived—that is, only with the use of the word. With
this, the relation of consciousness to itself and to other consciousnesses,
those relations within and among men that are congealed in language
or that pass through it, are introduced into the relation of consciousness and nature. Thus we saw the exchange with nature open out
on the social dimension of the world when we simply followed the
movement of Merleau-Ponty's treatment of perception. In "Un Inédit
de Maurice Merleau-Ponty" he said that he was working on two books
that treated the question of truth by means of an investigation of
the phenomenon of expression, particularly in language. One, *Origine
de la vérité*, was to be general; the other, *Introduction à la prose du
monde*, was to treat of literary communication. The "Inédit" is, to
our knowledge, the only place where he speaks of the latter. As for
Origine de la vérité, he also mentions this in "La Métaphysique dans
l'homme": "There would obviously be room to describe precisely the
passage from perceptive faith to explicit truth as one encounters it
on the level of language, concept and the cultural world. We intend
to do this in a work devoted to *The Origin of Truth*."

As for the theory of intersubjectivity, he makes it clear in the
"Inédit" that this will take the form, primarily, of a discussion of

history in the broadest sense, which, he makes equally clear, constitutes a single drama, though not in the sense that either intellectualism or materialism thinks. This project, which corresponds to the description of a humanist philosophy offered in his paper "Note sur Machiavel" (1949)—"a philosophy which attacks as a problem the relation of man with man and their constitution of a common situation and history . . ."—should lead him, he feels,

> to reflect finally upon that *transcendental man,* or that "natural light" common to all which emerges through the movement of history—on this Logos which assigns us the task of expressing a world which was heretofore mute,—as finally upon this Logos of the perceived world which our first researches encountered in the evidence of the thing. Here we rejoin the classic questions of metaphysics.[5]

It is not simply the inner dynamism of his own thinking, even in combination with the classic philosophical demands for total comprehension and with the exchange with his peers, that propels Merleau-Ponty toward the social. A variety of historical forces, he feels, is promoting the emergence of this dimension of being into the central position in the field of human attention. In "La Métaphysique dans l'homme" he interprets the development of the sciences of man in this way. Language study, sociology, and history are, like psychology, becoming "metaphysical or transnatural." In each the objectivist alternatives of fact and law are being scrapped—first for a notion of *structure* and then for one of *intersubjective behavior,* the very pattern that *The Structure of Behavior* revealed in the development of psychology. Language study, he says, for example, first made room among the facts and laws of language for a *speaking subject* among speaking subjects[6]—that is, for a

> general spirit which all constitute by their life in common, that intention already deposited in the given system of language. It is preconscious, since the speaking subject espouses it prior to being aware of it and raising it to the level of use. Yet it subsists only on the condition of being . . . assumed by speaking subjects.[7]

Sociology is being forced away from Durkheim's penchant for con-

---

5. *Ibid.,* p. 408.
6. He mentions the researches of men like Ferdinand de Saussure and G. Guillaume.
7. *Sens,* p. 176.

sidering social reality as a *thing* and toward a conception of it as "intersubjectivity, the living rapport and tension between individuals."[8] History, for its part, attentive to the individual event and yet requiring universality if it is going to be a science or even a coherent discipline, joins these two in this same dimension: "We do not reach the universal in leaving our particularity, but in making it a way of reaching others in virtue of that mysterious affinity which allows situations to comprehend each other."

What Merleau-Ponty saw accomplished in the intellectual history of his time by the progress of its various disciplines, he also saw in 1945 as having been accomplished in its general consciousness by World War II. In his article "La Guerre a eu lieu"[9] he said that people had "learned to recognize between each consciousness and all the others this general milieu where they communicate and which has no name in their previous philosophies." The task of giving this milieu its name is identical to that of formulating a humanist philosophy and no less identical to that of expanding the conception of reason. In addressing it Merleau-Ponty gives the impression that he looks out upon a surprising coherence of situation and resource. The intersubjectivity theme seems to permeate every level—philosophy, history, politics, art, religion, morality—opening up all of these to the one who discovers it no matter where the discovery is made. Speaking of the coexistence mentioned above, he says that *within* it "the various ethical positions, doctrines, thoughts, and customs, laws and works and words express each other: everything signifies everything." Like the body and the gesture the historical situation is to be regarded as a system of equivalences. It is envisioned as a vast and dynamic symbolic exchange, and this is the intelligible light that Merleau-Ponty will attempt to pick out, amplify, and make explicit in his reflection. With it he expects to reach an ultimate: "There is nothing beyond this unique fulguration of existence," he says of this symbolic complexus that is human coexistence.

For all the apparent coherence of problem and resource and for all the hope that it generated, *Origine de la vérité* was never written.

---

8. Such men as Mauss and Levi-Strauss are important here.
9. M. M.-P., "La Guerre a eu lieu," *Les Temps Modernes*, Vol. I, 1945, pp. 48–66. This article is also included in *Sens*, pages 281–310, and it is from this that we shall cite it.

Neither was *Introduction à la prose du monde*, nor was any single comprehensive work devoted to a discussion of transcendental man. What is to be made of this? Was he already committed to positions that blocked his effective management of these issues? Was the involvement in *Les Temps Modernes* basically a distraction? Did his energy fail him? Not the last mentioned, certainly. This period is filled not only with a remarkable quantity of work but also with intellectual advances and the alteration of alliances that quite obviously found in him the powerful spiritual resources that they demanded. As for the work with *Les Temps Modernes* and similar efforts, it must be remembered that Merleau-Ponty was determined his conception of history should be a product of an inventory of his time. It is best to see his efforts here in this light, though they terminated in articles rather than books and were very sensitive to the immediate developments in France and in Europe at large.

As for the questions of truth and of intersubjectivity, the fact that the anticipated books were not written does not mean that the issues were not dealt with. The reflection on history and its accompanying dialogue with the Marxists fill his two works *Humanisme et terreur* and *Les Aventures de la dialectique* and parts of *Sens et non-sens* and *Signes*. As we shall see, the attention given to the nature of the human community here was most serious and highly productive. As for the question of truth, it is our impression that no other preoccupies him quite so consistently and that however much it may elude the casual reader, his discussion of it is extensive, coherent, and ingenious. We shall consider his handling of the question of truth in this chapter and the following one and the questions of history and his alliance with Sartre subsequently.

TRUTH AND THE PRIMACY OF PERCEPTION

The lecture "Le Primat de la perception et ses conséquences philosophiques" to La Société Française de Philosophie contained nothing that had not been said in *Phenomenology of Perception* or elsewhere.[10] By its emphasis, however, it directed more attention to what

---

10. Preceding his lecture, a one-page summary of his position was circulated to members; a discussion followed it. Each is published along with the lecture itself in the Society's *Bulletin* for October–December, 1947.

still needed to be done to complete his position than did his previous writings, and this suggests that Merleau-Ponty was sensitive to the questions that were developing then among those who were becoming familiar with his work. The discussion that followed the paper brought the issue of the philosophical competence of his phenomenology to the surface immediately. In what we may be justified in imagining was a dramatic moment, Emil Brehier, then dean of the French historians of philosophy, took the floor first when the lecture was finished and, after the ritual compliments, outlined in broad strokes his own reservations, which were shared by many at the time and which have been adopted by many since:

> M. Merleau-Ponty . . . inverts the ordinary meaning of what we call philosophy. Philosophy was born of difficulties with perception: it is from perception and in taking up a distance from it that philosophy first came to be. . . . Plato, everyone's ancestor, philosophized in this fashion. . . . He moved from the inadequacies of that lived perception to a conception of the intelligible world which was coherent, which satisfied reason and which supposed another faculty of knowing than perception itself. . . . You follow the opposite path, attempting to re-integrate [Platonic idealism] in perception and I think that it is this which causes your difficulties.[11]

Just what are these difficulties? Let us schematize them in the interest of the clear focus that will be needed as this discussion proceeds. As we do, they will be recognized as stemming from the classic problem of unity of consciousness: can consciousness exist in the opposed forms of sensation and philosophical reflection without splitting into perception and "another faculty of knowing"? This first version of Merleau-Ponty's problem of intersubjectivity is the question of the relation of a given consciousness to itself (one might say *intra*subjectivity, though he does not). What is at stake is the thought or, as he says, the *reflection* necessary to philosophy—his own included. But what does philosophical reflection demand that the primacy of perception might seem to refuse?

Reflection of any kind requires a paradoxical presence and absence of consciousness to itself. The *absence* is the taking up of a distance (of which Brehier spoke) in order to survey perception and the thing perceived free of the flux and indetermination of either of them. But

11. "Le Primat," p. 136.

consciousness must also be *presence* to the perceiving and, by means of it, to what is *perceived*, if it is to be relevant to things. Most scientific and everday reflection aims at the expression of what is perceived. The psychologist's reflection may also aim at expressing the perceiving, and philosophical reflection will attempt to express the perceiving, what is perceived, and itself. If reflection is to be presence to *what is perceived*, the perceiving of what is perceived must have a structure definite enough for it to be the perceiving of one thing rather than another and stable enough that it not become something radically different while reflection dwells on it. Merleau-Ponty and other phenomenologists reject the *empiricist* tendency to guarantee the structural stability and definiteness of perceiving by making it some sort of *representation* of what is perceived. They consider such a conception to be at odds with the intentional nature of consciousness, because a representation in consciousness would have more the nature of a thing than of intentionality, which is a relation. What there is of perceiving in intellectualist views may find a guarantee for its consistency in what is perceived: in an intelligible essence dominating all the profiles in the way that a geometrical law dominates its application or that Platonic types dominate their participants.

Of course, the tendency in intellectualism is to reduce perceiving to thinking. This was the case with Descartes, for whom it was the consistency of the thinking consciousness above all, which the structures in the object tended to guarantee. The particular forms that such intellectualist reflection takes are simply the expressions of the mind's grasp of the essence of the thing perceived. We should notice, of course, that consciousness need be consistent with itself on the level of thought as well as on the level of perception in order that its expressing of the perceived not cease with each passing instant to be itself. If the evident fact of communication is also to be justified, this consistency must then be extended from one knowing subject to another. The intellectualist and idealist versions of the concept have a universality and a permanence—a consistency through time and space—which makes them indifferent to time and space and to the individuality of the particular knowing experience and even of the knower.

We have seen Merleau-Ponty refuse to concede that thought is endowed with such indifference to time and space. "All consciousness is in some measure perceptual consciousness," and every consciousness should be traced back to perception as to its root. Taken literally, Merleau-Ponty's remark might allow every—or at least some—consciousness to be also to some extent other than perceptual consciousness and to emerge above its perceptual roots. But, as DeWaelhens remarks, "the fundamental thesis of the philosophy of Merleau-Ponty: that all knowledge is rooted in perception, is itself ambiguous." For it might also be the case that every consciousness is compromised, as it were, by what is unstable and inarticulate in perception and that the phenomenological reduction, which led Merleau-Ponty to perception as the origin of each conscious act, in fact "unifies" consciousness by drowning it in perceptual immediacy. There are texts in his work that invite such an interpretation, and even though they are balanced out by other statements, they have been the cause of a line of criticism and reservation that embodies and extends Brehier's contention. Thus, we read in the Preface to *Phenomenology of Perception*: "the best formulation of the reduction is probably that given by Eugen Fink ... when he spoke of 'wonder' before the world" and again "to return to things themselves is to return to that world which precedes knowledge, of which knowledge always *speaks* ... " and yet again, further along in *Phenomenology of Perception*, "the task of a radical reflection, the kind that aims at self-comprehension, consists, paradoxically enough, in recovering the unreflective experience of the world, and subsequently reassigning to it the verificatory attitude and reflective operations, and displaying reflection as one possibility of my being." In 1951 DeWaelhens concludes his exegesis by conceding that "the major difficulty with Merleau-Ponty's philosophy [is] how one can make the possibility of writing a phenomenology of perception compatible with the thesis according to which one never leaves perception." Henri Lefebvre, perhaps the leading French Marxist intellectual during the early and middle 1950's, begins his careful appraisal of Merleau-Ponty's philosophy by saying that "the question is to know if one has the right to pose the problem *philosophically* on this level ... in a word, to know if on the level of the immediate there is philosophical reflection and

---

12. Henri Lefebvre, "M. Merleau-Ponty et la philosophie de l'ambiguité," *Pensée*, No. 68 (July–Aug., 1956), p. 50.

a problem."[12] Herbert Spiegelberg, in his extensive history of the phenomenological movement, asks of Merleau-Ponty's phenomenology,
"how far does the engagement in the body and history still allow
phenomenology to look upon itself from the necessary distance?[13]
Professor E. G. Ballard, commenting in 1961 on Merleau-Ponty's conception of the task of phenomenological or existential philosophy as
that of "formulating an experience of the world which precedes all
knowledge about it," says that "such an understanding comes . . .
perilously close to the border where philosophy is no longer or is
not yet."[14]

The very least that can be said is that Merleau-Ponty recognized
this problem from the beginning. His penultimate remark in *The
Structure of Behavior* asks, "can one conceptualize perceptual consciousness without eliminating it as an original mode; can one maintain its specificity without rendering inconceivable its relation to intellectual consciousness?" He responds to his own question with a
confident *yes*, saying to La Société Française de Philosophie, for
example, that his position "destroys neither rationality nor the absolute.
It seeks to bring them down to earth." This "bringing down to earth"
is not to be a burial: the unreflective consciousness to which he returns is "the unreflective understood and conquered by reflection. Perception left to itself forgets itself and its own accomplishments. Far
from philosophy's appearing . . . as a useless reduplication of life, it
is for us that without which life might be dissipated in ignorance of
itself or chaos." The structure of consciousness is such, then, that it
not only allows a distinction between reflection and unreflective consciousness—one that can be expressed in the conventional contrast of
intellectual and *perceptual* consciousness—but also such that one can
even speak of the *conquest* of the unreflective by reflection. But perhaps this is simply an expression of confidence in his ability to solve
an issue at a future date. It is ten years after acknowledging the
problem in *The Structure of Behavior* and two years after *Phenomenology of Perception* that he speaks of his intention to write *Origine
de la vérité*, which, as we said, never appeared.

---

13. Herbert Spiegelberg, *The Phenomenological Movement*, Vol. II (The Hague:
    Nijhoff, 1960), p. 560.
14. E. G. Ballard, "On Cognition of the Pre-Cognitive," *Philosophical Quarterly*,
    July, 1961, p. 224.

ESSENCE AND THE EXPERIENCE OF TRUTH

His confidence in the order of perception seems to have remained firm, however. He said in *Phenomenology of Perception* that it would supply the sources and the criteria for solving the problem of reflection: "It is in the experience of the *thing* that the reflective ideal of positing thought will have its basis," and also "that which is called an idea . . . is a cultural object." Thus the problem is to be worked out within the order of temporality and incarnation. And, as we said, he has more to show in this matter than the promise to write a work that never in fact appeared. There is a prolonged discussion of truth scattered through his various writings, particularly those that followed *Phenomenology of Perception*. The fact that it is scattered helps account for its not receiving the attention that it merits. An even more important reason for its escaping attention, however, is the form in which the question is posed. Merleau-Ponty conducts his discussion of truth most frequently in the form of a discussion of expressive behavior in general. In these treatments analyses of *painting* and *language* play a much more important role than any attempt to analyze a "concept" or an "idea" pure and simple. There is a basis for truth in temporality:

> There are truths just as there are perceptions: not that we can ever array before ourselves in their entirety the reasons for any assertion—there are merely motives, we have merely a hold on time and not full possession of it—but because it is of the essence of time to take itself up as it leaves itself behind, and to draw itself together into visible things, into immediately self-evident experiences.[15]

There is also an experience of truth, just as there is an experience of everything about which problems arise. It occurs, and truth emerges when consciousness pauses. There is truth for me only when consciousness ceases to plunge questioningly into the possible explanations of an event and comes to rest in it.

If we turn now to the experience of the thing—the "flesh and blood" criterion of *Lebenswelt* philosophy—to discover what might motivate a given pause, we encounter that most familiar of all candidates for the role of associating thought and thing: the essence. In *The Structure of Behavior* essence was viewed as a structure *for consciousness*, and

---

15. *Phenomenology*, p. 395.

Merleau-Ponty extends this view in the preface to *Phenomenology of Perception* and in Part I of his Sorbonne course *Les Sciences de l'homme selon Husserl*.[16] Establishing the *Lebenswelt* perspective in this issue in the preface of *Phenomenology of Perception*, he says that "our existence is too tightly held in the world to be able to know itself as such at the moment of its involvement. . . . it requires the field of ideality in order to become acquainted with and to prevail over its facticity." It is in turning to the *essence* that one achieves the needed "field of ideality." The essence is not an *object or goal* of philosophy. Rather "our effective involvement in the world is precisely what has to be understood and made amenable to conceptualization." The essence is a *means* of comprehending this involvement by making a knowledge possible. This knowledge that prevails over the facticity of existence invites speculation, because Merleau-Ponty is very careful to indicate that the essence is *not* an entity distinct from the existent thing of which it is the essence. In particular it is *not* a standpoint in thought equivalent, for example, to a concept. The word comes closest to being this. The essence is a structure of the appearing thing, "the core of primary meaning round which the acts of naming and expression take shape." This is another manifestation of the presence of the ideal in the "natural" dimension of phenomena, or at least of that quasi-ideality that emerged in *The Structure of Behavior* to distinguish what is phenomenal from what is "natural." More specifically, it is that "invariant . . . under the diversity of its aspects" that it is characteristic of human behavior to reveal, that intelligible minimum that "cannot be varied without the object itself disappearing."

Rationality seems to demand such an invariant and the profile-

---

16. Mimeographed notes for this course and for another, which he taught as Professor of Psychology and Pedagogy at the Sorbonne—*L'Etre avec autrui chez l'enfant*—were published by the Centre de Documentation Universitaire (Paris: Tournier et Constans). The "unofficial" nature of these dictates caution in their use, but in our opinion they merit confidence as an expression of Merleau-Ponty's work. For one thing, the positions offered in *Les Sciences de l'homme* follow quite closely those in *Phenomenology of Perception*. For another, it is probable that Merleau-Ponty approved their publication. Additional parts of the same courses are to be found in the *Bulletin du Groupe des Etudes Psychologique* in 1953. One lecture published there bears the explicit notation "Approuvé par M. Merleau-Ponty" (p. 681), and another, "supprimé sur l'avis de M. Merleau-Ponty" (p. 644). We shall hereafter refer to *Les Sciences de l'homme* as *Les Sciences*.

object structure appears to contain it. But is this not a structure that the doctrine of *Phenomenology of Perception* has blurred and softened to a point where it offers no stable meaning upon which reflection can focus? We think not. *Phenomenology of Perception* has certainly revised the way in which this structure should be conceived. The unity of the phenomenal object is symbolic: it (the phenomenal object) is a "system of equivalences" in which each part signifies all the rest. This type of unity allows the phenomenal object to offer a consistent meaning to reflection through a series of appearances. The gestalt notion of form—the model for this "system of equivalences"—certainly offers such consistency. That the meaning is conceived as permeating, or diffused in, the object rather than separable from it (a questionable contrast) or that the object is "correlative of my body and, in more general terms, to my existence, of which my body is merely the stabilized structure" does not eliminate that consistency. The correlation does mean that what is known is open to revision in the future and that the process or "teleology" that its revelation demands is not guaranteed from the outset. But this does not prevent the essence progressively revealed from dominating what the object says of itself until the moment of revision. In fact because of sedimentation the superseded essence would find a place in the truth about the object even after the revision that made it peripheral. It is doubtful that even a conservative epistemology would demand a guarantee of an individual experience that extended further. A conservative epistemology might not, of course, choose to express itself as Merleau-Ponty does when he cites Husserl to the effect that the essences that the Wesenschau reveals are "morphological essences . . . not susceptible to univocal determination . . . , inexact by essence" and at the same time that the vision of essences is an everyday experience, part of our dealing with any object. But any sense of the unity of the object would involve some appreciation of what Husserl, Merleau-Ponty, and so many others have called essence. If there is no divorce of essence from fact, neither is there a divorce of fact from essence: "The fact and the knowledge of the fact must always include a knowledge of essence, an a priori knowledge."

Experience of the thing, then, offers reflection a stable structure upon which it can focus. Persisting through the varying appearances of the object, it establishes that contrast—or contradiction—of perma nence and change, of the one and the many, upon which to build its paradoxical presence-absence. What is, from the point of view of the phenomenal object, the revelation of its primary core of meaning in every profile is, from the point of view of the consciousness knowing that object, the penetration of the latter to its core through each profile. But what is seen as penetration can also be seen as withdrawal: the presence to the essence in *every* profile frees consciousness from dependence on any given *one* and hence from any particular encounter. Its withdrawal is motivated by the same feature as its penetration. Its presence is absence and its absence presence. With this the knowing of the essence strains against perception with the same force with which the essence itself contrasts with what is perceived. Concept threatens to become detached from perception, and the movement toward "another faculty of knowing" gathers force. Merleau-Ponty refuses to give it its head: "there are not two knowledges but two different degrees of elaboration of the same knowledge." And yet the second degree of knowledge is to *conquer* the unreflective consciousness, to save it from chaos. Whence its redeeming force? An indication is found here: "Perception and thought have this in common, that each . . . appears to itself as temporal, *although they do not flow at the same speed nor in the same time.*" (Italics are ours.) This time of thought flowing at a different and, as it turns out, slower speed than perception is that of culture, and here Merleau-Ponty finds the dimension (locus) of thought. Not only is the idea a cultural object, but perception "reveals the permanent data of the problem which culture seeks to solve." Notice again, then, that the problem of the relation of consciousness to itself is interwoven with that of the relation of consciousness to that of other persons, the distinctive note of culture. The appeal at this level soon encounters the most remarkable of all cultural facts—*language.*

ESSENCE AND LANGUAGE

Merleau-Ponty gave so little attention to language in *The Structure of Behavior* that one suspects him of deliberately reserving it for later. The suspicion is deepened by the fact that the occasions for introducing it are there, and he does not avoid them. He treats the relation of thought to perception in his final chapter, for example, contrasting these levels in the interest of clarifying the objectivist error. Thus there is a level of thought that he calls "a tissue of ideal significations" where the perspectival character of the phenomenal object is overcome and where, in addition, all communication takes place. This level is inevitably part of our engagement in the world, because the moment a person as much as *names* what he perceives, he invokes it. Thought, conceived in this way, is integrated with the naturalist error of substituting objectivist things for phenomenal objects. It is, one can say, the behavior correlated with such things, and with them it suffers from the reduction of the natural attitude in favor of perception and of the phenomena. With them too it will require an explanation on the basis of phenomena. When Merleau-Ponty treats the behavior in virtue of which there are phenomenal objects for man—that is, the symbolic activity that places man at the peak of the behavioral hierarchy—he chooses to analyze not the concept nor any version of thought at all but the performing skill of typist and, especially, musician. Of course, the characteristics exemplified, since they belong to the symbolic order at large, will also be found in language, because the latter is rooted in this order. Speaking in *Phenomenology of Perception* of what animates this order, he says, "Speech is merely one particular case of . . . this irrational power which creates meanings and conveys them." The consideration of this "irrational power" in *The Structure of Behavior* introduced the characteristics that are later treated as essential to speech in *Phenomenology of Perception*: the capacity to improvise, for example, which becomes the most authentic dimension of speech, and the singular importance of the lateral relations among elements of the symbolic order. These not only gave that level its self-consistency, but allowed the phenomena to take on its profile-object relief by making man capable of managing both a single theme *and* its variations.

When he takes up the nature of speech in *Phenomenology of Perception*, Merleau-Ponty still approaches it almost exclusively through the *general* symbolic power of which speech is a particular instance. Thus the pathological evidence traces verbal failure of certain patients to a more general deficiency in the projection of meaning. In addition speech is comprehended on the model of the gesture. For all this, however, he sees in the attempt to understand speech an opportunity to move definitively beyond the classic dichotomy of subject and object.

For one thing thought is accomplished and delivered to its subject only by means of speech. At the same time, phenomenal objects take shape for me—they *are* for me—only by the action of speech as I denominate or name them. "For pre-scientific thinking, naming an object is causing it to exist or changing it." Thus it is a verbalized object upon which reflection turns, an object to some extent "idealized" by a naming that is at the same time a "materialization"—or better, an "incarnation" of thought. He compares this feature of the word with the esthetic expression that confers actual existence on what it expresses, while the vehicle of expression is effaced: "the actress becomes invisible and it is Phaedra who appears. . . . The meaning swallows up the signs."

The denomination of the object completes its being for me, but what of the relation of this naming gesture to the essence? Recall that in the preface of *Phenomenology of Perception* Merleau-Ponty maintained that the essence was a "core of primary meaning round which the acts of naming and expression take shape."[17] Taken as the center of organization, the essence can provide a focus for the signifying intention and at the same time not need to be thought of as eliciting the sort of univocal denomination that would leave no room for future development of experience. This suggests, of course, that the name would not exactly "fit" the essence and that there would always be something indirect and allusive about its reference. Merleau-Ponty maintains that this is the case.[18] The focus of language on the essence is apparently sufficient to prevent its being taken as (simply) arbitrary in its relation to phenomenal objects. When he described the persistence of words in experience, he said that they endured less as representations than as "a highly specific emotional essence, which is yet generalized, and detached from its empirical origins." It was also in "emotional gesticulation" that given languages were said to have their root. Treating this origin as emotional allows the experience both to endure and at the same time to enjoy a non-conceptual mode. These "emotional essences"

---

17. On page 388 of *Phenomenology* one finds the following remark: "What I call essence of the triangle is nothing but this presumption of a completed synthesis in terms of which we have defined the thing." The contrast between "presumption of a completed synthesis" and the "primary core of meaning," etc., is so striking that we assume the former to be simply a deviation by the author from the normal way in which he uses the term *essence*.

18. Cf. *Signes*, pp. 56 and 103.

persist as style, apparently associated with the words that pronounce them: "What remains to me of the word once learnt is its style as constituted by its formation and its sound." Their verbal uttering draws them into the web of language, where lateral relations are so important, with the result that their very triumph over what is arbitrary in their relation to phenomenal objects is supported by the context of expression. Thus, the original situation is conceived as "such as would make it not entirely arbitrary, if we designate night by the word 'nuit', to use 'lumière' for light."

If the established language combines consistency and indirectness in its relation to the phenomenal objects, the same is true in its relation with the fundamental signifying intention, something that could be taken as Merleau-Ponty's equivalent for thought. This intention comes to know itself—and *to be*[19]—by incarnating itself in words. By itself it is a "void," and by this he apparently means to designate the kind of relation that it has to the established words in which it is incarnated. It requires them and would be "empty" without them, but none fit exactly the intention that they embody any more than they do the essence to which they refer. They do not exhaust and fix the former any more than they fully and definitively reveal the latter. Rather they are polarized around the signifying intention to which they give a time-space deployment that is always capable of revision. Since the terms that the intention polarizes were generated with due respect for the essence that persists in the phenomenal object, the present intending of that object maintains its consistency with past experience and also contributes to the teleology or orientation of experience toward the future with the essence playing its structuring role at every point unless revised. Perhaps one can, then, speak of consistency on the part of language, the incarnate thought upon which reflection turns. Though it is conceived primarily as style, the word has a generality[20] that extends across the individual subject's experience and that is also shared by others in his culture.

---

19. "Thought is no 'internal' thing, and does not exist independently of the world and of words." (*Phenomenology*, p. 183.)
20. "Its generality is not that of the idea, but that of a behavioral style 'understood' by my body insofar as the latter is a behavior-producing power." (*Ibid.*, p. 403.)

STYLE, TRUTH, AND
THE PRIVILEGE OF LANGUAGE

But if conceiving speech as style permits it the combination of consistency and openness to development that it seems to demand, it still does not distinguish verbal behavior from any of the other expressive behaviors, nor does it account for the apparent clarity and universality of verbalized thought. Merleau-Ponty spells out only very briefly in *Phenomenology of Perception* the characters that he holds to distinguish speech from other forms of expression, and the distinction does not come through very clearly. Words can "sediment," he says, and become an intersubjective acquisition, can be reiterated indefinitely; and one can speak about language while one cannot, for example, paint about painting. But the first of these seems questionable, at least in his book's brief statement. Gestures certainly become traditional and characterize great cultural groups. He has himself drawn attention to the oriental inclination to smile in anger. Furthermore, there is a history of painting in which one age profits from its predecessor by a process that might also be regarded as a kind of sedimentation.

This leaves the fact that one can speak about language. This turning on itself is an aspect of the seeming detachability of language from its material instruments, a detachability that is less evident (if it exists at all) in other expressive behaviors. Merleau-Ponty associates it with the self-effacing of consciousness: "it loses sight of itself as a contingent fact, and takes to resting upon itself; this is . . . what provides us with the ideal of a thought without words." Perhaps there is something ultimate, something beyond all motivation in consciousness' losing sight of itself and in the fact that speech "implants the idea of truth in us as the presumptive limit of its effort." How are we to understand its doing this? One possibility appears momentarily in remarks that suggest that the ability of language to detach itself from its instruments lies in the fact that "speech is applied to nature, whereas music and painting, like poetry, create their own objects . . . and deliberately confine themselves within the cultural world." Is there a privilege to be accorded to speech because of some union that it enjoys with a *nature* that is established *beyond* the influence of expressive behavior? Is this the meaning of the criterion of "flesh and blood" presence of the object? We could think so only if we were to forget what has been driven home in both *The Structure of Behavior* and *Phenomenology of Perception*: that nature as well as art receives its meaning from man. Even then we could do so only for a moment, for a few lines later Merleau-Ponty stifles this possibility, which he introduced in the first place only to be stifled: "There is no fundamental difference between the various modes of expression, and no privileged position can be accorded to any of them on the alleged ground that it expresses a truth in itself." It is not surprising that one cannot give a privilege to one mode of expression as if it expressed a truth in itself; this would be to return to the objectivism and the natural attitude. But does speech enjoy no privilege at all? The difference between language and other phenomena of expression may not be fundamental, but it *is* striking, as striking as the natural attitude for which it seems to be the special vehicle and source. But it is also the vehicle of the philosophical reflection that breaks through the natural attitude. What does Merleau-Ponty do with this issue?

He does not sidestep it. Two additional writings (in article form) are directly addressed to the question of the privilege of language. They appeared at about the same time, indicating a period when the question was very much on his mind: "Sur la Phénoménologie du langage" in 1951 and "Le Langage indirect et les voix du silence" in 1952.[21] "Le Langage indirect et les voix du silence" compares verbal behavior with painting; its occasion was the appearance of *Les Voix du silence*, the work on the history and theory of painting by André Malraux. We are soon given a glimpse of Merleau-Ponty's conclusion: "It may be that the meaning of language has a decisive privilege, but it is in attempting the parallel [with painting] that we shall notice what makes this— perhaps—impossible at the end." The first few pages sum up and dramatize Merleau-Ponty's convictions about language. The most imposing thing about it to which he draws attention here is its self-consistency and independence. Language, he says, is "something like a being . . . , a spiritual power." It is "something like a universe capable of lodging in itself things themselves after having changed

21. "Sur la Phénoménologie du langage" was delivered as a paper at the First International Phenomenological Colloquy, which was held in Brussels in 1951, and then published with the other papers from that meeting under the title *Problèmes actuels de la phénoménologie* (Paris: Desclée de Brouwer, 1952). "Le Langage indirect et les voix du silence" was first published as a pair of articles in *Les Temps Modernes*, No. 80 (June, 1952), and No. 81 (July, 1952). Each is included in the collection *Signes*, from which we will cite them.

their meaning." In the face of the problem that learning poses to the view that makes language a single organic reality (we seem to learn it one expression at a time), he insists that language is whole from the beginning. Not as explicit words, of course, but as a single unarticulated attunement capable of seizing upon basic phonematic oppositions and affinities and upon these to found the ability to differentiate among signs. It would be interesting to know more fully the relation of the basic seizure of phonematic principles and the emotional gesturing that he placed at the root of language in *Phenomenology of Perception*. Even there, however, he spoke of the persistence of the emotional essence as style of sound and articulation. In any case what is first at this point are the principles introducing one to those *lateral* relations of sign with sign, the importance of which emerged in *The Structure of Behavior*. With this equipment the child is gradually caught up in the verbal ritual that unfolds around him: he is drawn into this self-consistent cultural universe. The language generated in this way maintains its indirect or allusive character with respect to object and intention, as one would expect. Merleau-Ponty exemplifies further in this connection: a meaning is expressed—a thought is uttered—when it is embodied in available terms. But these terms may express by what they leave unsaid as well as by what they explicitly say. Thus in Saussure's example the English *the man I love* expresses the sentiment delivered in the French *l'homme que j'aime* as well as the latter but without the use of the relative pronoun. Merleau-Ponty—and Saussure—hold that the gap expresses as well as the terms themselves. It is not to be denied, of course, that speech does allude to *thought* and *things*. As far as thought is concerned, words "are haunted at a distance by it, as the tides are by the moon . . . ,"[22] and as for things, real speech "delivers the meaning captive in the thing." Most important, however, "language is in itself oblique and autonomous and if it happens that it signifies a thought or a word directly, this is only a secondary power, derived from its interior life."[23] Taken in this way, speech is not likely to enjoy much privilege over the "mute" expressions, such as painting. Merleau-Ponty's discussion of painting reinforces the understanding of

22. In "Sur la Phénoménologie du langage" we will read: "the meanings of the word are always ideas in the Kantian sense, poles of a certain number of convergent acts of expression which attract the discourses without being properly given for its own count." (*Signes,* p. 112.)

23. It is difficult to evaluate the word "directly" here and in particular to know when or if a word did signify directly.

language by advancing knowledge of the expressive function that they *share*, but it tends to leave their distinctions obscure.

Turning directly to painting now, he attacks objectivist views according to a familiar pattern. Malraux has suggested that modern painting is the result of a historical transition from what is objective—a classic art taken as an attempt to *represent* nature—to the subject, the individual painter concerned with expressing himself. Merleau-Ponty challenges this. No painting was ever simply representative, and the "objective" techniques of classical painting—perspective, for example— are simply interpretations of a visual world that does not demand them any more than it would other interpretations. This, in fact, establishes what Merleau-Ponty regards as *the* problem posed by modern painting: how can we "communicate without recourse to a preestablished Nature on which all our senses would open; how are we involved in the universal by what is most particular to us"? The search for the unity required by communication in non-objective terms arrives at an important expansion of the understanding of *style*. Touched upon earlier, its clarification is the most important mission of this article, and its development leads to a revision of the notion of *truth*. For a given painter, style is a "system of equivalences that he establishes for his work, the universal index of the 'coherent deformation' by which he concentrates the meaning which in his perception is still scattered, and makes it exist separately." It is in virtue of the style realized in it that the individual painting coheres, its parts blending in its highly distinctive identity. Here lies the *true* expression of reality as the artist knows it and also the invitation to a revision of what we know as truth. Modern painters

> do not want a truth which is the resemblance of painting to the world. They would accept the idea of a truth which was the cohesion of painting with itself, the presence in it of a unique principle which affects each expression with a certain value in view of its use in the painting.[24]

It is precisely such a truth—truth as coherence of expression "without model or predestined instruments of expression"[25]—that modern painting and modern thought in general promote. This truth is not com-

---

24. *Signes*, p. 71.
25. Recall that early in *Phenomenology* he said that the "central phenomenon of perceptual life . . . is the constitution, without any ideal model, of a significant grouping." (*Phenomenology*, p. 53.)

pletely indifferent to things, of course. It does respond to them when called into play, for example, by a visual world that in turn helps sustain it. Renoir sits gazing at the Mediterranean as he paints in order to ask of the sea what it alone can give: "its fashion of interpreting liquid substance." But as he gazes at the sea he paints a small brook: he has drawn from what he has seen into his symbolic order, given it that "coherent deformation"[26] that results from style and that is a new level of explicit truth. Truth so conceived is not indifferent to the artist and his life either, but the style that is its principle of coherence normally is unconscious in the artist—appearing to others and himself in his paintings—and it does not simply reflect his life but transforms its events by giving them a role in his symbolic behavior.

The debate with Malraux carries beyond the particular painting and the works of a given artist. In an impressive demonstration of the versatility of his view, Merleau-Ponty extends the same conception of coherence in the form of style successively to the history of painting and to history in general. The move begins with the body, the original "system of equivalences" that explores, expresses, and unifies:

> We must recognize under the name of glance, hand, and in general body, a system of systems committed to the inspection of the world, capable of covering distances . . . of designing hollows and reliefs, distances and detours, a meaning in the inconceivable barrenness of being. The movement of the artist tracing his arabesque in infinite matter amplifies but also continues the simple marvel of directed locomotion and gestures of grasping.[27]

In addition to style conceived as structuring and orienting this extension of motility in a particular artist, there is "a unity of human style which gathers up the gestures of all the artists in a single endeavor and their productions in a single history, a single art." Beyond this lies the power of human signifying at its broadest: "the continued attempt at expression is the basis of a single history just as the grasp of our body on every possible object is the basis of a single space." The singleness of this attempt lies in "the intimacy of every expression with every other," which is the fundamental reality of history. It is a vast system of equivalences that is Merleau-Ponty's alternative to preestablished nature as a basis for truth.

---

26. The term is Malraux's; Merleau-Ponty endorses its aptness.
27. *Signes,* p. 83.

All of this has its relevance for language, a system like others, which accomplishes meaning by establishing it in the world, and Merleau-Ponty turns back to consider its claims to privilege again. What he does is to address the question of sedimentation, contrasting the "lateral" relations in painting with those in language and then relating this directly to what each has to say about things. A given painting may draw upon the history of painting, but once it does this, it takes its place among paintings without pretending to assume and replace its ancestors. But speech is different: "not content to go beyond the past, it pretends to recapture it, to contain it in substance . . . , to offer us its truth." Thus the human capacity to *assume* existence is greatest in language, whose "ductility" has no equal. But this sedimentation as recapture and assumption of past only comes into adequate focus when it is seen in the context of its revelation of *things*. Merleau-Ponty binds tightly together the revelation of the thing and the apparent absorption by speech of its own past along with its presumption of the future. Speech pretends to give us the thing itself and as it is. But utterance sufficient to express the thing itself would dispense with the need for any further speaking about it because there would be nothing left for this further speaking to contribute to the experience of that thing. Each previous formulation passes into the present one in an action that both sums it up and dispenses with it makes it present and absent. Thus there is a presence and absence of consciousness to itself in the temporal dimension—past, present, future—that is woven into the presence-absence of consciousness with object that is the condition for the reflection.

> When language is compared with the mute forms of expression— with gesture or painting—one must add that it is not content as they are to sketch out on the world's surface "a coherent deformation," a tacit meaning . . . . We do not have here the replacing of one meaning by another but the substitution of equivalent meanings. The new structure is given as already present in the previous one, the latter now subsists in the former, the past is now comprehended.[28]

In sedimentation the overlapping or contraction of time is brought to its highest degree and at the same time there is the great intensification of the present. But because it is this, sedimentation is also necessarily *presumption* (of total accumulation and total self-possession, for it does

28. *Ibid.*, pp. 101–02.

not acknowledge that it will develop further) and *forgetting* (of its origins and temporal conditions). Truths, in fact, can suffer as well as profit from their inclusion in this process. This is exemplified in the fate of the Cartesian *cogito* when it was assumed in the efforts of Descartes' successors. Hence Merleau-Ponty stands with the position that despite the seeming clarity of verbal behavior "meaning is implied by the verbal edifice rather than designated by the words."

LANGUAGE AND PHILOSOPHY

For philosophy the inseparability of thought from such a verbal edifice has a pair of consequences. The first is that philosophy must be taken as an attempt to substitute itself for all other meaning: to speak the word that terminates the need for further speaking, to be equivalent to non-reflective thought. The second is that the phenomenology of language becomes the discipline in which one judges the competence of philosophy, something that has historically fallen to metaphysics. In his article "Sur la Phénoménologie du langage" Merleau-Ponty assumes the task indicated by this second consequence and spells out his position on the nature of philosophical truth and the philosophical endeavor. The format of this article, more formally schematized than any other of his published works, reflects his intention to respond as definitely as possible to questions about his conception of philosophy and to bring Brehier's concern over his "inversion of philosophy" to a head.

He reaffirms the primacy of the order of incarnation, of the body, language, and history, because in its absence I simply could not come to know my belonging to a "pre-constituted world." But I do know this. He then refers to this order in which such knowledge is thrust upon me as that of "instructive spontaneity:" only given a body that "knows itself as constituted at the moment when it functions as constituting" can I comprehend my experience of another person, who establishes his presence in my life by what Merleau-Ponty calls *intentional transgression*. He introduces this theme in a manner that makes the comparison of the presence of the other persons to me and the presence of the past in my present by sedimentation simply irresistible. Then he proceeds to this comparison:

> Our expressive operations of the moment, rather than expelling those
> which preceded or annulling them quite simply saves them . . . ,

takes them up again insofar as they contain some truth, and the same phenomenon occurs as regards the expressive operations of the other . . . . Our present holds the promise of our past; we hold the promise of other persons.[29]

Thus the sedimentation model seems to apply to the relation *among subjects* as well as among the verbal expressions of the same subject, and the phenomena of truth can rest on this relation too.

To say that there is a truth is to say that, when I assume the former project or the foreign one and the successful expression delivers what had been forever held captive in being, an interior communication is established in the depths of personal and interpersonal time by which our present becomes the truth of all the other knowing events.[30]

Merleau-Ponty's treatment of the dialogue in *Phenomenology of Perception* wherein we think according to each other (the barriers between consciousness having become permeable) anticipates this dimension of the truth, this affinity of the various knowings. Thus does the present become more and more dense. Answering in a very limited way the problem to which he promised to devote the work *Origine de la vérité*, he says that "truth is another name for sedimentation, which is the presence of all presents in our own. . . . there is no light which surpasses that of the living present." As for philosophy "its ultimate move is to recognize what Kant called the transcendental affinity of moments of time and temporalities."

With this we find an echo of the remarks introducing the final section of *Phenomenology of Perception*, those to the effect that all problems are to be understood by attaching them to the paradox of time and that beyond this paradox there is nothing further to be understood. The work that followed these—on the issues that we have been viewing at least—has deepened and expanded what he said there but not basically changed it. The inversion of philosophy stands. In the matter of its philosophical competence and on the questions of the possibility of reflection and nature of truth, we have a view of what it can offer. Truth, according to this revised notion, is primarily the coherence of *expression*, though it is not completely indifferent to *things*. Above all, truth is the act that continually establishes that coherence. The origin of truth lies in that act, which is intimate with

29. *Ibid.*, p. 119.
30. *Ibid.*, p. 120.

every other expressive act, that draws from them and gives to them. The passage from primordial faith to explicit truth essentially demands the paradoxical combination of giving and receiving to which his term sedimentation is applied.

A question can arise, of course, over whether he is saying quite the same thing when he speaks of truth as *sedimentation* and when he speaks of it as *expression*. It is quite evident that he does not take sedimentation to mean simply the accumulation of experience. Though he must fight the term's own cultural weight to do so, he refers to it as presence, as we have previously noted. Still, it does seem to serve primarily to characterize the relation of the act of expression with other acts of expression rather than, for example, its relation to its own vital source or to the meaning that it asserts *now*. For the latter dimension of truth, the term *expression* itself seems to be the most appropriate one. For an adequate appreciation of his conception of truth one must hold together both the notion of sedimentation and the genetically more central idea of expression.

Merleau-Ponty does this in his *Eloge de la philosophie*, where he speaks of expression constantly and of sedimentation very rarely but where he is, nonetheless, still balancing the two. Thus he remarks that "I think neither according to the true *alone*, nor according to myself alone, nor according to other persons alone, because each of these three needs the other two. . . . A philosophical life always takes its bearings on these three cardinal points." Here, as is obvious, the vital context of philosophical life seems to take on a normative role, requiring that we honor it as we philosophize. However, the more active "expression" theme predominates: the duty of philosophy is to symbolize, "to substitute for the tacit symbolism of life a conscious symbolism . . . ," and it must extend its effort to the root of all symbolizing, that power "which other symbolisms limit themselves to exercising." Because it is expression "it is accomplished only when it renounces coinciding with what it expresses and when it sets it at a distance in order to see its meaning."

This returns us to philosophy and presence and absence. The ability to take up a distance is based on the minimal structure of the object expressed and on the process of sedimentation of experience in consciousness. These do support a significant degree of survey over the perceptual situation while seeming to make withdrawal possible only in a horizontal dimension—that is, toward the future. This would imply that the temporal bonds of a philosophy are such that there is no philosophy that cannot give way to another that is preferable, no word that does away with the need of further discussion. This, of course, is a fairly conservative position, particularly when one considers that on the other hand a philosophy once born has, like every event, a place that can never be nullified. The later and preferable philosophy will have the effect, then, of driving the predecessor from the center of attention but will always count it as part of its situation. We should ask, then, is this not sufficient? Does not every reflection lie open to challenge by yet another reflection and the truth that it utters to obsolescence? Is any philosophy taken seriously when it claims to have uttered the final word? Perhaps Merleau-Ponty is only introducing into philosophy and insisting that we constantly reckon with a point that others affirm and then ignore.

But we cannot yet have done with the question. There is the other and conflicting inclination of philosophy to substitute itself for all other meaning, to attempt to speak the word that eliminates the need for further speaking. Such a tendency is also built into our expressing. In *Phenomenology of Perception* Merleau-Ponty spoke of the *reduction*, the most basic phenomenological movement, as "the ambition to make reflection equal to the unreflective life of consciousness." Can the discussion of a cultural entity like language place us in a position to understand this? If we return for a moment to the meeting of La Société Française de la Philosophie we find M. Jean Hyppolite protesting that Merleau-Ponty has underestimated the dramatic character of the change that reflection introduces into consciousness. Reflection— Merleau-Ponty's as well as the next—raises the question of the "absolute being of all meaning." It results in "the projection of an eternal norm," which means "a passing beyond [perception] which may be formal or may be illusory, but without which there is no reflection." Merleau-Ponty agrees that this is so but in the following terms: "It is characteristic of man to think God, but this does not mean that God exists."

Chapter 6

The Absolute

Like Descartes, Merleau-Ponty *finds himself* with the idea of God. He finds this idea when he takes an inventory of consciousness, where it arises from the latter's objectivist behavior. He also finds it when he takes an inventory of his time, where it is part of the historical reality of religion. Though he does not give the question of God the lengthy and detailed treatment that he devotes to perception, language, and history, Merleau-Ponty does touch upon it with surprising frequency during his career,[1] at one time emphasizing the philosophical issue and at another, the religious, while never completely divorcing them. The most complete and most valuable comments from the philosophical point of view are to be found in "La Métaphysique dans l'homme" and *Eloge de la philosophie.* "Foi et bonne foi" attends chiefly to the historical and religious dimensions, examining Christianity as a humanism. Among the introductory sections that he wrote for the anthology *Les*

---

1. In *Phenomenology* the references to God are brief and usually in the form of allusions to the absolute consciousness involved in objectivism. Earlier, it will be recalled, his first article, "Christianisme et ressentiment," included his own observations on religion. After *Phenomenology* the issue is touched upon in various articles and papers: "Un Auteur scandaleux" (1945); "La Querelle de l'existentialisme" (1946); "Le Primat de la perception et ses conséquences philosophiques," particularly in the discussion that followed (1946); "Foi et bonne foi" (1947); "La Métaphysique dans l'homme" (1947); "L'Homme et l'adversité," particularly the discussion (1950); "Le Langage indirect et les voix du silence" (1951); *Eloge de la philosophie* (1953); and *Les Philosophes célèbres* (1956).

Philosophes célèbres, there is a remarkably perceptive meditation on "Christianisme et philosophie" that comments on the established positions concerning these institutions.

PERSONAL RELATION
WITH THE CHURCH

Christianity quite obviously meant Catholicism for Merleau-Ponty, and he managed its theological concepts with an ease that is conspicuous even in European circles, where familiarity with them is not at all uncommon. He spoke of his personal relationship with the Church at various times both in writings and discussion. "I have memories of a religion in which I was raised, and which I practiced beyond childhood."[2] His withdrawal from the Church took place in the 1930's gradually, one gathers, and apparently without outward drama. He tells us more about it in "Foi et bonne foi":

> Once there was a young Catholic whom the exigencies of his faith led to the "left." This was at the time when Dollfuss initiated the first Christian-Social party in Europe by a bombardment of the workers' quarter in Vienna. A Christian periodical had addressed a protest to President Miklas. It was said that the most advanced of our great religious orders supported the protest. The young man was received at the table of several members of that order. During the meal he was surprised to hear that, after all, the Dollfuss government was the established authority, that as regular government it was entitled to its recourse to police action and that, though they were free to blame him as citizens, Catholics as Catholics had nothing to protest about. As he grew older, the young man never forgot this moment. He turned to the father who had just said this—a man who was both generous and bold, as later events proved—and told him simply that this justified the opinion which the workers held regarding Catholics: in the social question, they could not be counted on to the end.[3]

The Dollfuss action occurred in February, 1932. Three and four years

---

2. M. M-P., "L'Homme et l'adversité," *La Connaissance de l'homme au XXᵉ siècle* (Neuchatel: Editions de la Baconnière, 1952), pp. 51–74. This was originally a paper delivered on September 10, 1951, at a session of the annual Rencontres Internationales de Genève. The discussion devoted to it is published in the same volume, pp. 215–52. The paper without the discussion is also included in *Signes*, pp. 284–308. We shall cite it from the former source and refer to it hereafter as "L'Homme."
3. *Sens*, p. 352.

later he published articles in the Catholic bimonthly *La Vie Intellec-tuelle* and in the first of these argued that the Church is not necessarily aloof from human affairs. One imagines him involved in an inner debate stretching beyond the time when the early articles were published. It is impossible to date the break exactly and not important to do so. In the period following *Phenomenology of Perception* his attitude toward Christianity was quite critical and at times severe. In the discussion following his paper "Man and Adversity," he was pressed hard on the significance of the *ambiguity* theme by, among others, Fathers Danielou and Maydieu (Catholics) and Pierre Thevanez and Charles Westphal (Protestants). He reacted with a certain amount of irritation to Thevanez's suggestion that the ambiguity of the human situation is an indication that this situation "opens out" on Christianity: "To me this is the height of confusion. To speak of ambiguity means that you are a Christian. No! This only means that you think there is ambiguity." At another point in the discussion he volunteers: "I do not spend my time saying that I am an atheist because that is not an occupation and because it would transform a quite positive effort of philosophical consciousness into a negation. But if after all I'm asked about it, I answer yes." This was in 1951. In 1953 in *Eloge de la philosophie* he declares the charge of atheism irrelevant to the nature of philosophy as he understands it,[4] In the years preceding his death, according to Sartre, he declined to be numbered among the atheists.[5] We shall take up the question of the Absolute from that point in the discussion of philosophical reflection at which it arose and allow the inevitable affinity of themes to lead us into the rest of its dimensions.

A PRESUMPTION
OF OBJECTIVIST CONSCIOUSNESS

Merleau-Ponty finds it "characteristic" of man to think God just as he found it "natural" for him to think things-in-themselves.[6] These constitute, in fact, two manifestations of the objectivist error. We pointed out before that one of the ways—the intellectualist way—for an appear-

---

4. This is repeated in *Signes*, page 171. We do not ignore the fact that denying the relevance of atheism to a philosophy may not be the same as denying its relevance to a philosopher.
5. "Merleau-Ponty vivant," p. 360.
6. Cf. *Structure*, p. 219.

ing thing to be in-itself-for-consciousness is for consciousness to embrace it in its entirety, to threaten it with *no* limitation of perspective or point of view. In *The Structure of Behavior* Merleau-Ponty called this taking the phenomenal object to be a thing in itself a motivated error—that is, an error that has an authentic phenomenal basis. He traced it back to a combination of *presumption* and *forgetting* on the part of consciousness: presumption of a complete synthesis and forgetting of the limitations of consciousness. When *Phenomenology of Perception* takes up the question of phenomenal objectivity, it builds a conception of the appearing thing as in-itself for a consciousness perceptually engaged in a world. His work on language extends and specifies this, making language the locus both of the forgetting of the past and the presumption of the future, which *The Structure of Behavior* first introduced. In its rejection of intellectualism *Phenomenology of Perception* also challenged the possibility of philosophy's operating from an absolute consciousness, saying,

> A philosophy becomes transcendental, or radical, not by taking its place in absolute consciousness without mentioning the ways by which this is reached, but by considering itself as a problem: not by postulating a knowledge rendered totally explicit, but by recognizing as the fundamental philosophic problem this presumption on reason's part.[7]

The "presumption of reason" is the one he acknowledged when he spoke of reflection's commitment to emulate the unreflective life of consciousness. This too he has associated with language, speaking in "Sur la Phénoménologie du langage" of the "vow to recover the world which was pronounced with the appearance of a language." Just as a particular verbal expression is the locus of a particular presumption and forgetting, which the speaker might imagine to be an idea summing up the *object*, language as a whole may be the locus of a generalized presumption and forgetting, which the philosopher might take as a system of ideas summing up the world. By substituting a strong phenomenological position and the priority of perception for the intellectualist stand, Merleau-Ponty feels he undoes the claims of absolute consciousness. Looking back on it from *Eloge de la philosophie*, he says that "to attain . . . the fundamental sound of the world in the face of every naturalist explanation and to free it from all sovereign necessity

---

7. *Phenomenology*, p. 63.

is one and the same thing."[8] Perhaps it is a sufficient managing of the "fundamental philosophical problem" to recognize presumption as presumption and to constantly recall philosophy to its beginnings and consciousness to its limits. "The meaning of philosophy is that of a genesis and it cannot be totalized outside of time . . . ," he remarks at one point, and earlier he said that metaphysics is "not a knowledge which would complete the edifice of knowledges. It is the lucid knowing of what threatens them and the sharp awareness of their price."

THE ABSOLUTE
AS A THREAT TO MAN

The writings immediately after *Phenomenology of Perception* do devote considerable attention to the description of the threat. This gives them a rather negative cast, which one does not expect Merleau-Ponty to continue. He does emerge from it eventually—and partially—but let us begin with these descriptions since he does. In "Foi et bonne foi" he says that "there is always a stoic component in the idea of God: if God exists, then perfection is already realized prior to the world. It cannot be augmented. There is literally nothing to do." When there is nothing to do, human liberty—which for the existentialist *is* human reality—is smothered. *Phenomenology of Perception,* incidentally, had made the same point, though with an emphasis on interhuman relations. With Spinoza in mind Merleau-Ponty says that the attempt to justify loving my neighbor as myself because each of us inheres equally in God will fail because in this case what might be claimed to be my love of the other person is really "the love which God has for himself through me. So that finally nowhere would there be love of others or indeed others, but one single self-love linked to itself beyond our lives, and nowise relevant, indeed inaccessible to us."

In "La Métaphysique dans l'homme" he generalizes about this, and the Absolute appears as a threat to all the relations of consciousness with consciousness. In a frequently quoted remark he says, "Consciousness, metaphysical and moral, perishes from contact with the absolute because it is itself . . . the living connection of self with self and of self

---

8. Previously, rejecting the absolute consciousness under another of its attributes, he said that "philosophy breathes only when it rejects the infinitely infinite thought to see the world in all its strangeness." ("L'Homme," p. 251.)

with others." I am not entitled, then, to assume that I am in contact with the Absolute because "whether there is or is not an absolute thought . . . I can judge only by my own opinions which remain capable of error however severely I discuss them." The point in this complaint seems to be the inability of the philosopher to be *certain* of the absolute. This note was also introduced into his discussion of essences and serves as a reminder of Merleau-Ponty's conviction that philosophy operates in the realm of the probable. Should I attempt to transcend that realm by invoking the Absolute despite my limits, my commerce with men is disrupted. If I introduce it into my theorizing, I can dispense myself from justifying my positions before other men and withdraw from the order of progressive experience, where these positions have their meaning. If I rest my practical behavior on an Absolute, whatever I do is justified, even if I "piously slaughter my adversaries." When he is more specific about the nature of this Absolute that would make those who invoke it such a detriment to human community, we find that he has in mind certain rather familiar philosophical versions of God: the creating God in the Leibnitzian sense and the Kantian idea limit. He takes these, incidentally, as the form in which religion also understands God and not as simply belonging to philosophy. He rejects both versions abruptly and for the most venerable reasons: the notion of a creating God is irreconcilable with the presence of evil in the world, and the idea limit substitutes what we *wish* the world to be for what it actually *is*.

So far we face the conclusion that *any* Absolute is quite foreign to all that is human, and foreign with that foreignness of ideas and things that Merleau-Ponty rejects when he rejects objectivism. But at the same time and on another level the issue is developing somewhat differently. When in "La Querelle de l'existentialisme" he argues with Catholic critics of Sartre's opposition of consciousness and thing, he appeals to both Pascal and Malebranche in order to show the presence of such a distinction in the tradition of the critics themselves. With Malebranche this distinction is reflected in his conception of God, for he insisted that the "glory of the architect" that God receives from *things* is quite different from the glory given by men who labor to reclaim the world for Him. "This is to distinguish in striking terms between a God of things and a God of men. It was the assertion that the human order began with freedom." At the beginning of "Le Primat de la perception et ses conséquences philosophiques" he said that the primacy of perception would not destroy the absolute any more than it would destroy rationality but would attempt to bring both down to earth. At the end of that paper he did admit that his position meant destruction for a "separate Absolute," obviously one beyond the process of human history. Now the Absolute that we have watched him reject up to this point has certainly been that separate Absolute, that God of things. But what of the Absolute brought down to Earth, the God among men? This is of great importance both from philosophical and religious points of view. Merleau-Ponty usually discusses religion, incidentally, with allusions to the doctrines of the *incarnation* and *death of Christ* and a regret that Christianity is not more attentive to their implications. We shall return to this.

PARADOX OF AN ABSOLUTE INCARNATE SUBJECT

"La Métaphysique dans l'homme" attempts to indicate the status of this incarnate Absolute: "Metaphysics can only seek a God that is *for himself* as well as *for us* behind consciousness, behind our ideas, like the anonymous force which sustains each of our thoughts and our experiences." When metaphysics *does* seek this God, however, its efforts merge with those of religion and become inarticulate, as he says religion inevitably is: the role of religion seems to be to mark the place in our culture for what is foreign and enigmatic,[9] a role that religion carries out "not insofar as it is dogma nor even as belief, but as a cry." Any attempt to characterize this Absolute would be *contradictory*. Merleau-Ponty is not usually ill at ease with contradiction. He has, in fact, taken it to be an essential of consciousness whose very being is to assume it. But now he distinguishes a fecund from a sterile or "inert" contradiction:

---

9. This is not quite as clearly stated in "La Métaphysique dans l'homme" as it is in his "Lecture de Montaigne," which appeared at approximately the same time. In the latter he sees Montaigne holding what is obviously his (Merleau-Ponty's) own position on the matter: "The value of religion lies in this: that it reserves a place for what is foreign to us, and that it knows our fate to be enigmatic. All the solutions which it gives of the enigma are incompatible with our monstrous condition. As a questioning, religion is justified as long as it remains without answers." (*Signes*, p. 257.)

> I have the right to consider as ultimate and true the contradictions of my life as thinking and incarnate subject because I experience it and because they are connected in the unchallengeable experience of a thing or in the experience of a truth. I cannot introduce behind me a "transcendence in immanence" because I am not God and cannot verify in an unchallengeable experience the coexistence of these two attributes.[10]

I am not God. I cannot therefore be God, for this would be a sterile contradiction. I can not-be my world and at the same time be it.[11] The same is true of my relation with my body, my past, and the other dimensions of my being. This is all essential to that ambiguity that the description of experience prompts me to attribute to myself, that identity in difference that I can understand if I attach it to the paradox of time. But the paradox of time will not support the presence of the Absolute. If, as my role as symbolic function seems to demand, I am implicated in the meaning of what I experience and particularly if what I experience finds its phenomenal conditions in my consciousness, then it would seem to follow that I could not experience or express a being whose meaning is that it owes me nothing. Merleau-Ponty has not limited this conception of my *lending* phenomenal conditions simply to things but extends it to persons as well. Thus the experience of the other person involves one's finding in him "a miraculous prolongation of my own intentions." Later he says this even more sharply: "I lend myself to another person. I lend him my thoughts: this is not the defeat of the perception of the other person. It is the perception of the other person." At another moment, as he describes the crucial experience of dialogue, he suggests that in a certain sense the other lends himself to me: "There is . . . an ability to think *according to others* which enriches our own thoughts." The experience of the other person, then, is described (in part at least) when I speak of our crossing the gap that separates us, inhabiting each other so that in a genuine sense each *is* the other.

When he thinks on the question of the Absolute, Merleau-Ponty quite evidently has the possibility of this sort of identity in mind. In "La Métaphysique dans l'homme" Leibnitz is said to have "claimed the point of view of a God without a world. . . ," and those generally who

---

10. *Sens*, p. 193.
11. "I am all that I see." (*Phenomenology*, p. 452.) "I am my body." (*Ibid.*, p. 198.)

referred to God in their thinking were held to be "rejoining the absolute principle of all thought" and withdrawing problems from discussion. Speaking of Lavelle in *Eloge de la philosophie*, he mentions the latter's admission that in regard to the Absolute "we cannot place ourselves in it to watch the derivation of the world." In this work, of course, he also insists that the great philosophers "refused themselves the right to install themselves in an absolute knowledge." We shall see in a moment that Merleau-Ponty's critics will insist that a knowledge of the Absolute is not necessarily an absolute knowledge, and reference to it is not an identity of the sort that would cause the death of consciousness.

But Merleau-Ponty is, not inconsistently, posing the question within that framework of identity and non-identity that is his, and his position does seem incompatible with the Absolute. When I cross the gap that separates me from the other person and think according to him, the gap I cross still remains. If it did not we would not be *other* than each other. I contribute to this gap and to his being other than I by the opacity of my consciousness, which leaves him his privacy,[12] and by my passivity, which allows me to experience him as active. In short the *other* person that I "am" remains *other* thanks in part to the things in me that mark the failure of my strict identity with myself. It is this that Merleau-Ponty has related to the paradox of time, that accommodates so well the opacity of consciousness, past and present, and also the being constituted that is part of every present. Here, then, in the description of the experience of self and of other person, being and non-being cohabit with ease. They support rather than threaten each other, and the contradiction is now in fact that dialectical opposition that, as far back as *Phenomenology of Perception*, he made essential to metaphysics.[13] But the attempt to extend this metaphysics to God—and from his manner of posing the question of the Absolute, this *is* what Merleau-Ponty feels is at stake—

---

12. Given our mutual implication, total clarity about myself would require total clarity about him.
13. We take the liberty of repeating this quotation: "The dialectic is not a relationship between contradictory and inseparable thoughts; it is the tending of an existence towards another existence which denies it, and yet without which it is not sustained. Metaphysics—the coming to light of something beyond nature—is not localized at the level of knowledge: it begins with the opening out upon 'another' and is to be found everywhere, and already, in the specific development of sexuality." (*Phenomenology*, p. 168.)

would be futile. God's total transcendence would, on the one hand, make the gap between us total, and his total immanence would make our identity with him complete. In addition if I were certain of God, I would be fully identical with myself and no longer temporal. This would be sterile contradiction, irreconcilability and not dialectical relationship.

PROBLEM OF GOD INERADICABLE

But serious questions persist and arise from our experience: "it is characteristic of man to think God." If men did not think God, there would be no problem in the first place. In the face of questions about the inadequacy of his conception of experience to allow for the *other* person and for reflection Merleau-Ponty asserted that *in fact* the other person exists for me and *in fact* there is reflection, and so the conception of experience must and can accommodate them. Might not its being characteristic of man to think God indicate that the Absolute has *in fact* some place in our experience of things, a role that both demands and allows for some analogous accommodation? Consider, for example, the way in which we have seen him describe the relation of words and ideas. Merleau-Ponty said that words are "haunted at a distance" by ideas and again that "the meanings of words are always ideas in the Kantian sense, poles of a certain number of convergent acts of expression which attract the discourse without being properly given for its own count." This certainly seems to be the integration of the idea into the experience of the thing named, where it seems to stand as the necessary goal of that transcendence of consciousness beyond any particular profile, the transcendence that gives the thing its relief as in-itself-for-me. As such it might be taken to be as "real" as the transcendence, and one might regard the "presumption" of reason to be as "real" as reason. Perhaps the Absolute is a pole attracting all philosophical discourse (or even all human endeavor) without being "properly given for its own count." Perhaps it too is as "real" as the transcendence of consciousness and as indispensable if I am to account for the being-for-me of all else.

Something of the sort was the sense of the intervention of Hyppolite that we noted as we introduced this question at the end of the previous chapter. It is certainly the central theme of the reaction of Catholic critics like DeWaelhens and Jolivet.[14] They attempt to associate God with the movement of transcendence itself, insisting that this movement and the human process of justification that it conditions are only comprehensible in relation to an Absolute toward which consciousness tends without ever fully arriving. DeWaelhens chides Merleau-Ponty for introducing into the discussion of the Absolute the very interior-exterior distinction that he has himself done so much to render suspect. He then asserts that reference to the Absolute need not be identification with it and does not necessarily remove questions from the human process of justification:

> To accept the notion that experience must be able in some fashion to be absolutely grounded is not to admit a truth that transcends every form of justification if, really, that admission only pushes to its extreme the very effort upon which every justification of which we are capable lives and constitutes the final meaning of such justification.[15]

Jolivet later states the matter even more sharply: "if there is no 'absolute knowing,' it does not thereby follow that there is nothing absolute in knowing, for there is at least that drive toward the absolute [*exigence de l'absolu*] that alone gives knowing its meaning." In order to dissociate absolute knowing from an Absolute in knowing (which can be known), he and other Catholic thinkers point to a certain inevitably negative character in the knowledge of God, by which they mean that there is no exhausting the God known and consequently no philosophical conception of God that is entirely satisfying and none that cannot be replaced with a better one. Merleau-Ponty is suspicious of such tendencies, which are certainly common among Catholic thinkers, perhaps feeling that they are an attempt to ride the existentialist bandwagon: "It is striking to observe that today one rarely proves God as did St. Thomas, St. Anselm, and Descartes. The proofs ordinarily remain understood, and one merely refutes the negation of God . . . in seeking in the new philosophies some fissure through which the idea of necessary being can reappear." As far as he is concerned, the limitless transcendence of human existence is not such a "fissure" in his own work. If description of the transcendence in the objectivist position uncovers a

---

14. DeWaelhens, *Une Philosophie de l'ambiguité*, pp. 384–89. Régis Jolivet, "Le Problème de l'absolu dans la philosophie de M. Merleau-Ponty, *Tijdschrift voor Filosofie*, Vol. XIX (1957), pp. 53–100.
15. DeWaelhens, *op. cit.*, p. 394.

negative side, this is not the inexhaustibility of a real being toward which consciousness tends but rather the forgetting by consciousness of its own origin, its situation, and itself as event. Neither does the philosophical consciousness tend toward God as toward an ideal being: he has already challenged this as an unwarranted projection of human hope.

COMPREHENDING GOD

But is the phenomenal basis of this thinking of the Absolute nothing more than an illusion, a presumption that does not recognize itself? Merleau-Ponty does offer something more in "La Métaphysique dans l'homme": "my belief in the absolute, to the extent that it is solid, is nothing other than my experience of an accord with myself and others." The positive meaning of this thinking of the Absolute eludes us still as we are returned to the being of communication.

Eloge de la philosophie has more to say about the negative consciousness and also about the being of communication as a philosophical ultimate. This work will, incidentally, supersede "La Métaphysique dans l'homme" as *locus classicus* of Merleau-Ponty's discussion of the Absolute. Written six years later, its tone is sure, even serene, and the phenomenology that it advances does not contrast but rather blends in with what it takes to be the best in the previous philosophies. They too are held to have seen philosophy as expression, which like every other expression presupposes someone who expresses himself, a truth expressed, and others before whom it is expressed. As the question of the Absolute is taken up again, he speaks with warm approval of the philosophical greats who declined to situate themselves in an absolute knowing, saying rather that they taught "not this knowledge but its becoming in us, not the Absolute but at most, as Kierkegaard says, an absolute relation between it and us." In both Lavelle and Bergson, upon whom he comments, he finds versions of the exterior God irreconcilable with man *and* the God among men, with a clear option for the latter. The following remark about "Bergsonian theology" applies also to Lavelle, to Socrates (who is later discussed), and, without doubt, to Merleau-Ponty himself: in this theology "there is a sort of fuzziness [*bougé*] as a result of which one never knows whether it is God that sustains man in his being-human or the reverse, because in order to recognize his [God's] existence, we must go through our own, and because this is not a detour."[16] The understanding of God, then, is irrevocably qualified by the fact that it is *my* understanding. Continuing to interpret Bergson along lines set down in "La Métaphysique dans l'homme," he points in Bergson's work to a "God among men to whom will correspond a prospective history that is an experience seeking its own accomplishment." This God "cannot be fixed, known, or be apart from our duration and for itself." The progress of the experience with which he corresponds is defined "not by an idea but by an orientational constant."

In the system self-self-others-truth, which, according to *Eloge de la philosophie*, is the fundamental dimension of philosophy, the affirmation of God cannot occupy the position of *truth*. Merleau-Ponty underscores this by introducing a distinction between philosophy and theology such that this affirmation defines the latter, and the refusal to make it defines the former. The distinction emerges when, for instance, he refuses to consider the charge of atheism as relevant to a philosophy: "This is philosophy as seen by a theologian."[17] He turns then to remarks made by Henri de Lubac in his work *The Drama of Atheist Humanism* to the effect that twentieth-century atheism intended to "suppress the very problem that brings God to mind." Answering in

---

16. A question can arise here over the legitimacy of regarding remarks by Merleau-Ponty about Bergson and others in *Eloge* as applicable to his own position. We have indeed done this on certain occasions but regard it as justified because 1) *Eloge* is quite evidently a comment on what he has *in common* with Lavelle, Leroy, Bergson, and Socrates, and 2) the distinctions he makes and develops here have been made elsewhere when he was obviously speaking of his own view. The distinction of exterior God and the God among men is a prime example of his prolongation of categories previously introduced.

It has occurred to us that Merleau-Ponty has given some of the more striking statements of his *own* position in the process of commenting on the philosophy of others. *Eloge* is one example of this. The Preface to *Phenomenology* is another and his comment on Husserl's work in "Le Philosophe et son ombre" (*Signes*, pp. 201–28) yet another. The articles on Montaigne and Machiavelli (*Signes*, pp. 250–66 and pp. 267–83) are also examples.

17. He continues: "If we recall the history of the word atheism and that it was even applied to Spinoza . . . we have to admit that any thought that . . . defines the sacred differently is called atheist and that the philosophy that never places it here or there as a thing but rather places it at the juncture of things or words will always be target for this reproach without the latter's ever being able to touch it." (*Eloge*, 63–65.)

the name of the philosophy he advances, Merleau-Ponty says "this *problem* is so little ignored by the philosopher that . . . he radicalizes it and places it beyond 'solutions' that smother it." One might wonder, in connection with this important remark, whether the problem is being placed beyond *all* solutions or only beyond certain classic "solutions that smother it." As Merleau-Ponty himself continues, he seems at first to have a particular version in mind, but then he allows this version to subsume all the rest: turning to Maritain and to his claim that the saint is an "integral atheist" when it comes to rejecting such caricatures of God as an "emperor of the world," Merleau-Ponty says that "the philosopher will wonder if the natural and rational concept of God as necessary Being is not inevitably that of Emperor of the world, if without this the Christian God would not cease to be author of the world." This was to be expected. When we consider that *radicalizing* for Merleau-Ponty is a turning back to the point at which meaning is generated, to the dynamic present, it is evident that any problem directly attached to this moving and self-constituting consciousness will stand beyond any definitive and certain solution.

It is important now to see the relation between the present and that equilibrium of self with self, other selves, and truth that orients philosophy. This equilibrium is accomplished when developments in all three of its dimensions intersect to reinforce each other and to present philosophy with an optimum moment upon which it can henceforth take its bearings. Any such optimum moment is, of course, a present where *presence* is most intense and where meaning takes shape spontaneously and without a model. As the present becomes the seminal moment, the rejection of the notion of God conceived as goal of human tendency or as creator is immediately indicated, because to conceive God as goal would be to establish the source of meaning in the future and to regard God as creator would place it in the past. But where the present is origin, as we saw in *Phenomenology of Perception*, one goes toward his antecedents and sustains them, and the future is opened by an ecstatic move of the present toward it. The priority of the present thus leads one directly to the rejection of the classic notions of God as an Absolute, standing at either the beginning or end of time. But it is much less directly suggestive about the stubbornness of consciousness in presuming such absolutes. In fact when Merleau-Ponty radicalizes the problem by placing it beyond the solutions that stifle it, he is indicating quite clearly that the question is *not* to be stifled, which is to say that it is to stay *alive*. However much it outstrips my capacity for expression, it will nonetheless continue to tempt and mobilize this capacity, and this too must be ultimately due to the nature of the originating present. This *now* from which meaning springs is *my* present and so marked by my finitude that an Absolute outside of time altogether, an eternal God, cannot be justifiably maintained. Yet there is a dynamism in this present that so qualifies my finitude that Merleau-Ponty will say at one moment "I am the *absolute* Source." At other and later moments this dynamism seems to transcend the "I." In "La Métaphysique dans l'homme" he speaks of "an anonymous force sustaining each thought and experience . . . ,"[18] and in *Eloge de la philosophie* he seems to be expanding the same notion when he speaks (approvingly) of God for man in Bergson and says that man "encounters at the root of his constituted being a generosity that is not compromised by the adversity of the world and that works with him against it." How much can Merleau-Ponty concede to this dynamism (in order to make sense of the persistence of the issue) without violating his priority of the present? In "La Métaphysique dans l'homme" he gave us a clue to his attitude when he said that the most solid thing in our acceptance of an Absolute is our experience of accord with ourselves and others. He can also admit the extension of the present into every moment an *omnitemporality*[19]—but he cannot divorce it from *every* moment, for the eternal God implied in such a divorce would be incompatible with the experience mentioned above. My present can as well extend into the present of other persons, into the social dimension, but again it cannot go beyond this without *apparently* dissolving it. Thus does the transcendence of the present find its limits.

For the philosopher the central way in which this finitude seems to take hold is in its bearing on certitude. Recall that in "La Métaphysique dans l'homme" Merleau-Ponty insisted that my maintaining the Absolute was compromised by the fact that "I can judge only by my own opinions which remain capable of error."[20] But of *what is* the philos-

---

18. He says that philosophy cannot express this, as we noted. He does not deny, however, that it can seek to express it and so keeps the item alive as a problem that is, in one sense, a way of expressing it.

19. This is Husserl's term. Merleau-Ponty endorses it and the notion that it expresses in *Les Sciences*, page 8.

20. The same note is struck in *Eloge:* "The philosopher cannot be asked to go beyond what he himself sees or to give precepts of which he is not sure." (*Eloge*, p. 46.)

opher certain? The flesh and blood criterion of evidence—and certitude —operates in the present. But *what* would satisfy this criterion enough to authorize *complete* certitude? Given the mutual involvement of phenomena and the contextual character of the truth, this would demand a kind of presence to everything, and Merleau-Ponty seems to agree that it would: "There is the absolute certainty of the world in general, but not of any one thing in particular . . . ," he said in *Phenomenology of Perception.* The present in which this certitude could be had would be total immediacy, lived at the perceptual source and ruptured by the transcending movement of consciousness as it institutes meaning. Once divorced from this level (and divorce occurs by *any* act of reflection or affirmation), then one leaves the possibility of absolute certitude and enters the field of the *probable.* Here, conclusions would not have the ultimate coercive power of the primitive engagement, but it is here that every work of reflection—philosophy included—dwells. Merleau-Ponty, again differing from Sartre, has always demanded respect for the probable. This was evident in the last chapter of *Phenomenology of Perception.* In *Les Aventures de la dialectique* he will say that "the probable is another name for the real. It is the modality of what exists."

Philosophical positions, then, are probable. Philosophical conviction is not and never can be absolute certitude. Whatever *verification* is to be had on the basis of our experience of thing or truth, it is not to be secure against eventual overthrow. It is doubtful that Merleau-Ponty believes he said the word that ends the need for further speaking when he announced, for example, that consciousness is intentional or even that the subject is finite. Why should he demand more of the philosophical affirmation of the existence of God as he certainly does when he poses the problem in terms of absolute certitude and absolute knowing? It is true that at various points in history men have ruptured the human community in the name of the God of whom they had an "absolutized" conviction. But this is not the only form that conviction can take. Furthermore, the human community and its philosophical community is able not only to admit but to draw great profit from philosophical positions put forth with that tenacity and sense of appropriateness that is philosophical conviction. Indeed, it would be hard to imagine a philosophical position taking hold without the impulse of such a conviction. Why, then, not allow the philosophical affirmation of the existence of God to stand as a *philosophical position* required to justify itself like any other and subject only to philosophical conviction rather than absolute certitude?

These questions can be taken to embody a theist protest against Merleau-Ponty's handling of the question of the Absolute. Yet their theme can just as well be taken as his response to them, reminding them that *philosophically* their position is simply one among others that have emerged in the historical process of philosophy and that his posing of the question in terms of absolute certitude and absolute knowing has the effect precisely of rejecting the attempt to make it something destructive of that process and community. Merleau-Ponty does not deny the philosophical significance nor even the greatness of a Descartes or Augustine, a Malebranche, a Hegel, nor their place in the philosophical community. He does not deny the significance of religion nor its interest for philosophy. He does insist, however, that the affirmative of the existence of God rides the momentum of a presumption on the part of consciousness and rides it out of the range of evidence. For their part theist critics will feel entitled to remind him that he too admits the existence of this drive that he calls presumptive and that he has yet to account effectively for it. They will find it unlikely, along this same line, that he will ever be able to propose an adequate notion of the *ideal* order, in which such presumption is so important. Under the circumstances, then, they will wonder, and seriously, about the ability of philosophy to "comprehend" itself in any meaningful way and certainly about its "comprehension" of religion, a task that Merleau-Ponty clearly assigns it: "it is in the universe of the philosopher that one saves the gods and the laws by comprehending them." Merleau-Ponty does not, in our opinion, leave himself in a good position for offering an eventual understanding of the ideal order.

As for that stubborn presumption of consciousness with its forgetting of itself as an event, that presumption of the Absolute, which he said in *Phenomenology of Perception* was the "fundamental philosophical problem," we must recall that we have just heard him say that the very problem that gives rise to the thought of God has been placed beyond stifling solutions. The presumption is not to be explained, where "explain" means solve. Rather, is it apparently an *ultimate*, another face of temporality or of that fundamental generosity to which he has alluded. Such problems are not solved, though they are profitably meditated and even, in some sense or other, "comprehended." This will, of course, be unsatisfactory to the theist, who will wonder what "comprehend" can mean in this case. For Merleau-Ponty it will not mean to absorb intellectually but to enter into an effective dialogue *with*. We shall follow him in his attempts at comprehending religion here and in the comprehension of philosophy in the final chapter.

CRITIQUE OF RELIGION

The attempt to comprehend religion includes a critique of Christianity's worth as a vehicle for the incarnation of value among men. In his very first article he insisted that during the great epochs of faith the kingdom of God—though it was "not of this world"—was never an excuse for indifference to injustice on earth. Whether it is because the post-World-War-II period was not a great age of faith or because he had changed his mind about the concrete significance of Christianity's "unworldliness" (and it is in fact both), he says in his 1947 article "Foi et bonne foi" that the Church is a "reactionary institution." The article itself is a remarkable encounter of Catholic thought and spirituality with phenomenological existentialism. It tends more to block out in broad strokes an accommodation of the former with the latter than to draw the issues out to a highly refined point, and it includes a confrontation of existentialist faith with the Christian version as well as existentialist readings of certain key Catholic dogmas. A fundamental equivocation, he feels, is typical of the Christian position in history: at times it is generous and progressive but more often conservative and indifferent to social need. From its spiritual life the Church feeds both of these tendencies, which can create such tensions within the individual believer: "Catholicism believes in both an interior God and an exterior God. Such is the religious formula for its contradictions."

A question immediately arises here about the relation of this distinction with the one already made between the God of things and the God among men. One would expect the exterior God to be the God of things and the interior God to be the God among men, but in fact the *reverse* is the case. The key to this particular handling of the distinction lies in Merleau-Ponty's present focus on the *individual* and on the point at which the individual accomplishes his relation with God and with his own reality rather than in the perceptive realm as a whole and on God's transcendence of it. Thus the interior God is discovered when one turns away from the world and toward one's own soul. He communicates directly with this individual soul and in fact *is* really more myself than I am. Otherwise he answers the description of the God of things: perfection already accomplished, absolute and oppressive. For the individual there is nothing to do, really, save identify himself by knowledge and obedience with this being. This is accomplished by a movement *away* from the world, which terminates in an identity with self because it is union with God. This accomplished *self*-identity is what existentialists regard as *sincerity:* the sincere person tries only to be himself. Sartre made much of this in *Being and Nothingness.* The achieving of this at a distance from the world presents the picture of an impregnable Christian rectitude that is at the same time quietism, for action among men is meaningless.

The development that makes the self-identity of sincerity the characteristic of the Christian stands in contrast with Christianity as the religion of the exterior God. The religion of the interior God is the religion of God the Father, and that of the exterior God is the religion of Incarnation, of God the Son. The "exterior" character of the latter lies in the fact that its center of action is not within the soul but among men. The kingdom of God is not to be contemplated but constructed by the free action of men turned outward toward the world and each other. Such men are not capable of sincerity in the sense of confident and lucid "being themselves," because they are so involved in the world that they are not to be accomplished before it is. Their rule is not sincerity but *faith*, considered as adhesion to what one does not clearly see and extending beyond specific guarantees, and *responsibility.* The God in whom they believe and who is for them a call to action is consistent, he feels, with the dogma of the Incarnation but radically different from the interior God.

> the God-Man and the death of God transform the spirit and religion. It is as if the infinitely infinite God no longer sufficed; as if something stirred in him; as if man and the world, rather than being the useless degradation of an original perfection, became the necessary moments of a greater perfection. God can no longer be God and creation can only be accomplished if man freely recognizes him and renders him back the world in Faith . . . . there is something to do.[21]

Catholicism attempts to honor at once both this tendency and those

---

21. *Sens,* pp. 358–59.

of the religion of God the Father. Merleau-Ponty censures not their failure at this but the attempt itself, measuring it against his existentialist reading of the significance of Pentecost. "Pentecost means that the religion of the Father and that of the Son should be fulfilled in the religion of the Spirit; that God is no longer in heaven but in society and in the communication among men. . . . Catholicism stops and freezes this development."[22] It nourishes that aloofness from the human situation that is part of the religion of the Father, and the effect of this upon the Church, the institution that regards itself as the prolongation of the Incarnation and hence as the contemporary actuality of God-among-men, is that it slips out to the periphery of human affairs. Undervaluing social action, it accepts existing evils too readily and too quickly seeks privileges for itself in the status quo. While the human situation demands the overturning of the status quo in the interest of a future where the great masses of men can share in the accomplishments of civilization, the Church sanctions revolt only when it is itself threatened and "the Catholic as Catholic has no sense of the future."

There is a more tenable notion of sincerity in the existentialist conception of action and a far more tenable equilibrium between the demands of personal integrity, orthodoxy, and the human situation in the Marxist view of the individual, the party, and history. For the existentialist the identity with self occurs only in action, never in reflection, as the theme of the interior God demands. When the action is of historical significance it engages one's fellow men, with whose positions one must reckon. Merleau-Ponty feels at this point that Lenin's notion of "democratic centralization" allows in a uniquely adequate way for reconciling the demands of individual conviction and the institutional demand for unity. Without going into detail about this conception he says that it holds disagreement and tension between individual and party to be inevitable but to be transcended by the life of the individual in the party that is *his* party. "What differentiates the Marxist notion of party from any other and makes it a new cultural phenom-

---

22. Four years later in his *L'Homme et l'adversité* he presses this dilemma even more sharply upon Catholicism. Speaking on the point that there was an acceptable atheism that only rejected the God of philosophers (cf. also references to Maritain and *Eloge*), he says that "without an ideal God (*Dieu en idée*), without the thought that is infinite and that created the world, Christ is a man. His birth and passion cease to be acts of God and become symbols of the human condition."

enon . . . is that conception of an exchange and of a vital communication between individual judgment and historical reality through the intermediary of the party."

In 1947, then, preferences were definite, particularly on the question of the historical incarnation of values. The examination of Marxism is to continue and, as we shall see in the following chapter, occupy a great amount of his effort. His relations with it fluctuate. Like Christianity it will raise for him the problem of the Absolute. The Marxist Absolute would be, of course, that of a classless society lying at the term of the development of history, and it is not unusual for those thinking out this situation to attempt to distinguish basic philosophical options by speaking of the need to choose either the Absolute in the vertical dimension—the transcendent God of Christianity—or the one in the horizontal dimension—the shining future in Marxist thinking. Commenting on this posing of the question in "Le Langage indirect et les voix du silence," Merleau-Ponty says that "no philosophy has ever consisted in choosing between transcendences—for example, between the transcendence of God and that of the future of man. Philosophies are all concerned with mediating them, with understanding for example, how God becomes man or how man becomes God." The term *mediation* appears with increasing regularity in Merleau-Ponty's later works, and one of the interests in the remark just quoted lies in its making mediation a matter of learning how something came to be. To the extent that this remark is indicative of its meaning, mediation is that return to the genetic instance with which we have already become familiar. The attempt at such mediation can, he feels, be a work of great value for philosophy: "The confrontation with Christianity is one of the occasions in which philosophy best reveals its essence."

This remark is drawn from his short piece "Christianity and Philosophy," which introduces a section of *Les Philosophes célèbres*. This is in 1956, and though Merleau-Ponty has maintained his distance from Christianity (something to which he will allude in this article), the tone in which he addresses the question has lost much of its impatience, and the calmness that characterized his discussion of God and the Absolute in *Eloge de la philosophie* continues to prevail. As he begins, he offers a concise and very perceptive comment on a classic discussion of the possibility of a distinctly Christian philosophy that took place in France in 1931 and in which virtually all of the major figures in the French philosophical community participated.[23] Beneath the decisions as to whether there is or is not a Christian philosophy, he divines a series of attitudes regarding whether or not philosophy has an essence that can be considered in a pure state, and he notes that positions on this do not correspond with positions on whether there is or is not a Christian philosophy. (Some who hold that there is an isolable *essence* of philosophy maintain that there is a Christian philosophy, and some deny this.) Merleau-Ponty rejects the conception of a pure essence in favor of a relation with culture and maintains that there *is* a Christian philosophy. He insists, in fact, that there are many and that they are Christian because they stem from Christianity as cultural matrix. Some pages earlier he said that Christianity is "the recital and the meditation of an experience, of a group of enigmatic events which, themselves, invite several philosophical elaborations and have not ceased to elicit [*susciter*] philosophies."[24] The remark underscores the matrix character of instituted Christianity, and he moves then to address what he calls the central problem, which is the relation between this matrix and "Christianity effectively lived and practiced in positive faith."

This sounds as if it might introduce a discussion of his own religious position, and in a sense it does. But the self he considers is subsumed, so to speak, by his function as philosopher. The philosopher may view Christian culture with approval and may respect Christian philosophers, but "because he comprehends them the philosopher is not one of them. . . ." To comprehend is inevitably to set at a critical distance. For itself, he remarks, Christianity is "not a symbol but the Truth." This cannot be the case for the philosopher for whom any truth can be overthrown. Yet he insists upon the reality and the intensity of the dialectical relation between such a philosopher and Christianity.

> In a sense, the tension is greater (because the distance is less) between the philosopher who understands all on the basis of human interrogation and the strict and profound practice of the very religion that he "comprehends," than between a rationalism which pretends to explain the world and a faith which is in its eyes only nonsense.[25]

---

23. Cf. "La Notion de philosophie chrétienne," *Bulletin de la Société Française de Philosophie*, report of the Session of March 21, 1931.
24. This meditation on Christianity and philosophy closes with the remark "Christianity has nourished more than one philosophy, whatever privilege one of them may have acquired. In principle it does not admit of a unique and exhaustive philosophical expression, and in this sense, whatever its acquisitions, Christian philosophy is never a completed work."
25. *Signes*, pp. 179–80.

The philosophy that Merleau-Ponty understands as interrogation does not maintain the sterile contrast with religion that rationalism does. This could be seen in what he has already said. In "Foi et bonne foi" he noted that faith, the distinctive note of religion, was to be understood as "an adherence which goes beyond given guarantees." But philosophy, with presumption built into every concept, also includes this note. It is no accident nor is it inappropriate that the primordial relation to the world, the perceptive engagement, is often called *faith*. With such an affinity between philosophy and religion in mind, it is not surprising that he feels that the way of comprehension lies in seeing both philosophy and Christianity not as opposites but "ridden with the same contradiction." Or again: "Philosophical and religious relations with God should be of the same type. Philosophy and religion must symbolize." This is to insist that religion must have a place in that system of symbolisms that is the ultimate *logos*, rather than standing beyond it. When he looks into the history of the question to find the position that best approximates what he hopes for, it is toward Malebranche again that he turns. Without being *completely* satisfactory Malebranche had the outstanding merit of "substituting a transverse cleavage for the longitudinal division of a philosophical domain of pure understanding from the created existent world, domain of natural and supernatural experience. He apportioned to reason and religion the same typical structures of light and sentiment, of ideal and real." With such a view we have the invasion of one domain by the other with, one supposed, some consequent possibility of transcribing the experiences of one into the terms of the other. The analogy with his conception of other domains—perception, painting, history—is, of course, obvious. As in these other cases, however, he insists upon the contrast as well as the affinity among the areas that penetrate each other—thus his reservations on Malebranche for insisting on the ultimate identity of, say, the eternal Word and the incarnate word; thus his rejection of Blondel's position that the relation between philosophy and theology as that of interrogation and response. Each area, he insists, has its own negative *and* positive characteristics, its own interrogations and its own responses. The relation between them must respect this if it is to be the exchange essential to comprehension. He sums this up cautiously and from the side of philosophy: a genuine exchange between philosophy and Christianity would be possible only "if the Christian, with his reservations over the ultimate source of his inspiration which he alone can judge, accepted without restriction the task of mediation which philosophy cannot renounce without destroying itself." Philosophy, accepting the mediation, is apparently open to the exchange. Merleau-Ponty, accepting the validity and importance of Christian philosophy, embodies this position. What is left seems the task of the *Christian*—reconciling himself with philosophical mediation.

Chapter 7

Marxism

Merleau-Ponty's reflections on communism are part of an inventory of his time that he urged on all French intellectuals after the war.[1] It was a matter of finding a responsible and fruitful position in the political and social area, a duty incumbent on him as a responsible human being, as an intelligent French citizen, and as an editor who determined the political position of a major publication. But there is a good deal more to his interest in communism than this. As philosopher, he takes the communist problem as a means of extending his phenomenology into the questions of the nature of society and history and as an occasion to expand his reflection on intersubjectivity toward the forming of what DeWaelhens calls an "ontology of humanism." Quantitatively, his work on this issue is more extensive than that on any other subject with the single possible exception of perception. In form it is more difficult to survey because, as we said previously, there is no single treatise but rather various articles and essays published from 1945 to 1960. We might call these occasional, but if we do we must remember that for a thinker devoted to an inventory of his time there is nothing

---

1. "French intellectuals are not called upon to maintain the atmosphere of devotion and panic, the enthusiasms and vague terrors which give French politics a mythical and almost childish character. They are called upon to conduct an inventory of this century and of the ambiguous forms which it offers us." (M. M-P., "Pour la vérité, *Les Temps Modernes*, I, 4 (Jan., 1946), pp. 577–600.) This article is included in *Sens*, from which we quote it and where the above remark is found on page 347.

of the trivial or the superficial in the notion of occasional. In adjusting itself to the polemical reaction that it often draws—and in occasionally becoming polemical itself—the form of these writings reflects the climate of the discussion of the communist issue through most of these years in France.

As we consider the two series of articles that appeared under the titles *Humanisme et terreur* and *Les Aventures de la dialectique* and the material scattered through *Sens et non-sens* and *Signes,* we shall see Merleau-Ponty's position on communism shift from an early endorsement of its critique of capitalism and a refusal to oppose its politics to a "secularizing" of communism that denied it any favorable prejudice. His position on the nature of history alters from an emphasis on the proletariat as embodying the meaning of history and the acceptance of revolution as the process for its fulfillment to an acceptance of non-proletarian features of civilization as true and of non-revolutionary means for accomplishing the meaning of the human drama. The theme of intersubjectivity is led through its social and political dimensions, and the conception of *truth* is given some of its most striking expressions.

The themes in which one can see the central affinity between Merleau-Ponty's position and Marxist thinking began to emerge in the middle chapters of *The Structure of Behavior.* Here the *things* of experience were recognized to be objects-for-man. The *symbolic activity* in virtue of which they are such is treated as a practice—he usually says praxis—which brings things to their fulfillment. This view is certainly similar to that conception of the relation of consciousness with thing that Marx spoke of in his theses on Feuerbach, where he said that the question of their relation was a practical one (compare Theses II and III).[2] Merleau-Ponty prolongs this conception of praxis into the description that is given of work—"the ensemble of activities by which man transforms physical and living nature . . ."—and on beyond this to that giving of meaning that *Phenomenology of Perception* found to be *the* definitive character in man. He feels that such a position accentuates that "human productive activity" that Marx and Engels placed at the heart of their materialism.

His reflections on Marxism in *Phenomenology of Perception,* it will

2. K. Marx, "Theses on Feuerbach," *Marx and Engels,* Lewis Feuer (ed.) (New York: Doubleday, 1959), p. 243.

be recalled, take the form of an extended note on historical materialism, which appears at the end of the chapter on sexuality, and several pages on class and history, which are located in the chapter on liberty. The note promises a restatement of Marxism, gathering up its valuable insights and reformulating them in the non-objectivist terms anticipated for an existentialist conception of history. Just as existentialism's conception of consciousness rescued Freudianism from objectivism by integrating sexuality with existence rather than reducing existence to sexuality, the existentialist conception of history "consists just as much in making economics historical as in making history economic." There is an ambiguous identity of economics and history like that of existence with each of its other dimensions with the result that "there is no one meaning of history: what we do has always several meanings, and this is where an existential conception of history is distinguishable from materialism and from spiritualism." The analogy between social and individual existence is continued so that the "system of equivalences" notion is introduced into the former: "Conceptions of law, morality, religion and economic structure are involved in a network of meanings within the unity of the social event, as the parts of the body are mutually implicatory within the unity of the gesture."

So much attuned to the conception of symbolic activity, this "system of equivalences" theme also appeared in Merleau-Ponty's first article in *Les Temps Modernes* and then in *Humanisme et terreur*. Like the function of symbolizing and even interchangeable with it, this theme is a constant of his thinking, and he presses it even further now when he says of historical materialism that "one is tempted to say that [historical materialism] does not base history and ways of thinking on production and ways of working, but more generally on ways of existing and co-existing, on human relationships." One need have penetrated Marxist literature no further than the *Communist Manifesto* to know that Marx always refused to substitute mankind at large or general "interhuman relations" for particular classes and the specific relations found among classes in conflict when discussing the basic categories for understanding history.[3] Nor is there any point more consistently at

---

3. The *Manifesto* condemns German or "True" Socialism for orienting itself toward "the interests of human nature, of man in general, who belongs to no class, has no reality, who exists only in the misty realm of philosophical fantasy." (K. Marx and F. Engels, "Manifesto of the Communist Party," *Marx and Engels*, p. 34.)

issue between Marxism and its critics than the role and position of the proletariat. Eventually this will determine Merleau-Ponty's distance from Marxism. At the moment, it can be said, however, that both he and the Marxists are at least *rejecting* the same notion of mankind, that of an inert and separate *genus*. When Marx accepts the human essence as "the ensemble of social relations" (Thesis VI), the conception of the meaning of social that is implied converges with Merleau-Ponty's where he says that "man is but a network of relationships, and these alone matter to him." In the final chapter of *Phenomenology of Perception* he does turn to class and in particular to the proletariat. The questions he considers are those of class consciousness and personal initiative in history, and he challenges objectivist concepts here as he did when discussing individual consciousness and action. Like much of individual consciousness class consciousness is mute and unformed. Even at its point of greatest articulation—at the moment of revolution, as we pointed out earlier—its condition is not one of lucidity about historical conditions but rather unanimity in the sentiment that things must change. History for its part does not impose the revolutionary change automatically, and revolutionary practice demands human initiative even more than the perceptual praxis. Historical conditions ripen, and the situation proposes roles that must be taken up at given moments by individual men who may accomplish them, and with them the revolution, or may fail at both.

The themes of *situation* and *practice*, present in *The Structure of Behavior* and *Phenomenology of Perception*, provide a basis for his "existentialist" reading of Marx. They are "incarnational themes," and he says at one point that "the principal thought of Marxism . . . is of an incarnation of ideas and values" and at another that "in Marxism, 'matter' like 'consciousness' is never considered apart." But Merleau-Ponty feels that the French communists who were his contemporaries in the mid-twentieth century have rehabilitated the metaphysical materialism that Marx and Engels rejected.[4] In his article "Marxisme et philosophie" he taxed Marxist intellectuals Roger Garaudy, George Cogniot, and especially Pierre Naville for philosophizing in a way that simply suppresses the distinction between men and things. Those who have read Sartre's popular lecture "Existentialism Is a Humanism" may recall, in the pages devoted to the discussion that followed the lecture,

4. Cf. F. Engels, "Ludwig Feuerbach and the End of Classical German Philosophy," *Marx and Engels*, pp. 226–32.

texts of the sort Merleau-Ponty has in mind. In presenting the Marxist view of reality, which he prefers to call "naturalism" rather than "humanism," Naville says there that "the first reality is natural reality, of which human reality is only a function. . . . There are laws of operation for man as for every other object of science, laws which, in the fullest sense of the word, constitute his nature."[5] It would be hard to imagine a text more completely exemplifying the "legend of Marxist positivism." Marx himself lent credence to the legend, for he fought idealism with such ferocity that he drew attention away from the rejection of metaphysical materialism of which Naville's "naturalism" is an obvious example. Engels admits as much.[6] Merleau-Ponty fights the legend at every turn: consciousness, he insists, cannot be reduced to nature any more than history can be reduced to economics. The *dialectic* in *dialectical* materialism does not occur in things in themselves but in things as perceived by men. His constant preoccupation during his dialogue with communism is with the opposition of the legend and human presence: "is communism willing to integrate the subjectivity?" This is its major problem.

The central attack on the problem takes the form of a phenomenology of communist political and social behavior. He turns to it in *Humanisme et terreur*, where his thought moves from a set of crucial events—the 1935 trial by the Soviet regime of Bukharin and other well-known communists—out across the political, social, and to some extent ethical dimensions of Marxism. His conception of political and ethical existence—at least an early version of it—can be glimpsed in a remark drawn from his first essay on Marxism:

> the political problem is to institute social structures and real relations among men such that liberty, equality and law become effective. The weakness of democratic thinking is that it is less political than ethical, because it poses no problem of social structure and considers the conditions for the exercise of justice to be given with humanity.[7]

---

5. Sartre, *Existentialism* (New York: Philosophical Library, 1947) Bernard Frechtman, trans., pp. 75–76.
6. "Marx and I are ourselves partly to blame for the fact that the younger people sometimes lay more stress on the economic side than is due to it. We had to emphasize the main principle vis-à-vis our adversaries, who denied it, and we had not always the time, the place, or the opportunity to give their due to the other elements involved in the interaction." (F. Engels, Letter to Joseph Bloch, London, Sept. 21–22, 1890, *Marx and Engels*, pp. 399–400.)
7. *Sens,* p. 205.

The difference between what is *political* and what is *ethical* is based on the difference between the social and the individual dimensions of human endeavor. Ethics is the realm of individual behavior in the interest of value, and in it choice, intention, and motivation are the issues of greatest importance. Politics too is a realm of behavior—"Political criticism is not concerned with ideas alone; it is concerned with the behavior which ideas mask rather than express"—collective behavior in the interest of values common to many. One would not expect the reservation on "democratic thinking" to be a simple option for the political at the expense of the ethical—that is, for the social in opposition to the individual. If his underscoring of the importance of human initiative and his existentialist attention to freedom did not mitigate its being this, his notion of the incarnation of individual behavior in things and in institutions that are accessible to all would do so. In his very first writing—the article on Scheler in 1935—he protested Scheler's apparent reduction of personal morality to intention as a *disincarnation* of such morality brought about by freeing it from the responsibility for its consequences. In time he will make the same protest against Koestler and Sartre. This consideration of communism's historical behavior is led into the ethical because of the ethical consequences of the political order. Actually the political dimension dominates in his discussion because of Merleau-Ponty's desire to take communism on its own terms. The problem of communism is the opposite of the one attributed to Scheler: it is that of a political order threatening to stifle men because of the consequences of their behavior.

HUMANISM AND TERROR

Humanism is the recognition of man by man. Terror, as we shall see shortly, is anything that stands in the way of this recognition. These two are the good and evil of the human order. The phenomenology of communist behavior leads beyond the event toward them with that momentum of description seeking its foundation that we saw when the description of perception led to being-in-the-natural-*world*. Just as we had to ask there if the foundation was adequately revealed by the behavior examined, we shall have to ask now if problems of recognition of man by man is adequately manifest in its communist form. There is an additional question of whether the term *terror*, so fitting in postwar

Europe, is not too limited a term to express what stands between man and his recognition of and by his fellow man. In any case Merleau-Ponty is convinced as he begins *Humanisme et terreur* that anyone who deals with the communist problem must reckon with the terror (or *violence*, a term he uses even more frequently) that is part of its fabric. But nowhere in the political order has evil been banished, and the Western powers—"liberal powers," as he calls them—which oppose Russia under the banner of freedom, have a violent history also. Their freedom, he feels, is a matter of abstract principle or at most of constitutional declaration. Like that of Christianity it has not passed into historical reality: American constitutional guarantees coexist with racism and the suppression of strikes; those of Britain rest on colonialism. West does not face East as good vs. evil, as humanism vs. terror, then, in 1946. Wherever there is humanism, it will be alloyed with terror. As a result "the question for the moment," he says on the opening page of his first chapter, "is not to know if we accept or reject violence, but if the violence with which one forms his pact is 'progressive' and tends toward its own suppression or if it tends to perpetuate itself." Communism cannot be studied according to Western liberal principles (conditioned by quite different historical circumstances) but must be viewed according to its own: "Communism should be considered and discussed as an attempt to solve the human problem," he says at one point, and at another, "Is communism equal to its humanist intentions? That is the real question." This real question takes concrete form as the problem of the status of the proletariat, the actual nature and importance of its role in communist society. The *subjectivity* that communism must integrate is an *intersubjectivity*: "the proletariat is the only authentic intersubjectivity." His verdict after detailed consideration is negative.

Humanisme et terreur is divided into two parts, *Terror* and *The Humanist Perspective*, followed by conclusions.[8] The first part is a search for the structure of the communist problem, and this is found in a balance of logic and contingency, an ambiguity that makes initiative —personal or collective—significant. Koestler and Trotsky in his later years overstate in different ways the logical or objective aspect. In the

8. There are three chapters in the first part and two in the second. Four of these five appeared previously in *Les Temps Modernes* as articles. The fifth, a chapter on Trotsky that concludes the first part, is new.

second section the terms of the problem are located in the proletariat, which, Merleau-Ponty feels, contemporary communism abuses. This abuse is another triumph of objectivity over the subject.

KOESTLER'S DILEMMAS

The first chapter is a discussion of the writing of Arthur Koestler, particularly of his *Darkness at Noon,* which was exciting considerable attention in France at the time. *Darkness at Noon* is the tale of a devoted Marxist, Rubochov, one who had been a central figure in the communist revolution. Once in command of the nation, the revolutionary regime takes a direction that is at odds with Rubochov's conception of the meaning of history and of the needs of the proletariat. It is at odds with everything, in fact, to which he had given his life. In particular he could not be reconciled with the revolutionary regime's sacrifice of international proletarian interests to the more restricted interests of the "land of the revolution." The scene is obviously that of Stalinist Russia. Rubochov is arrested, broken down, publicly tried, and executed as were Bukharin and others in the 1930's.

In his first few pages Merleau-Ponty traces Rubochov's recovery of himself from an immersion in history that had lasted forty years. Even though they may not themselves have realized it, Rubochov and others like him had originally begun with an affirmation of the value of men. But their attempt to establish this value ran against a history that was impermeable to it, a history whose logic is not "that living logic of history that Marx had described and which is expressed indivisibly by objective necessities and by *the spontaneous movement of the masses* [but] the summary logic of the technician who deals only with inert objects." Merleau-Ponty feels that Koestler has placed his hero in a situation whose structural components are not drawn from Marx's notion of history at all but from sociological scientism: the opposing absolutes of a history *in itself* and pure consciousness. Between these no dialectic is possible. In such a framework there would be no possibility of the incarnation of human intention, and one would have to choose between complete withdrawal from history and society —the role of the yogi—and becoming a part of it—the role of the commissar. "Because he was only a mediocre Marxist," Koestler has missed the profound Marxist idea that "interhuman praxis is the absolute."

THE AMBIGUITY OF HISTORY
ACCORDING TO BUKHARIN

The Marxist structure of the problem—the interhuman praxis—appears more clearly if one turns more directly to Marxist behavior. *Humanisme et terreur* moves behind Rubochov to Bukharin, upon whom Koestler's hero was modeled,[9] and from *Darkness at Noon* to the actual account of the trial of 1938.

In the middle and late twenties Bukharin, a member of Lenin's inner circle, had led the opposition to Stalin's drive to establish those economic bases for Soviet society that were lacking at the time of the revolution. This drive meant the simultaneous and immediate development of heavy industry in Russia and the collectivization of Russian agriculture. When Stalin prevailed, Bukharin was expelled from the party and eventually—in 1938—was leading defendant in the first public trial of the famous series. He was charged with treason, with spying, and with various terrorist activities. The treason consisted in his opposition to the course Stalin was taking. Though it had occurred years earlier, it was now considered a crime. The espionage and terrorism charged involved liaison with German Intelligence service and attempts to kill Lenin. He pleads guilty to treason but denies at the same time being a traitor, a spy, or a terrorist. One gains an interesting view of the situation that Merleau-Ponty has in mind from Bukharin's own last plea: "I refute the accusation of having plotted against the life of Vladmir Ilyich, but my counter-revolutionary confederates and I at their head endeavored to murder Lenin's cause."[10] How is one to understand that what was at the time of its occurrence a quite precedented opposition to a direction of policy then under discussion comes to be viewed as a *crime* some years later? At the same time how make sense of the fact that the person who acknowledges himself guilty of treason denies that he is a traitor? This question of political responsibility seems to threaten the accepted order of past and present as well as the conventional relation of the subject with his own acts.

---

9. In a note Merleau-Ponty remarks that "it is known that Rubochov has the physical traits of Zinoviev and the moral character of Bukharin."
10. Report of Court Proceedings: The Case of the Anti-Soviet Bloc of Rightists and Trotskyites (Moscow: People's Commissariat of Justice of the U.S.S.R., 1938), English edition, pp. 778–79, quoted in Robert V. Daniels, *A Documentary History of Communism* (New York: Random House, 1960), Vol. II, p. 65.

What Merleau-Ponty insists upon first of all is that the trial must be taken as revolutionary in style. To be revolutionary is

> to judge what is in the name of what is not yet. . . . Revolutionary justice . . . judges in the name of a truth which the Revolution is in the process of making true . . . . This is why it is not concerned with the intentions or motives of the accused, be they noble or ignoble: it is a matter of learning if in fact his conduct . . . is or is not revolutionary.[11]

By the mid-1930's the "truth" that the revolution had accomplished was the Stalinist situation, so that the question of whether Bukharin's behavior in the preceding twenty years was revolutionary or not is the question of whether he did or did not work to promote the Stalinist situation. He did not, of course: he recognized this himself and pleaded guilty to counterrevolutionary activities. From the point of view that he himself accepted he is guilty, no matter what his intentions were. Now there is nothing unprecedented about judging human acts according to their consequences and without regard for intention. This is the normal thing in political life—Marxist and other: The statesman, as Merleau-Ponty says, "is defined . . . by the forces upon which he counts." Though he does not bring these forces into being, he selects certain ones as most important. By giving them their place in the determination of policy he becomes responsible for them. Thus Bukharin, reckoning on the hardship of collectivization and the resistance of the Kulaks differently from Stalin and previously having viewed the threat of Germany and the defeatism among the Russian military differently from Lenin, worked to make the commanding policy accommodate these. His option was neither personal nor private; to promote the view that accommodates these is to enter into a certain alliance with them. There are *no* indifferent acts in politics.

But if there are no indifferent acts in politics, one can, it is usually said, distinguish intention and good will on one hand from bad judgment on the other and at least allow the erring man to continue to live. One of Merleau-Ponty's basic protests against communism is its refusal to legitimate its opposition. He does not make his argument about the death penalty in Bukharin's case, however. Rather does he remind his French readers that after the liberation they punished German col-

---

11. *Humanisme et terreur*, p. 30.

laborators, some of whom might have been guilty of nothing more than believing that the Germans were there to stay and that the only alternative had been to cooperate. And the wartime conditions that come to mind as an extenuating circumstance for the punishment of the French collaborator were also present in the judgment on Bukharin, so that the explicit issue of his execution is lost in attention to world history. The latter said in effect that the threat of fascism in 1938, a threat that made Stalin's industrialization appear so important a protection for Russia, justified the verdict: guilty of counterrevolutionary activity. In his final statement Bukharin points to this and says, "World history is a world court of Judgment."

"Historical responsibility outstrips the categories of liberal: intention and act, circumstance and will, objective and subjective." Bukharin must be viewed quite differently from the way in which Koestler views Rubochov. Like Oedipus he finds that he has acted against his own intentions and promoted the very condition he wished to avoid. He is not an individual moral subject at odds with a great objective history but a tragic figure: the man at odds with himself:

> there is not simply Fate—an exterior force breaking a will—but genuine tragedy—a man at grips with exterior forces of which he is *secretly the accomplice*, because the opponent of the power can neither be completely for nor completely against it. The division is no longer between man and the world but between man and himself.[12]

This tragedy reveals the *contingency* in history, the fact that history is neither fully accomplished nor clearly known by those who must read it and even gamble their lives on the reading. This contingency permeates both its political and its ethical dimension. One of Merleau-Ponty's protests against the Russian behavior in connection with the trials of the mid-1930's is the refusal—exemplified by Vishinsky, Bukharin's prosecutor—to admit this ambiguity without which, he feels, one could not have a revolutionary perspective. The communists behaved as if the defendants were purely and simply guilty of violating established law clearly promulgated and understood, which would make their acts a matter of intention rather than historic responsibility.[13]

---

12. *Ibid.*, p. 71.
13. "The Moscow trials are revolutionary trials presented as if they were ordinary trials. The prosecutor attempted precisely to prove that the accused are criminals against common law. But on this level there is not even a hint of proof." (*Ibid.*, p. 31.)

TROTSKY'S RATIONALISM

Trotsky also said that the trials were not tests of historical responsibility for counterrevolutionary activities. But his protest was based on the view that the Stalinist situation in Russia was itself counterrevolutionary—that, in short, history in Russia had itself ceased to be revolutionary. Merleau-Ponty finds this attitude yet another example of a refusal to concede to history its *ambiguity*. There is no doubt that there was profound change in Russia from the time of Lenin to that of Stalin, but Merleau-Ponty refuses to accept the idea that this should be read as a swing from revolution to counterrevolution. The fact that it fails to maintain the strict revolutionary form does not give it a definite counterrevolutionary character. Because of the ambiguity of history the revolution can be preserved and prolonged in quite unexpected forms—even that of Stalinism. Trotsky himself on an occasion in 1926 had conceded that Stalinism was acceptable as a situation of fact, during which there could be forged the ideological instruments and organizations for a new revolutionary push at some time in the indefinite future. To move from such a position and later to judge the Russian communism of the mid-1930's as counterrevolutionary is to invoke very abruptly a standard of rationality in history that history can never be expected to show.

In summing up the first section of *Humanisme et terreur*, Merleau-Ponty associates terror with this contingency in the very historical situation: "history is terror because there is a contingency." In its most basic realization it is that "fundamental *terror* that in each of us is the consciousness of our historical responsibilities." This identification of the consciousness of historical responsibilities with terror makes the issue of the use of this term acute. We should recognize first of all, however, that the term is used in the typical existentialist way: the identity in question is that ambiguous identity that we previously saw between sex and existence or body and existence. It is certainly not suggested that terror is the total content of one's consciousness of historic responsibility, its complete meaning. Rather would the terror theme be a constant and permeating one that would not exclude other themes any more than sex excludes body or time. But even understood this way problems about its appropriateness remain. Postwar existentialism was given to the selection of words that tended to express a situation in a negative and emotionally heightened way. This often resulted in gaining for previously unappreciated themes the attention they deserved, but it also resulted in "deadening" the effect of the term by overextending its range. Thus the use of the term *terror* here underscores the great personal urgency of the task of humanization, but at the same time the thrust of the term is sapped by the fact that some people quite evidently regard their historical responsibility with joy, as a challenge that exhilarates, while others treat it in a matter-of-fact way. In fact the term diminished rapidly in importance in Merleau-Ponty's political vocabulary after *Humanisme et terreur* as the world situation tended to stabilize and to call for a less intense reaction.

FROM PROLETARIAN TO COMMISSAR

Humanism, of course, is the ultimate historical responsibility; violence is a basic dimension of the human condition. "Violence is our lot insofar as we are incarnate," Merleau-Ponty says at one point, and "the problem of violence is posed only for a consciousness originally involved in a world, that is, in violence." He then introduces the political perspective onto the scene in a way that gives it an ontological resonance: "The problems of politics come from the fact that we are all subjects, but we see and treat others as objects." Thus "violence is the situation with which every regime begins."

But if it is so deeply rooted in man, is it not also the terminal situation? According to Merleau-Ponty it may be, but this is not inevitably the case. The domain of political action is as extensive as that of political problems; man can alter his basic condition for the better, and the recognition of man by man is the goal of a course that can be advanced. Marx felt that it *could* be advanced to a solution, and his original reference point was the proletariat. "The theory of the proletariat as bearer of the meaning of history is the humanist 'face' of Marxism." When Marx describes the proletariat in the *Manifesto* and elsewhere, he depicts an objective condition: total dependence on a productive system that strips the proletariat more and more of individuating and particularizing features. This he conceives as promoting a consciousness on the part of the proletariat of its condition and at the same time as promoting a refusal of that condition. This refusal would be an affirmation of human freedom in the face of proletarian dependence. Marx's position points to a movement of *negation and detachment* from actual conditions, a movement that is accomplished by life and not by thought. Such a proletariat embodies the philosopher's dream of a concrete universal.

> It accomplishes what is valuable for all because it alone is beyond particularities, it alone is in a universal situation. It is not a sum of consciousness each of which would choose revolution, nor is it an objective force like weight . . . . *It is the only authentic intersubjectivity* because it alone lives simultaneously the separation and the union of individuals.[14]

So conceived, the proletariat is the very core of history. Merleau-Ponty rejects the version of Marxism that centers upon the proletariat as fulfilled in the classless society to come. He opposes this as a reading of the nature of history—it always emphasizes the *necessity* of historical development—and for its ethical implications—it gives human behavior a single final end that justifies every means. Marxism is "much less the affirmation of a future as necessary, than the judgment of the present as intolerable and contradictory. It is in the *thickness of the present* that it acts and with the means of action that this present offers." (Italics are ours.) The affinity of this emphasis on the present with that considered in the relation of man with the natural world is heightened by the use of the expression we have italicized and that is almost identical to the one concerning the individual situation in *Phenomenology of Perception*.[15] Communist violence must find its justification, then, not in a bourgeois-rationalist scheme of separate means and ends but in the *proletariat*, where the terms of this scheme fuse. The proletariat, if it is the end—its own domination *is* sought—is also the starting point —"a new humanity already prefigured"—and it is also the means to its own accomplishment: "history includes a logic such that non-proletarian means cannot lead to proletarian ends." With this, the proletariat becomes the politician's standard, the regulator of the Party's behavior and the norm for judging the meaning of terror. The Party must behave and terror be practiced according to the same dictum that Lenin offered for valid compromises between revolutionary and bourgeois regimes—that is, "in a manner which raises rather than lowers the general level of consciousness, revolutionary spirit, capacity for struggle and for the victory of the proletariat." The proletariat acts

---

14. *Ibid.*, p. 125. Italics are ours.
15. Cf. *Phenomenology*, p. 433.

as "regulator of the dialectic" in history as long as these interests are honored, and this means, as Merleau-Ponty eventually maintains, that the various basic policies must be explained to the proletariat in a manner that allows it both to understand and be convinced.

But as far as he is concerned communism no longer shows this face of Marxist humanism; it has cast the regulator overboard: "the proletarian movement itself as conscious and spontaneous movement . . . has ceased to be the term of reference of communist thought." In the decisive Russian situation the advent of revolution where economic bases for socialism were not available led to a subordination of everything to their construction, and this upset the equilibrium necessary to Marxist humanism: "the present phase . . . compared to the traditional perspectives . . . overestimates the objective factor of economic bases and underestimates the subjective factor of proletarian consciousness." Citing a few available statistics on such factors as salary structure and educational opportunity, Merleau-Ponty concludes that what the revolution has produced in Russia is in fact a hierarchized society in which proletarian interests are subordinated. Twenty years after its beginning, the revolution has become "an almost purely voluntary enterprise," a matter of decision and directives by the party chiefs.

THE YOGI AND THE PROLETARIAN

This said, Merleau-Ponty turns in his last chapter to define his own attitude toward communism. He decides on "comprehension without adhesion and free examination without denigration." Why does he show such patience with a system that fails as humanism? For one thing no other system has succeeded better. For another there are certain definitive accomplishments to Marxism's credit, in particular its philosophy of history. In this matter and at this time it is either Marxism or nothing, because every philosophy of history postulates in some form or other "the idea that morals, conceptions of law and of the world, modes of production and work have an interior connection and express each other," and this idea is "a kind of dialectical materialism." At the same time, it is the "system of equivalences" notion realized in the domain of intersubjectivity. It makes for a distinctive broadening of Marxism —beyond the lines of economic determinism and class conflict—but one that is accomplished by a distinctive narrowing in content, because

Merleau-Ponty also divorces Marxist negation from Marxist affirmation. As criticism of the existing situation, Marxism is not just one hypothesis replaceable by another but the simple enunciation of the conditions without which there will be no humanity, in the sense of a reciprocal relation among men, nor any rationality in history." On the strength of this and because the Communist Party in fact maintains the allegiance of the greatest number of European workers, Merleau-Ponty felt that communism should have its chance to work out its consequences. In particular it should be allowed to call the proletariat to its real fulfillment if it can. Communism must proceed without a guarantee of its success, however, and despite a humanist failure in Russia—two things the communists have refused to admit. Merleau-Ponty's attitude—*Marxist anticipation*—is incorporated in three precepts: (1) Criticize Marxism only on its own terms; (2) give no support to the notion of a preventive war; (3) do not approach the question of communism as if war actually existed at that time (1947).

If there is patience here, there is detachment also, and the latter seems to be growing. In 1945, just two years earlier, his espousal of the cause of the proletariat involved more than the "comprehension without adherence" to the communists. If he made it clear that he shared communist illusions about inevitable success, he nonetheless said that the best policy for the time was the "prevailing politics [*la politique effective*] of the communist party." A remark by Sartre helps place this increasing detachment in its context:

> From several conversations we had later, I gained the impression that prior to 1939 he had been closer to Marxism than he ever was later. What drove him away? The trials, I suppose. They must have struck him for him to discuss them at such length ten years later in *Humanisme et terreur*.[16]

It should not be thought—and Sartre is not trying to suggest—that in focusing on the 1938 trials in *Humanisme et terreur* Merleau-Ponty is simply acting out a youthful memory. For one thing the Russia of 1946–47 is still Stalinist Russia as it was in 1938, and the reflection on the trials is thus a way of gaining genuine insight into actual orthodox communism. In addition they offer an example of what Communists

---

16. J-P. Sartre, "Merleau-Ponty vivant," *Les Temps Modernes*, No. 184–85 (Numéro spécial, 1961), p. 315.

have regarded as reconcilable with their system. Merleau-Ponty's detachment from Marxism will grow, and his patience with it will lessen. But his attention to the communist phenomenon will not cease, and his inventory of his time will continue to select most of the events that it analyzes from communist behavior.

In 1949 he complains in *Les Temps Modernes* that the self-criticism forced upon the communist writer Georg Lukacs must be regarded as a passage of communism "from Marxism to superstition."[17] In January, 1950, he comments on the revelation of the existence of forced labor in Russia for persons who might number ten million.[18] This, plus the development of a social hierarchy in the Soviet Union, raised again the question of whether one could really call the system socialist at all. He criticizes this situation sharply, then, and at the same time refuses to take the U.S.S.R. as the only enemy. The concentration camp, he reminds everyone (and particularly David Rousset, whose exposé of the Soviet situation began the furor), is to be found in Spain and Greece as well. In *Eloge de la philosophie* he condemns Marxism for having given up on a truly human notion of the historical dialectic and having espoused a position that makes of all philosophy ideology and mystification. This is an echo of the philosophical reservation on materialism that he expressed earlier, but now for the first time he admits that Marx himself moved in this objectionable direction after his early works.

This, however, is in 1953, and by now Merleau-Ponty's attitude of Marxist anticipation has not only been worn thin by Soviet behavior, it has simply been destroyed and by a single culminating event: the outbreak of the Korean War in June, 1950. In the years that immediately followed this, his position in the political order shifts from Marxist anticipation to what he calls *acommunism*. During this time also (in 1952) he breaks with Sartre and leaves *Les Temps Modernes*, primarily

17. M. M-P., "Commentaire," *Les Temps Modernes*, V, 50 (Dec., 1949), pp. 1119–21. This article is included in *Signes*, from which we quote it, under the title "Marxisme et superstition," pp. 328–30.

18. M. M-P., "Les Jours de notre vie," *Les Temps Modernes*, V, 51 (Jan., 1950), pp. 1153–68. In this appearance it was offered as the editorial at the beginning of the issue and was cosigned by Sartre. In "Merleau-Ponty vivant," however, Sartre asserts that it is Merleau-Ponty's alone, and it is included in *Signes* under the title "U.R.S.S. et les camps," pp. 330–42, with no reference to collaboration by Sartre.

over the political issue. His philosophical position shifts and broadens as well, but to comment on all this it is best to consider his *Les Aventures de la dialectique*, in which it is exposed. It is well to recall as we consider this book that though it was published in 1955, its essays were written in 1953 and 1954, and that one of the most significant events in its genesis occurred in 1950.

The brief preface of *Les Aventures de la dialectique* warns the reader to expect only "samples, soundings, anecdotes from the philosophical life." But after this disarming beginning one encounters a series of four compact, closely reasoned studies that, however valuable taken separately, form together an impressive single study, united by the movement of Merleau-Ponty's reflection on history that reaches its most refined stage in them. He begins with a consideration of history in general, a consideration that takes the form of a dialogue with Max Weber. Then he advances to his own conception of Marxism in a pair of essays dealing with the work of Georg Lukacs and with its alternative, which the party adopted. After this he discusses the Trotsky situation in Marxism as an example of the actual state of communism. These four studies occupy what amounts to a distinct first section of *Les Aventures de la dialectique* even though the book is not explicitly divided into two sections. The second half is devoted to a critique of Sartre's position on the communist problem. It does not have the closely reasoned and compact character of the previous studies, nor, in our opinion, does it add substantially to what he said in them. Its significance lies elsewhere: in the fact that it set in public opposition the thoughts of the two most striking figures both in French existentialism and non-communist Marxism. We shall divide our treatment of this section between this chapter and the one that follows. In the Epilogue, with which *Les Aventures de la dialectique* concludes, Merleau-Ponty summarizes his own position and recapitulates the changes in his thinking on the communist problem across the previous ten years.

Les Aventures de la dialectique like *Humanisme et terreur* poses the problem of communist willingness to integrate the subjectivity, and for it too the subjectivity in question is intersubjectivity. Again, in short, the role of the proletariat is central. *Les Adventures de la dialectique* is more "theoretical" than *Humanisme et terreur* was, however. The latter, choosing as its central event the fate of individual revolutionaries

—Bukharin and his companions—has an existentialist tone and an ethical dimension which is not in evidence in the former. *Les Aventures de la dialectique* moves through theories of history to the terms of the problem, and the behavior under consideration is not the making of revolution but the making and judging of *theory*. It moves in the order of what primitive Marxism termed "ideology." *Dialectical materialism in various forms is what is being judged. The problem of communism here is whether a philosophy can be both dialectical and materialist at once. The verdict is that they cannot.* Contemporary Marxism has chosen to be materialist—and this is its *failure*.

THE CRISIS OF UNDERSTANDING

Weber's famous work *The Protestant Ethic and the Spirit of Capitalism* seems to embody a tenable theory of history. It allows one to focus first upon the *present*, that *point* at which the subject, which must be integrated in any tenable conception of history, intervenes. "Perhaps it is the definition of history to exist completely only thanks to what follows, to be suspended to a future." The future in this remark turns out to be the period following the historical past—that is to say, it turns out to be the *present*, the point at which an agent can intervene. While the subjectivity that must ultimately be accommodated is *intersubjectivity*—particularly the proletariat—the subject with whose intervention he begins is that of the *historian*. Actually, Merleau-Ponty maintains that the historian or theorist is not basically different from other historical agents like party and class, and this similarity permits quite easily a shift from one of these "levels of praxis" to another.

If history is completed by the intervention of an agent, then the historian's choice of perspective in which to view the past must be taken as *contributing* to whatever objectivity he achieves rather than threatening it. Thus while other Protestantisms are available, Weber selects Calvinism. He also selects a young, industrious, and independent capitalism rather than a later speculative version or one supported by political forces. He chooses these because they seem to provide a key to a variety of events, and his selection—obviously a choice—is not *arbitrary*. They are the components of a certain historical situation showing themselves first to him as a certain "style." As the study advances, the choice is justified as these elements resolve into a complex of themes that permeate every level of history. Capitalism, for example, is a structure that such themes constitute: a "rationalization" of history. Weber also calls it a "prodigious cosmos," and Merleau-Ponty feels that this view of the scheme justifies crediting Weber with a renewed conception of historical matter: "a human choice become situation."

Now the choice referred to here is *not* the selecting of themes by the historian but that to which his choice is attuned, what it is that he selects. *This* choice is rather the project characterizing an epoch and advanced, often in spite of themselves, by historical agents. Rejecting as always the position that this project is an *idea* at work in history, Merleau-Ponty represents it as a version of that more obscure and active consciousness to which he alluded in *Phenomenology of Perception* when he spoke of "productive imagination" and in *Le Langage indirect* . . . when he discussed painting. It is a sort of

> *imagination in history* which sows here and there elements which are capable of one day being integrated. The meaning of the system at the beginning is like the pictorial meaning of the painting which directs the gestures of the painter less than it develops with it and results from it.[19]

It is no less akin to the development of the meaning in language or in perception. Compare, for example, this remark from *Les Aventures de la dialectique*:

> History does not work on a model; it is precisely the coming to be of meaning.[20]

with this one from *Phenomenology of Perception*:

> the central phenomenon of perceptual life . . . is the constitution without any ideal model, of a significant grouping.[21]

A particular historical system takes shape only when historical agents —a class or leaders—take up its themes and advance *them* rather than the themes that would generate other systems. Capitalism required the initiative of the seventeenth century's historical agents, and its structure manifests their option. With the movement of history Calvinism eventually atrophied, but the cultural system (capitalism) that it helped create remained and still remains a major historical structure.

---

19. *Les Aventures de la dialectique,* p. 26. This work will hereafter be referred to in footnotes as *Les Aventures.*
20. *Les Aventures,* p. 27.
21. *Phenomenology,* p. 53.

Whether it will endure or perish cannot be known, for although history eliminates false solutions, it does not guarantee the institution of true ones. Capitalism's survival or replacement depends on the *present* initiative of historical agents just as its theoretical comprehension demands that of the historian like Weber.

Like everyone else Weber stands in his present and looks *back*. But he is part of the historical movement influenced by the past: it is *his* past, and it helped structure him *and* his present. Thus he is not in principle prevented from confronting the past with its own criteria, which is all that objectivity demands. At the very heart of this ability of the historian to comprehend is that root affinity between situations and freedoms that for Merleau-Ponty animates everything: "What we postulate in the attempts at historical comprehension is simply that freedom understands all the usages of freedom." Speaking of Weber as a man, Merleau-Ponty says his basic strength was "not to seek to have an image of himself and his life . . . ," and this description presents in terms of a personal life that "operation without a model" that is the exercise of the freedom that generates all meaning and understanding. The proletariat, conceived as without particularizing loyalty or other features—that is, as pure freedom, operates in the same way, and so both person and class can be said to exercise "the art of inventing what later appears required by the times." This reading of history that Weber inspires allows Merleau-Ponty's conception of history to be integrated with the previous themes of his *philosophy of signification* in an impressive way. The former now becomes a real prolongation of the latter though with results that remain to be judged. There can be no doubt, however, that it accommodates the varied dimensions of subjectivity, and it does so in the way that is claimed for Marxism in its great early period. It allows him to say that "what makes a given politics important . . . is the human quality thanks to which the leaders genuinely animate the political apparatus, and thanks to which their most personal acts belong to everyone."

OCCIDENTAL MARXISM

Though Weber's historical practice implied this position that converges so nicely with Merleau-Ponty's, his methodological and theoretical work does not formulate it. In his theoretical work the integration of subjectivity remains a problem: Weber felt that the fact that the understanding of history was itself a historical fact—that the subject was included in its object—was a wholly unacceptable relativism. Merleau-Ponty says in this connection that Weber seems to have remained dominated by the idea of an *unconditioned truth*. But the problem of relativism in history is also acute for the Marxists, and they too have a preferred reading of it. In 1923 this issue was attacked by Georg Lukacs, a Marxist and student of Weber, in the book *Geschichte und Klassenbewusztsein*.[22] The work and its theses were almost immediately rejected by orthodox Marxism, and Lukacs thereupon gave up the position. But Merleau-Ponty finds it to be the version of Marxism closest to maintaining the original and distinctive philosophical virtues of the dialectic materialism. Lukacs takes as a *fact* the relativity that frustrated Weber. As *Les Aventures de la dialectique* put it: "There is only one knowledge [*savoir*], and it is knowledge of our world and its becoming. This becoming, in its turn, englobes knowledge itself." This is a genuinely *dialectical* conception in Merleau-Ponty's eyes; and in it a position—dialectical materialism, for example—can become *radical* without being absolute, according to his earlier prescription "by considering itself as a problem."

The *matter* in such dialectical materialism is *human matter*: men in their concrete circumstances. Its historical development reveals the presence of consciousness. This development is not inevitable and mechanical as it would be in the bourgeois notion of progress but rather a process in which it can at least be said that a later stage of society—capitalism, for example—is more integrated than previous stages. Basically this integration is an intensification of the presence of man to man, which to Merleau-Ponty *is* the meaning of becoming in history. Now this intensification of interhuman presence is not to be found in the operation of a universal consciousness but rather in "the consciousness that in principle is to be found in each man [and that] finds in the structuration that history has realized a complicity that permits it to become knowledge of the social." The dimension in which this is accomplished is neither that of subject nor object but "that of the relations among men inscribed in tools and social symbols. These relations have their development, their progress, and their regressions. In this generalized life there is the half-seen, the doubling back or diversion, the reaction of the result upon what was envisioned."

---

22. G. Lukacs, *Geschichte und Klassenbewusztsein* (Berlin: Malik-Verlag, 1923).

This third order is *history,* and Merleau-Ponty uses the term *sedimentation* in speaking of the building up of structures that serve as vehicles intensifying the presence of man to man. The results of the process are visible only in retrospect, after historical inertia has been overcome by the human initiative that has intervened to solidify them or to institute a perspective in which they are manifest. The meaning of history, then—its *truth* (the term is used very frequently in *Les Aventures de la dialectique*)—demands that its accessibility to consciousness be maintained. Many contemporary communists support a doctrine of ideology that makes all consciousness false and confused and all literature, for example, suspect. Merleau-Ponty argues that the very claim that a consciousness is *false* indicates the presence in it of a connection with a truth that serves as norm for judging and rectifying it. He turns then to Lukacs' theory of *ideology,* which maintains the openness of consciousness to history in its entirety. This is to be seen in Lukacs' recommending bourgeois writers—Goethe, Balzac, Stendahl— as literary models to communist artists. The accomplishment of truth at the literary level, then, can move at a pace different from that on the political level. In the absence of a most direct relation between these levels, even the bourgeois origin of events in literature does not make such literature a form of false consciousness. With this, the decisive consciousness of history seems to outstrip its proletarian origins.

On the other hand if we turn to Lukacs' understanding of philosophy, we find that the consciousness in virtue of which history has its meaning is given its strict Marxist form as proletariat. Reporting this, Merleau-Ponty says: "History gives itself its own interpretation in producing, with the proletariat, the consciousness of itself." Generated by capitalism and maintained as a distinct class by the constant pressure of the bourgeois oppressor, the proletariat is part of history. Indeed, its conflict with capitalism is the central meaning of contemporary history: it *is* the very embodiment of criticism of its own historical situation. As the sociopolitical form of criticism it is revolutionary, and one must see the revolutionary behavior of the proletariat as the generator of truth. In carrying out this role the proletariat is neither pure subject—completely conscious of itself—nor simply an *object* for the *theorist.* Saying this, Merleau-Ponty returns to history as the *third order* of reality. Still drawing on Lukacs' early work, he now centers on what he regards as the central concept, in relation to which previous discussion of history has only been an approximation: praxis.

Praxis is a difficult notion but one in which Merleau-Ponty's philosophizing about history reaches a climax as, in a sense, did his conception of perception and speech. Attention to it not only underscores the themes that make Marxism a valuable philosophy, it makes the most impressive case for Marxism's convergence with phenomenology and existentialism. Thus in describing praxis Merleau-Ponty draws upon the existentialist vocabulary of *Phenomenology of Perception*. Praxis is "the inner principle of activity, the global project that sustains and animates the productions and actions of a class, that outlines for it an image of the world and its tasks in this world, and that . . . assigns it a history." It is not, quite obviously, the idea of any one person or the plan of any given group. An existential project, it need be remembered, is not voluntary and deliberate or fully conscious, even though the term "choice" is often applied to it. Again praxis is said to be "the situation common to the proletariat, a system penetrating all the orders of action. It is supple and can be deformed . . . but always eventually makes its weight felt. It is there, a vector, a solicitation, . . . a principle of historical selection, a scheme of existence." Finally, praxis is an order *beyond* the rivalry of consciousnesses. "The profound and philosophical meaning of the notion of praxis is to install us in an order that is not that of knowledge but that of communication and exchange."

This said, Merleau-Ponty articulates his conception of *truth* in the political order. It is a matter of the relation of the various dimensions of praxis—their adjustment to each other—and this is conceived according to the *Fundierung* model. Party and theorist are each superior levels of praxis where the truth generated by the proletariat receives its explicit formulation as politics and theory respectively: "Class consciousness is not an absolute knowledge of which the proletariat has miraculously become the repository. It must be formulated and corrected." To the extent that clarity and distinctness are achieved, it is the work of the superior levels. But the ground for this explicit truth is the life of the proletariat, and the *sine qua non* of its value is its adjustment to this life. There must be a "recognition by the proletariat of its own action in the politics that the Party presents to it." The proletariat must not only be consulted but *convinced*, and their acceptance with conviction is the "seal of truth" for the Party, assuring it at least of the "non-falsity" of its position. For the theorist there is truth when there is not disaccord with the proletariat. In both cases this explicit *truth* is a commitment to known facts but is never closed to alteration in the face of further facts. The proletariat as it is now—the empirical proletariat—is open to development. In this development history offers truth in the form of "an indefinite process of verification" that is identical with revolutionary praxis and that underlies these explicit truths as their genetic impulse.

It was, then, the very essence of Lukacs' thought, as Merleau-Ponty saw it, to place the meaning of history within history, and this opened his thought to convergence with the model developed in *Phenomenology of Perception*. This is, of course, a relativizing of any theory of history and as well of any class. But it was always true of the proletariat that it was to suppress itself as class when it accomplished its own fulfillment by revolution. This much relativism seems built in, so to speak. Merleau-Ponty—and Lukacs in 1923—hold it also to be "proper to dialectical materialism to apply to itself." It could become radical by taking itself as a problem and could even yield to a more competent successor. In short the relativizing of the meaning of history does lead one beyond relativism, but to a unique absolute *present* that is more comprehensive than class consciousness and, according to Merleau-Ponty, not limited to revolution as its mode. This would be a historical praxis, adequate to the generation of *truth* beyond class.

PRAVDA

Official Marxism preferred something else and rejected Lukacs' view in favor of what Merleau-Ponty holds to be metaphysical materialism. It confronted Lukacs with certain doctrinal "fundamentals" and particularly with the definition of *truth* that Lenin offered in his *Materialism and Empirico Criticism*: "the accord of representation with objects outside itself." The effect of this placing objects—in this case, history—outside consciousness is that as one does it one places the conscious subject outside of history. This in turn "dispenses Marxism from applying its own principles to itself" and makes it the observer of a dialectic now installed in objects. This attitude can be traced back further than Lenin, however, and *Les Aventures de la dialectique* points to its roots in the work of Marx himself: "the Marxism that wished to integrate philosophy was that prior to 1850. Afterward came 'scientific socialism,' and what was given to science was taken from philosophy." In the struggle between dialectic and nature Marx opted for nature, and with this Marxist positivism was born. There is even a remark in the second preface of *Capital* in which Marx calls *dialectical* "the positive knowledge of existing things." Marx's turn in this direction, Merleau-Ponty feels, was dictated by his difficulty in dealing with the *inertia* of historical infrastructure and the resistance that it posed. He lacked a conception of institution, particularly one modeled on language: "This order of 'things' that teach the 'relations among persons,' which is sensible to the weighty conditions connected with the order of nature and which is open to whatever personal life can invent: in modern language this is the *milieu* of *symbolism*, and Marx's thought should have culminated here." But Marx's thought did not culminate in the realm of symbolism, whose balance of inertia and agility might well be the best hope for the incarnation of the *dialectic*. It ended in *nature*, and even Lukacs finally declares himself willing to treat history as a second *nature*. Though Lukacs still maintains some elements of his dialectical philosophy in his theory of literature, Merleau-Ponty thinks that they too are doomed eventually: the internal literary criteria will fall before the demands of "class literature." Dialectic and naturalism simply do not mix. This is the fate of Lukacs and the story of communism, which in the elimination of opposition places its conception of dialectic "beyond challenge, but also beyond use."

THE DIALECTIC IN ACTION

Trotsky's career offers Merleau-Ponty an example drawn from communist practice of the disruptive effect of the opposition of dialectic and materialism. When he spoke of literature, politics, or morality, Trotsky maintained the central and regulating position of the proletariat. But in philosophy and in action—at the extremes of his thought—he slipped into naturalism. The latter showed particularly in that period when tension grew between himself and the Stalinist direction of the Central Committee in Russia during the twenties. Trotsky not only did not place his case before the proletariat as one might have expected him to but defended the Central Committee, joining with it, for example, in the concealment of Lenin's will and in branding as liars those who published it. In addition he was extremely hesitant and equivocal about his diagnosis of the thermidor stage in the Russian development of communism. Although in 1935 he insisted that the thermidor was ten years old in Russia, in 1926 and 1927 he had rejected the idea and turned only slowly toward it in the following years.

Merleau-Ponty believes these behaviors to have stemmed from a deeply ingrained Marxist inability to conceive of the party in *conflict* with the *proletariat*—and this particularly in the land of the revolution, where domination by the proletariat was taken to be assured by history. Thus even in exile Trotsky declined to refer to the bureaucracy—the seeming embodiment of counterrevolution—as another *class*. Certain of his critics (Merleau-Ponty debates with Claude Lefort on this point)[23] hold that his inability to separate the accomplishment of collectivization and planning from a framework in which it worked *for* the proletariat is due to his Bolshevik habits, those of the professional revolutionary whose frame of mind grew in illegal conspiratorial groups and who rarely hesitated to force a position. But Merleau-Ponty traces it back again to Marx himself and to scientific socialism, pointing now to its political consequences:

> When in the second half of the nineteenth century Marx moved over to scientific socialism, that idea of a socialism inscribed in the facts rose to guarantee yet more energetically Party initiatives. For if the revolution is in things, why hesitate to eliminate resistance by any means whatever, since resistance now would only be apparent. If the revolutionary function of the proletariat is engraved in the infrastructure of capital, the political order that expresses it is as justified by it as the Inquisition was by Providence.[24]

Trotsky's "permanent revolution" is a version of this objective revolution. It is at work in being beyond human initiative and is the point of proletarian rallying only where it has already become dominant. To admit that the revolutionary suppression of capitalism was a triumph of the party but *not* of the proletariat—or even that it was simply not of the proletariat—would run against the fundamental order of reality and "take from the dialectic its realist foundation and from the revolutionary party its authority." Trotsky's Marxism was *not* ready for this.

Stepping away, then, from Trotsky—and at the same time posing the

---

23. Lefort's position was put forth in his article "La Contradiction de Trotsky et le problème revolutionnaire," *Les Temps Modernes*, IV, 39 (1949), pp. 23–36.
24. *Les Aventures*, p. 116.

problem in another way, more philosophical and more Hegelian—
Merleau-Ponty says that Marx saw the proletariat as the embodiment
of the negation of its own historic situation and eventually of itself as
class. But such negativity would require the proletariat to be *always*
that fluid, self-conscious dimension of history that it actually comes to
be only at the privileged moment of revolution. At other times "one
does not find a proletariat that exists as 'self-suppression.' One only finds
proletarians who think this or that, are enthusiastic or discouraged, right
or wrong." They are, in short, a quite positive reality represented by
functionaries whose day to day activities are no less positive. Such is the
weight of history that Marxists—and Marx himself—have been unable
to integrate with dialectic. Their failure here is driven home by the
actual rupture of the dialectic at every level. Where the revolution was
installed as a *regime* (in Russia), it smothered its opposition and thereby
destroyed an essential dimension of historical process. The very process
that eliminated capitalism was supposed to bring the proletariat to
power inevitably. But the elimination of capitalism in Russia did not
bring the proletariat to power, only the Party. The fact that the revolution itself has occurred not where capitalism was mature, as Marx pre-
dicted, but in backward nations even raises the possibility that it might
be "essentially bound to the structure of backward nations." In sum in
the actual movement of history the "perspectives of the proletarian revolution have been shifted to a point where there is not much more reason
to preserve them and to force facts to fit them than to set such facts in
the framework of Plato's *Republic*." Dialectic in the hands of communists plays the role of *ideology*—that is, "it helps communism be
something other than it imagines itself." Historical fact has ruptured
the Marxist historical framework as surely as psychological fact ruptured Pavlov's psychological framework.

SARTRE AND ULTRA-BOLSHEVISM

There is objectivist disruption of the dialectical conception of history
from another quarter besides materialism. Sartre is anything but a
materialist, and the fact has always stood between himself and communism. It has not prevented him from endorsing communist action
in various areas and at various times, however. There is an example of
this in a series of articles that appeared in 1952 and 1953 in *Les Temps*

Modernes under the title "Les Communistes et la paix."[25] In it Sartre analyzes communist practice, as he says, "according to my principles, not theirs." Merleau-Ponty compares Sartre's position at length with that of an ideal Marxist in the second half of *Les Aventures de la dialectique*. Since it does not extend his own conception of Marxism and since Merleau-Ponty has already disavowed actual Marxism as a departure from its original promise, one must see the comparison as basically devoted to situating Merleau-Ponty in relation to *Sartre*. (Reaction to the work tended to support this idea, with Marxist critics— Garaudy, for example—concentrating on the first half and existentialist criticism—Simone de Beauvoir—on the second.) We shall briefly outline his position here and return to it again in the following chapter.

As Merleau-Ponty sees them, Sartre's *principles* are two: "there are men and there are things." Sartre has said this sort of thing often enough and offers some textual basis at various points in his works for the rest of this interpretation of his position. Men are defined by their consciousness of things, which are in themselves taken as opaque and beyond meaning. This consciousness of things is pure negation of the things of which it is conscious, and this negation is the *liberty* that Sartre places at the very core of man. Because it is the negation of things, it is bound to the things it negates and ultimately to the world at large. On the other hand it is only through consciousness as negation that any meaning whatever comes into the world. Thus this liberty is necessarily involved in the world, and in its involvement meaning arises. But, at the same time, Sartre insists that this freedom is in no way compromised, structured, or affected by this involvement. Consciousness remains as *pure* action or pure creativity. Merleau-Ponty feels that such a freedom must remain *impotent*, for it can never "take hold" in history, never gather its resources. Above all does it compromise that middle ground between subject and object that *is* praxis. Its meaningful contact with things would have to be conceived as *momentary*, for its purity allows neither dependence on a past nor commitment to a

25. J-P. Sartre, "Les Communistes et la paix," *Les Temps Modernes*, No. 81 (July, 1952), pp. 1–50; Nos. 84–85 (Oct.–Nov., 1952), pp. 695–763; No. 101 (Apr., 1954), pp. 1731–1819. Compare also his "Réponse à Lefort" in *Les Temps Modernes*, No. 89 (Apr., 1953), pp. 1571–1629, which defends the position of the first two articles against Claude Lefort, a friend of Merleau-Ponty's, who challenged it in the article "Le Marxisme et Sartre." Lefort's article preceded Sartre's in *Les Temps Modernes*, p. 89.

structure in the future. In such a framework historical truth—an institution, for example—simply could not find its grounds.

Where Merleau-Ponty contests Sartre's position most sharply and where he feels justified in speaking of ultra-Bolshevism is with regard to the latter's conception of the Communist Party and the proletariat, a conception that seems to be modeled on his notion of consciousness. The party is taken as center of consciousness and initiative, and its spontaneity is regarded as the source of the historical existence of the proletariat. It is "their continuous creation and the emblem of their nothingness, itself pure act or relation." With this intimacy of Party and proletariat guaranteed "the Party . . . is substantially the proletariat because prior to it there was no proletariat. Any divergence between the two is obviated, then, and in principle. The proletariat does sustain the Party, but this sustaining takes the form of strict and unquestioning obedience to orders. It lies not at all in the typical positive features of a worker's life. To reflect or to question is to hang back, to withdraw from the party into individual isolation. Lenin's Bolshevism lay in the fact that, despite all attempts to maintain the initiative of the proletariat, it was ultimately only the leaders who understood the situation and their spontaneity that was the key to history. Sartre's ultra-Bolshevism lies in his even more radical identification of historical consciousness with spontaneity—that of the Party—with the result that whatever is not the Party is the *enemy*. Opposition must be suppressed, and as a result the dialectic conceived as self-negation is once again stifled.

THE PROSPECTS OF MARXISM

The Epilogue of *Les Aventures de la dialectique* is a summary of its argument and the announcement of *acommunism* as a platform for political action. First we are reminded of what dialectic is, then of the "illusion" that has crippled it, and finally of the terrain of historical praxis that can be glimpsed beyond the contradictions of the illusion.
Dialectic is

> the global primordial cohesion of a field of experience where each element opens out on the others. It is conceived as the expression or *truth* of an experience where the commerce of subjects among themselves and with being was already established. . . . It has a past and a future that is not simply the negation of itself . . . . The natural and

human world is unique . . . because our differences open out on it, because we are imitable and participable by each other.[26]

The *illusion* that led to the banishment of such dialectic from history—save to the extent that is still preserved as "myth" or point of honor—was that of "precipitating into a historical fact, the birth and growth of the proletariat, the total significance of history. . . . It was to believe that the proletariat alone was the dialectic."

To exorcise the illusion, Merleau-Ponty turns briefly to revolution—proletarian praxis—to insist that it is not dialectical but equivocal or contradictory. Every revolutionary movement that has succeeded and become the dominant political institution has ceased to be both movement and revolutionary and has attempted to stifle each. The Russian Revolution and regime upon which he has dwelt so long and the French Revolution that he now mentions briefly are powerful examples of this. One must begin to suspect that the so-called betrayal of revolutions is not an anti-historical behavior of the bourgeoisie but rather an insurmountable historical fact. In every historical situation, even where capitalism has been banished, one faces some analogue of the dominant and oppressing class. Since this is the case, proletarian revolution must be regarded as an ingenuous form of historical praxis because it takes change and resistance to change as the *content* of history destined to be overcome together in the surge of revolution. But change and resistance to it are the *structure* of history and not its content, and they will not be overcome. As a result a shift in attitude toward the relation of historical action with institutions is in order. If history is inevitably structured, then it makes no sense to be against a set of institutions because they structure certain epochs—as capitalism does, for example—and to imagine that their overthrow would assure the recognition of man by man.

The first move in addressing the situation in which the Marxist perspectives are challenged is to "secularize communism"—that is, "deprive it of the favorable prejudice to which it would be entitled if it had a philosophy of history and in addition give it an attention that is all the more fair for not expecting from it the end of history." One of the major pillars of Merleau-Ponty's earlier policy of Marxist expectancy was Marxist philosophy of history, whose critique of capitalism he called

26. *Les Aventures*, p. 274.

a definitive accomplishment. Now he concedes that the acceptance of Marxist critique accompanied by a rejection of its action was itself an equivocal and ahistorical position because this critique and action form a single concrete movement. It was communist action itself, given the occasion, that made the unity clear. With the Korean War—which Merleau-Ponty felt that the Russians could have prevented—a situation of force suddenly prevailed in which the *criticism* of the anticommunist position could *only* be regarded as the acceptance of communist behavior.

The acommunist position, which he hopes will rally the non-communist left, is a withdrawal of a preference accorded to one of the two major alternatives of the time, but a withdrawal in the interest of a more candid examination of each and a different involvement in history. Acommunism is "the strict condition for the understanding of the U.S.S.R. because it confronts its ideology with what we know of its reality . . . , condition of a modern criticism of capitalism because it alone poses in modern terms Marx's problems." Its action is a positive seeking, for one thing, to develop an area of coexistence for the two major powers so that the ultimate question of war or peace does not arise. When one reads that "it anticipates a generalized economy of which [communism and capitalism] are particular cases . . . ," he gathers that acommunism is an option for *history tout simple*, rather than one side or the other, and that it found in its situation the structures that allow the hope that this transcending of alternatives is not a loss of grip but a deepened penetration of the historical process. On the level of political institutions parliament is reconsidered. In 1945, when he was urging that the politics of the Communist Party be adopted while one hoped for the revival of the proletariat, Merleau-Ponty disparaged any form of parliament as a means of social reforms. Now he sees it as a means of legitimating the necessary historical opposition. It is "the only institution that guarantees a minimum of opposition and truth." One of the things that he is struck by in 1956 as he comments on the de-Stalinization move of the Russian Communist Party's Twentieth Congress is Khrushchev's affirmation that the parliamentary method could be used as a way to socialism. Apparently, then, parliament can count as a proletarian means to proletarian power as Marxist logic demands. This seems to be an expansion of communist logic in the face of historical reality, though Merleau-Ponty has some doubts about the effect of a communist parliamentary majority on the freedom of a non-communist minority. Now *beyond* the need to appeal even to an *expanded* communist logic, Merleau-Ponty insists that the non-communist Left give up any tendency to regard political liberty as bourgeois and primarily a defense of capitalism. He seems to have taken it as bourgeois himself at the time of *Humanisme et terreur.* Now he sees it as indispensable to the dialectic in history. In this endorsement of freedom we see that the tension between the existentialist and Marxist perspectives is resolved in favor of the former. The original description of dialectic in *Phenomenology of Perception* made it a matter of the relation of man with man, and the note on history in the same work made it a matter of the full scope of human coexisting rather than simply of productive relations. Each set of remarks anticipated the humanism—the recognition of man by man—for which the Marxist class-dominated perspectives were simply too narrow.

The Marxists of course, did not agree, but one would not have expected them to. From the very beginning Merleau-Ponty's reflections on history and on the communist problem must have appeared as an attempt by an outsider to protect their own doctrine against them and their weaknesses. Pierre Hervé, communist editor of the periodical *L'Action,* wrote a typical response to Merleau-Ponty's article "Pour la Vérité," where the latter urged that the politics of the Communist Party be carried out but without illusions as regards the relation of this politics to original Marxist inspiration.[27] He referred to Merleau-Ponty as a conventional type of leftist intellectual: "both fascinated and repelled by communism." Reflecting on the latter's attention to earlier periods of communism, especially those prior to 1917, he says of Merleau-Ponty's work that "it is less a matter of political thought than the fascination exercised by the language and gestures of a bygone day." He is in "an agony of political romanticism." The preface to *Humanisme et terreur* devotes about fifteen pages to an ironic musing over the reactions of both Right and Left to the articles collected there when they first appeared in *Les Temps Modernes.*

The most notable communist reaction followed *Les Aventures de la dialectique,* however. At a public meeting held in Paris on November 29, 1955, the task of responding to Merleau-Ponty's actual rejection of

27. Pierre Hervé, "Sommes-nous tous les coquins," *L'Action: Hebdomadaire de l'Indépendance Française* (Feb. 15, 1946), p. 3.

Marxism was portioned out among France's leading communist intellectuals, and the product of their efforts was subsequently published under the predictable title *Mésaventures de la dialectique.*[28] The first and lengthiest piece was by Roger Garaudy,[29] and in it one finds a vehement and sweeping critique of Merleau-Ponty's position. Garaudy challenges the originality of *Phenomenology of Perception*, for example, and of the conception of the cultural world of which it offers a glimpse: "all the essential themes of *Phenomenology of Perception* . . . are to be found in five pages of Karl Marx, and the allegedly new 'cultural world' is really one hundred and ten years old." The pages in question are from manuscripts of 1844, very early in Marx's life and the period that most interested Merleau-Ponty. "But," says Garaudy, eager to rule out even the similarity that this lack of originality might suggest, "Marx went well beyond that first explosion of the 'cultural world.'" Beginning with *Eloge de la philosophie*, Merleau-Ponty conceded that Marx himself had moved away from the themes that were the most promising part of Marxism. He feels, of course, that this was a loss; Garaudy takes it as gain. Before he completes his attack upon those parts of *Les Aventures de la dialectique* that bore on Marxism, he has drawn upon a list of thinkers ranging from Shakespeare and Descartes through Anatole France, whom he puts to work in the censure of a book whose purpose he finds is "to give a philosophical foundation to anticommunism and to shore up the metaphysics of Mendes-France."

Garaudy was followed by Jean Desanti, who treated *Phenomenology of Perception* as a return to Berkeley, and by Maurice Caveing, who insisted that historical praxis must be conceived as class struggle. Victor Le Duc and J. Kanapa (the latter wrote in the first issue of *Les Temps Modernes*) then considered the practical political manifestations of the new Left. In doing this they focused on one theme that virtually all the other speakers included in the form of epithet. This was Merleau-Ponty's contribution of political commentary to the weekly paper *L'Express* and his respect for Pierre Mendes-France, the radical Socialist, whom it supported. Invoking this along with the remark in *Les Aventures de la dialectique* that stated "if the major crime of the bourgeoisie today is stagnation, and if the enlightened fraction of the bourgeoisie is for an extended period the only group in a position to

---

28. *Mésaventures de la dialectique* (Paris: Editions Sociales, 1956).
29. The subtitle is "Aventures de la dialectique ou dialectique d'une aventure."

struggle against stagnation, should one not ally himself with them?" Le Duc protests that such a position cannot be called a leftist position at all. One *is* brought to wonder at this point why a position that refuses the established Left and Right for history as a whole should regard itself as *Left* rather than "neo-capitalist," as the communists claim. The response is available, however: Acommunism will be a position to the *Left* because it is devoted to the political and social problems that were the concern of Marx and have always been identified with the Left. *Mésaventures de la dialectique* closes with a letter from Georg Lukacs, who speaks of Merleau-Ponty's use of his (Lukacs') early position as "disloyal," characterizes acommunism as reactionary, and concludes that "one must protest publicly against such a deformation of all the facts, against such a reversal of true relationships."

His political commentary in the period following *Les Aventures de la dialectique* stays abreast of the development of the coexistence theme in communism and the consequent adaptation of established Marxism to the demands of the history of the period 1955–60. This adaptation must have given him satisfaction. In "L'Avenir de la revolution," written in August, 1955, he analyzes the encounter of Marxist political and social practice with an advanced economy: that of East Germany. Marxism was strikingly unsuccessful here, and Merleau-Ponty guesses that its failure may have helped prompt the policy of coexistence, which was then developing. In the policy of coexistence, as far as he is concerned, "the revolutionary system admits for the first time that it doesn't cover all of history." Perhaps the proletariat outside Russia will be allowed to fashion its own—even non-revolutionary—means. His article "Sur la Déstalinization" of November, 1956, on the occasion of the Hungarian revolution insists that the *de-Stalinization* movement places in question the "two fundamental principles of the (Russian) system: that of the dictatorship of the proletariat and authoritarian direction, which is the modern form of the first." Finally, in 1960, he says of Marxism: "with the events of recent years, Marxism has decidedly entered into a new phase of its history where it can inspire, can orient analyses, can maintain a serious heuristic value, but where it is not *true* in the sense that it believes itself true." It is a valuable philosophy but not a practical grasp in history. History and philosophy have been divorced by the failure of existing philosophies of history. Yet the failure of the philosophy of history up to this point has not meant a complete failure of humanism. The last paragraph in the preface to *Signes* makes this clear.

> The world is more present to itself in all its parts than it ever was. More truth circulates today than twenty years ago in world capitalism, world communism and between them.[30]

---

30. *Signes*, p. 47.

Chapter 8

Merleau-Ponty and Sartre

On the opening page of her rejoinder to *Les Aventures de la dialectique* Simone de Beauvoir says that Merleau-Ponty

> has known Sartre long enough for the public to imagine that he also knows Sartre's thought. There was a time when he exhorted his adversaries to "learn to read" with such force that one might suppose that he knew how to decipher a text without prejudice and to quote one without mutilating it. In such circumstances, his misrepresentation is an abuse of confidence and it must be denounced.[1]

She does denounce it. Speaking, without doubt, for Sartre, she conducts a lengthy and detailed analysis designed to refute the attack upon him through what she asserts is a straw man: a pseudo-Sartre. Again and again, in a reply as bitter as the attack was harsh she charges bad faith and dishonesty.[2] With this, the level of the relations between Sartre and Merleau-Ponty reached its lowest point, and drama on the

---

1. Simone de Beauvoir, "Merleau-Ponty et le pseudo-sartrisme," *Les Temps Modernes*, Vol. 10, 1955, pp. 2072–122. This article is also included in *Privilèges*, a collection of three of Mlle. de Beauvoir's essays published by Gallimard in 1955. We shall cite it from the latter. The reference to the "learn to read" exhortation by Merleau-Ponty has in mind his reaction to the varied interpretations given his *Humanisme et terreur* when it first appeared in article form in *Les Temps Modernes*. This reaction was itself first published as an article: "Apprendre à lire," *Les Temps Modernes*, No. 22 (July, 1947), pp. 1–27. It then became the introduction to *Humanisme et terreur*, where the exhortation is found on p. xxx.
2. Cf. "Merleau-Ponty et le pseudo-sartrisme," pp. 222, 229, 242, and 264.

French intellectual scene one of its highest. It could not have been otherwise: if one of these men was not the most important philosopher in France at the time, the other was. Simply in terms of the individual talents involved their dispute would have been notable. But then it could not have been taken simply as a clash of highly talented individuals. Everything prior to the time—existentialism, non-communist Marxism, *Les Temps Modernes*—had operated to make them a single phenomenon. Their dispute shattered a unity well established in the eyes of their public and was all the more startling for that reason. What was its background? Merleau-Ponty wrote on Sartre the man[3] three times: twice early in their association and again the year before he (Merleau-Ponty) died.[4] Sartre wrote just once on Merleau-Ponty, an extended and often moving testimony after his death.[5] The light it sheds on their relationship, particularly during the periods of tension, is invaluable.

THE FRIENDSHIP

"At school we knew each other without being close friends." This is Sartre speaking. Merleau-Ponty recalls their association at L'Ecole Normale in connection with a particular incident: he and a friend faced a threatening group of fellow students who had been angered when Merleau-Ponty and his friend whistled their disapproval of certain particularly crude student songs. Sartre, three years older, "slipped between us and our persecutors and managed to extricate us without concessions or damages from the heroic and ridiculous situation into which we had gotten ourselves." After L'Ecole Normale events established a distance between them. Sartre, with his three-year start, taught at Le Havre, spent a year at Berlin (1933–34), and published his "La Transcendence de l'égo," *Esquisse d'une théorie des émotions, L'Imagination,* and his novels *Le Mur* and *La Nausée.* Merleau-Ponty taught

---

3. We prescind at this point from the philosophical commentary in *Les Aventures* as well as the earlier comments in *Phenomenology* and a few in "Les Sciences de l'homme selon Husserl."
4. M. M-P., "La Querelle de l'existentialisme," *Les Temps Modernes,* I, 2 (Nov., 1945). This is included in *Sens,* pp. 141–64; "Un Auteur scandaleux," *Sens,* pp. 83–96; *Signes,* 1960, pp. 32–47.
5. J.-P. Sartre, "Merleau-Ponty vivant," *Les Temps Modernes,* No. 184–85 (special issue devoted to Merleau-Ponty).

at Beauvais and completed *La Structure du comportement* (in 1938) but published only the two review articles in *La Vie intellectuelle*. For both men it was a time for the discovery and development of the instruments that they needed: "until 1939 we pursued our readings and research at the same rhythm, but separately." As it turned out, they discovered and developed the same instrument—phenomenology. By September, 1939, each was in military service, Sartre as an enlisted man in a meteorological unit and Merleau-Ponty as a junior officer in the infantry. Demobilized after the defeat of France, they met again in 1942 as members of a resistance group of intellectuals called "Socialism and Liberty." The group did not last, but their association did. "Husserl became both our friendship and our distance." Phenomenology, in short, drew them toward each other, but their versions of it differed; and their research, begun separately when they were less aware of each other, remained separate as their friendship grew. Their discussions were apparently profitable despite a normal complement of misunderstanding due to the personalities involved: Sartre felt that his own tendency to leave reservations unexpressed often contributed to Merleau-Ponty's assuming agreement where it did not exist and then his later irritation when he found that it did not.

Those who have read Sartre's political commentary and heard him call the bourgeoisie "slimy rats" may be inclined not to take seriously his reference to himself as a person given to leaving his reservations unexpressed. The articles that drew Merleau-Ponty's polemic—"Les Communistes et la paix" and "Réponse à Lefort"—are examples of a public tone become intensely provocative because of a quasi-personal thrust. It is not that Sartre habitually impugns the intentions of his adversaries but rather that he regards them—and himself—as responsible for situations that they do not intend. The "slimy rat" expression, for example, is not *pure* invective but a term with a definite moral meaning: "it is a term which designates that category of individuals, quite widespread in our society, unfortunately, who are guilty but who can be reproached for nothing." Sartre includes himself in the category, which originated with the communists. Still one cannot pass over the fact that he selects *this* type of expression rather than a less abrasive one. Curiously, though, Merleau-Ponty agrees with Sartre's judgment on Sartre's habit of the unexpressed reservation. In "Un Auteur scandaleux" he defends the latter against a breed of postwar critic who took certain ugly situations from his novels and used them as ground for dismissing him as an intemperate man, preoccupied with what was disgusting. Personally, he says, Sartre is the least provocative of men. For example, "literary confreres . . . at times attempt to anger him by proposing those theses which they believe to be the most contrary to his own. He reflects, nods, agrees, and gives his interlocuters a hundred good reasons for persevering in their positions." This is said without irony and included in a list of reasons for acknowledging Sartre as an estimable human being, which began with the incident at L'Ecole Normale. It *was* said several years prior to "Les Communistes et la paix," but its tone returns later in the preface to *Signes*, and the list is extended at this time.

Sartre concedes that he owes his political awakening to Merleau-Ponty. *Humanism and Terror* was the occasion: "This dense little book led me to the object and method: it gave me the push I needed to tear myself away from my immobilism." Apolitical before the war, this was still his attitude when he wrote the opening presentation of *Les Temps Modernes*,[6] despite his insistence there that the intellectual was concretely situated, that his situation was a call to voluntary action, and that the major threat in this situation was from the bourgeoisie. The intellectual in question was the writer and primarily the novelist; the voluntary action was an inventory of the time, which took responsibility for itself as an influence on the time, but which was not oriented toward direct political action; the bourgeoisie was far more the locus and matrix of pernicious cultural values than the possessor of political power destined to be seized by violence in a proletarian revolution. Sartre confesses that, at the time, he had placed "an abyss between the vague phantasies about collectivities and the precise ethic of my private life." Merleau-Ponty had learned much sooner that one must expect to be judged not only on one's intentions but also upon what history makes of them. This lesson, one of the most important in the appreciation of history, was learned in what Sartre calls the latter's "full and painful appreciation of passing time."

In any case, as the original editorial board of *Les Temps Modernes* drifted away,[7] "Merleau saved the journal by agreeing to take charge

---

6. Cf. *Les Temps Modernes*, I, 1 (Oct., 1945), pp. 1–21.
7. Though the resistance brought them together, Raymond Aron, Albert Olliver, and Jean Paulhan never really shared the views of Sartre and Merleau-Ponty.

of it: he became editor-in-chief and political director. It happened by itself . . ."—that is, it was not deliberately decided: things just took the shape in which *Les Temps Modernes* was coedited. But he refused to be formally acknowledged as coeditor (that is, he refused to put his name beside Sartre's on the cover) and simply initialed the brief editorials with which certain issues of the review began as *Les Temps Modernes*. Longer articles simply committing himself were signed. Sartre puzzles at some length over this and concludes that Merleau-Ponty was not confident of his (Sartre's) stability in dealing with the issues to be faced by the review. The political line taken by *Les Temps Modernes* during these years—and accepted by both men—was a familiar middle position. It promoted sympathy for the social aims of communism but kept up a criticism of its political behavior. Together, the two men made a single venture into active politics as members of the committee directing the Rassemblement Democratique Revolutionaire, an organization that attempted in 1948–49 to crystallize a political third force in France. It soon collapsed from the pressure of both Right and Left, and henceforth its two disillusioned supporters conducted their political activity in *Les Temps Modernes* and in the form of criticism and commentary.

POLITICAL DEVELOPMENTS AND ESTRANGEMENT

During this period Merleau-Ponty's reservations on the communists were growing. The proletariat showed no signs of rallying for the establishment of world socialism, and the nation in which socialism was established resembled more and more a classic dictatorship. His article on Russian forced labor camps appeared in January, 1950. In June the Korean War began and "Marxist anticipation" died. The one who had insisted that communism be allowed to work out its own conclusions saw it conclude in imperialism. The secularization of Marxism that he was soon to urge on everyone took place in him. The moment must have been a grim one, however: capitalism was already condemned, and communism was now lost. The likelihood of a meaning in history, of an intelligibility that might serve as vehicle for the incarnation of values that he believed political action to be, seemed slight indeed. With others dropping their neutrality to move left or right, he was extremely isolated. Politically, he grew silent, regretting some of his prior patience with communism. Curiously, though, *Les Temps Modernes* had gathered enough momentum to continue in its course without deliberate direction. Articles were submitted, accepted by Merleau-Ponty as a matter of professional conscience, and printed. Competent persons joined the staff, so that, according to Sartre, "between 1950 and 1952 a ship without a captain recruited the officers who saved it from perdition."

But the drifting bothered the now politically awakened Sartre. While Merleau-Ponty was silently grappling with his secularization of Marxism, the tensions generated in Europe because of the Korean War were building in the latter a pressure to speak out, to take a personal position, and to see *Les Temps Modernes* committed. The non-communist Left was simply breaking up and, in the face of what it thought to be the renewed threat of Russian imperialism, sided with the government, the Atlantic Pact, and the U.S.A. The political Left was manned by the communists alone. General Ridgeway, who had commanded the United Nations forces in Korea, came to Europe to direct those of the Atlantic Pact. The communists demonstrated (unsuccessfully) and the French government took repressive measures, arresting Duclos and other communist leaders on charges that were quite vague and arbitrary. At the same time, one Henri Martin, neither a leader nor a communist but a sailor, was imprisoned for the distribution of literature opposing the war in Indochina.

These things, which themselves loom rather small against the immense forces at play and grand-scale questions posed, triggered Sartre: "I swore a hatred for the bourgeoisie which would last until I died. . . . An anti-Communist is a dog. I hold this and always will." Inevitably, the fury seized his pen, and "The Communists and Peace" was written. "I had to write or smother. I wrote day and night . . . with rage in my heart, gaily, without tact. . . . Not for an instant did I . . . spare him." It appeared in the July, 1952, issue of *Les Temps Modernes* along with the final installment of "Le Langage indirect et les voix du silence." Sartre says that it started out to be a single article, though in fact it does close by posing a question to which the following article responds. The focus was upon the communist "political" demonstrations and strikes against Ridgeway and the Atlantic Pact in late May and early June, 1952, and upon their failure, which was caused by worker refusal to obey party directives and turn out. Anti-communists—the non-communist Left included—saw this as a worker rejection of the party because of its domination by Moscow and as demonstrating the possibility of a change in their political allegiance. Convinced that the only possible political Left required the Party as a rallying point, Sartre argued that the communist relation to Moscow did not compromise the revolution in France (the relation was a historical fact but not a necessity, and much was left to local initiative); that Moscow did not want war (if the Russians had wanted to conquer Europe, they would have already done so); that the Party had not damaged worker manifestation as a device for action by using it for political rather than economic purposes (workers do not live by economics alone); and that one cannot blame the Party because it promotes violence (violence is part of the condition of the worker qua worker). Neither Merleau-Ponty nor Korea is explicitly mentioned, and one might wonder why Satre feels called upon to say that he did not "spare" him. But he did say this in connection with the non-communist Left: "what is beyond my understanding is the imbecilic satisfaction of certain persons and newspapers of the 'Left,'" satisfaction at the supposed rupture between Party and proletariat. He says that these have had an unhappy love affair with the Party, followed by an estrangement according to the following uneven steps:

1. The Party is wrong, but still one cannot go against the proletariat;
2. I love the working class, but still one has to admit that it isn't very perspicacious;
3. I am no longer interested in the workers since they tolerate . . . Soviet concentration camps;
4. . . . alliance with U.S.A. . . . atomize Russia . . . hang all the Communists . . . reconstruct the real, international, democratic, reformed socialism on the ruin.[8]

The blanket charge certainly included Merleau-Ponty. Still "Merleau . . . seemed surprised at my zeal but encouraged me to publish the essay. . . . As a friend, he preferred to be amused rather than offended at my fury."

The fury then abates somewhat: "I was out of wind." The following (August) issue of *Les Temps Modernes* apologizes for the delay in

---

8. J.-P. Sartre, "Les Communistes et la paix," *Les Temps Modernes*, LXXXII, 81 (July, 1952), p. 2.

appearance of the second part "for technical reasons"[9] and promises it for September. It is not published until the October–November issue. The third part will not appear until April, 1954, a year and a half later. Sartre is fighting a number of battles at this time[10] and is also working hard to get his thoughts in order. The second and third articles explore the relation of Party and proletariat, the second attempting to clarify its nature and the third its status at that time in France. Now, in Part II, he makes clear the nature of his endorsement of the communists: "the aim of this article is to declare my agreement with the communists on precise and limited subjects, and reasoning from my principles, not theirs." He declares himself a sympathizer, a fellow traveler but not a Party member. It is in this article that he puts forward the theme at which Merleau-Ponty directed most of his fire, feeling that Sartre was operating on a consciousness-thing model, which is simply not adaptable to the social relations that exist between Party and class.

If Merleau-Ponty overplays this complaint—and he does—it is not without Sartre's having offered him an occasion. Sartre *does* argue that the proletariat only exists because of the Party. In doing this he distinguishes between a great mass of workers whose objective condition makes them workers and a proletariat: a real class from which a

9. *Les Temps Modernes*, Vol. LXXXII (Aug., 1952), p. 384.
10. The August issue of *Les Temps Modernes* does include an exchange between Sartre and Camus, in which Camus accuses the magazine of a travesty in the review of his *l'Homme révolté*. The tone of Sartre's response can be judged from his remark, "I shall answer, then, without anger, but, for the first time since I have known you, without sparing you." The review of Camus' work had actually been done by Francis Jeanson, and Sartre is involved because Camus addressed his reply, not to Jeanson (who adds his own response, pp. 354–61), but to the "Directeur des Temps Modernes." Alliances are being smashed everywhere, but one which might be expected to grow at this time does not—or at least proceeds only with the greatest difficulty. We refer here to a possible alliance between Sartre and the communists. Jean Kanapa, a communist who wrote an article for the first issue of *Les Temps Modernes*, conducts a slashing attack upon the review because of a favorable view that Colette Andry, a regular writer for *Les Temps Modernes*, took of a book by a former communist, one D. Moscolo. Kanapa accuses her and the magazine of serving American interests and of being "intellectual cops." Sartre rages: "It is not enough that one agree with you on the major chapters of your politics. He must cover the books you like with bouquets and drag the ones you don't in the mud. . . . Are you crazy? Haven't you learned anything? Are you going to sacrifice another alliance to that imbecilic arrogance that you maintain toward your allies?" (*Les Temps Modernes*, Vol. C, p. 1728.)

revolution might be expected. Then he notes Marx's insistence that the workers require a political party in order to be effective in history. Putting the two together makes the difference between atomized massified workers and a proletariat something the Party brings about: "if the laboring class wishes to detach itself from the Party, it can do so in only one way: by crumbling into dust." If the laboring class wishes to remain a class and disavow the present Party, it can do so only "if it affirms its unity against the communists, if it manifests itself as a class by the disavowal of the Party." This, he adds, would require other chiefs and another discipline. In each instance, it is the Party that makes the class a class. The first version emphasizes the giving of meaning by the Party and the second the fact that this is exclusively a matter of negation. Such is the behavior of consciousness in the *pour-soi* and *en-soi* relation, and there is little doubt that the latter model does operate. For Merleau-Ponty, who rejects the distinction between massified workers and a proletariat (or at least Sartre's use of it), it dominates the scene.

The final article in the series appeared in 1954. It attributed the actual indifference of workers to the Party primarily to divisions among them, divisions traceable to the development of capitalism. In particular does he emphasize the growth of a worker elite among technically skilled men, a group distinguished by its industrial *merit*. It has pulled away from the unskilled mass, which is distinguished by its *want*, and has often taken the best worker energy with it into other organizations.

We are obviously not doing Sartre complete justice here. This would require many pages that would actually belong in a book about Sartre, rather than one about Merleau-Ponty. Our goal is simply to make the meaning of this disagreement accessible. Sartre is now well beyond the position in "Les Communistes et la paix." Simone de Beauvoir said:

> Sartre wrote "The Communists and Peace" in given circumstances and for a precise purpose. Merleau-Ponty decided to look in it for a complete and definitive philosophy of history and found none. Rather than admit that Sartre hadn't put one there, he treats deliberate silence as evasion and undertakes to reconstruct on the basis of Sartrian ontology what Sartre must be thinking.[11]

What is one to say about this complaint of reconstructing a philos-

---

11. "Merleau-Ponty et le pseudo-sartrisme," p. 204.

ophy of history from Sartrian ontology? The picture of Sartrian philosophy given in *Les Aventures de la dialectique* is fundamentally that
of *Being and Nothingness*, which was published in 1943, nine years
prior to "Les Communistes et la paix" and twelve prior to *Les
Aventures de la dialectique*. Merleau-Ponty's criticisms are basically
those outlined in the final chapter of *Phenomenology of Perception*,
and they culminate in the problem that virtually everyone has with
Sartre's work: how does one reconcile the conflicting extremes of a
being and nothingness ontology with Sartre's own psychology and
phenomenology, which include conceptions of situation, engagement,
and facticity? The indispensable theory of social reality demands this
reconciliation that, Simone de Beauvoir herself admits, raises problems.
She says, however, that "Merleau-Ponty knows perfectly well that
Sartre is preparing a philosophical work directly attacking the question." This would be Sartre's *Critique de la raison dialectique*,[12]
which appeared in 1960 and which as reliable an observer as Ricoeur
says "vindicates him of any voluntarism. . . ."[13] But Sartre had not
attacked the question in 1952–54 when "Les Communistes et la paix"
was written or in 1955 when *Les Aventures de la dialectique* was published, and the sections of the former dealing with the relation of
proletariat and Party *do* suggest the categories of 1943. It is demanding
a great deal of a reader to expect him to make the necessary allowances
when Sartre admits that he is shouting in order to be heard. Is it
asking too much of a close friend? Perhaps not. But one is forced to
the conclusion that Merleau-Ponty was secularizing Sartre at this
point as he had previously secularized Marxism.

   The two went through a period of personal estrangement. The
exchange between Sartre and Lefort, the written version of which,
modified on both sides by Merleau-Ponty's good offices, finally appeared
in *Les Temps Modernes* in April, 1953, touched off a series of lengthy
arguments in which the hitherto silent reservations of both men were
voiced. It came to a head over a trivial affair. Sartre had accepted an
article by Pierre Naville that eventually appeared under the title
"Etats-Unis et contradictions capitalistes." After having read it,
Merleau-Ponty—in Sartre's absence—wrote an introductory note to

---

12, J-P. Sartre, *Critique de la raison dialectique* (Paris: Gallimard, 1960).
13. P. Ricoeur, "Le Philosophe foudroyé," *Christianisme Sociale* (May–June,
   1961), p. 393.

accompany it and to express editorial reservations that he felt were in order. Later, Sartre—now in Merleau-Ponty's absence—became irritated about the note and removed it. Merleau-Ponty learned of this only when he read the issue of *Les Temps Modernes*. He reached for the phone, a two-hour argument followed, and he resigned. The issue of the journal is dated December, 1952,[14] and this would be the approximate date of the split. Looking back on it, Sartre calls the whole thing "idiotic" but also inevitable in view of the accumulated reservations and in the interest of *Les Temps Modernes*.

THE WORK OF RECONCILIATION

The estrangement did not take the form of personal enmity. They met from time to time and spoke briefly. Sartre says that the work of reconciliation was underway when, in 1953, Merleau-Ponty lost his mother and withdrew from circulation. "I did not see him again until 1956. His best friends saw him even less." *Les Aventures de la dialectique* was published during this period and in it Simone de Beauvoir's response, "No doubt we had tried too hard to avoid violence. Some was necessary if we were to liquidate our differences." The violence died quickly, and in the following five years they met at various times, particularly at conferences. In 1961, a short time before his death, Merleau-Ponty went out of his way to attend a lecture by Sartre at L'Ecole Normale, and the latter was quite moved. But even prior to this, when he wrote the preface to *Signes* in 1960, he took an initiative to close the breach on an occasion that Sartre offered. The occasion was ideal—a reflection by Sartre on his own youth and on that of a mutual friend of his and Merleau-Ponty's—Paul Nizan. The reminiscence is Sartre's preface to a work by Nizan, *Aden Arabie*[15] published posthumously in 1960.

Nizan had been a close friend of Sartre—his roommate in L'Ecole Normale—and an acquaintance of Merleau-Ponty. His life was a prolonged tragedy: an extreme sensitivity subjected first to an impossible childhood and then to what he found to be an impossible society. Attempting to find his way—to "save his soul"—he left L'Ecole Normale

---

14. We attribute the seeming inconsistency in the relation of dates to stages in the argument to an editorial lag in the publishing of the Lefort–Sartre exchange.
15. P. Nizan, *Aden Arabie* (Paris: François Maspero, 1961), p. 188.

to take a tutor's position in Arabia. This failed him, and he returned to France to join the communists. He labored for them for a number of years, finally becoming an editor of one of their periodicals. They failed him too: he was horrified at the German-Russian pact in 1939 and quit the Party. A little later, during World War II, he committed suicide. The communists treated him as a traitor; others were indifferent. Sartre, however, wanted to reclaim him from oblivion and proposed him as model for the young people of the 1960's in France: "Who will speak to these 'angry young men'? Who can illuminate their violence? Nizan, he is their man . . . ," Nizan, not Sartre! Sartre accuses himself of an easy optimism at the time when Nizan was writing, "I am twenty years old. I shall not allow anyone to say that it is the most beautiful age in one's life, . . ." Sartre accuses himself too of having later capitulated with his time so that, with the rest of his generation, he makes a poor figure beside "Nizan, the man who said *no* right up to the end." Merleau-Ponty considers this and esteems Nizan but urges: "read Sartre too." As for the latter's regret at not having begun his life by revolt, Merleau-Ponty says that this was not weakness but rather a "precocious lucidity [that] does not come off badly when compared with the vehement errors of others." Sartre may disparage it, he continues, but we must remember that it is Sartre writing and that "his constant rule, since he is his freedom, is to refuse himself the excuses which he allows others."

Nothing here or elsewhere in these pages suggests the harshness of the preceding years. As he continues to discuss Sartre and Nizan, he makes some observations on youth that Sartre will pick up and echo in his eulogy. He says:

> There are two ways of being *young.* . . . Some are fascinated by their childhood. It possesses them, holds them enchanted in an order of possible privileges. Others are rejected by it toward adult life. They think themselves without past and within reach of every possibility. Sartre was of the second kind . . . ,[16]

and he had to learn that everyone has roots. One is tempted to say that in speaking of the first type Merleau-Ponty has abruptly turned from the relations between Sartre and Nizan to those between Sartre and himself. Nizan's childhood was hateful, and one expects fascination and enchantment only over the kind of joyous period that Merleau-

16. *Signes,* pp. 34–35.

Ponty knew. But that is much too simple. One can be fascinated by ugliness and emerge only with the greatest difficulty from a bad childhood. The first way of being young applies not exclusively to Nizan, but also to Merleau-Ponty himself and those "who continue their childhood or who wish to preserve it even as they transcend it . . . ," to those, in short, "who have never been cured of an incomparable childhood," as Sartre said of Merleau-Ponty. "They had to learn that what one transcends one does not preserve and that nothing can give them back the totality which they long for." If he had not said this himself, it would be difficult to take Sartre seriously when, in commenting upon Merleau-Ponty's seclusion after his mother's death, he says, "In seeing his childhood disappear he understood himself; he had never hoped for anything more than to rejoin it, and this impossible desire was his singular vocation, . . . his destiny."

INDEPENDENCE

As they balance accounts in their fifties, each reveals a surprising nostalgia for youth. At the same time, each finds the other not his enemy but his complement. Merleau-Ponty underscores Sartre's acuity and self-possession, while Sartre focuses on the unity of Merleau-Ponty's life, his rootedness and traditionalism. It was this traditionalism, he holds, that led Merleau-Ponty in 1945 to seek out the company of certain communists, a group with its own traditions. Earlier it had held him in the Church longer than might have been expected for a French intellectual. In each case an attempt to find a community failed, and he was thrown back upon himself. When the death of his mother drove home the tie between his search for a community and his attempt to regain a past that was irrevocably past, he was thrown back once again upon himself. After a period of retreat he appropriated this experience as he had the others. The seclusion breaks; friendships are renewed. Considering Sartre's self-criticism at this time, he says that "what is uncompromised in him is the sense of newness and freedom." Considering the point at which Merleau-Ponty had arrived, Sartre designates it as "Virtue without illusion." Deliberately, no doubt, the remark echoes what Merleau-Ponty says in the final paragraph of the Preface to *Signes:* "The conclusion is not revolt, but virtue without resignation."

This remark is directed at history, but it also applies very well to the moral and philosophical dimensions of Merleau-Ponty's own life. One's philosophizing is not out of touch with moral and emotional life, of course. No one could doubt that Merleau-Ponty's feeling for the past and his taste for community had their impact upon, for example, his conception of the intimate relation between the experience of the past and the experience of other people. It is also legitimate to see a process of purification accomplished in him by the various ruptures and disillusionments that he underwent. Thus the failure of Marxism threw him back upon himself, and his appropriation of it led him decisively beyond its class-dominated categories to a more coherent view of history as human coexistence, something that he had previously acknowledged but had not previously faced single-mindedly. The break with Sartre and the death of his mother without doubt occasioned a rectifying of his relation with his contemporaries and his past. We must be careful, however, not to mismanage the relation between the events of Merleau-Ponty's life and his philosophizing. The former did not just happen and impose their effect by impact upon a passive thinker for whom appropriation was a defensive reflex. The philosophical life has its own traditions, community, and labor of appropriation. As he will soon say, it "lives on everything that happens to a philosopher and to his time. But it reorients [*décentre*] this or transfers it into an order of symbols and of expressed truth." The *Fundierung* relation is certainly the relevant model here. If his feeling for the past and for community influenced his conception of these experiences, who can doubt that his conception of the relation between the experiences of the past and of others—already asserted in *Phenomenology of Perception*—was a resource in the moral and emotional struggle he faced during the period of retreat and silence. He did not discover human coexistence with the secularization of Marxism; he had it in mind and used it as a norm for Marxist performance from early in his career. Anyone skeptical of the relative independence and consistency of Merleau-Ponty's philosophizing should know that *philosophically* there was no silence, no period of retreat. From 1950 to 1952—the period of *political science* and withdrawal—he not only taught regularly at the Sorbonne; he wrote constantly. His two major articles on language, for example, date from this period, as does *Eloge de la philosophie*. As for 1953–55, he wrote *Les Aventures de la dialectique*—not only its polemical section, but the highly refined and lucid preceding chapters on history.

Merleau-Ponty was independent in his relation with these influences, then, and actively assumed the events in which they had their impact. This was part of his living out the movement of radical comprehension that is philosophy. Philosophy is itself a constantly unfolding event whose dimensions are self, the other person, and the truth. In 1953 it reached a climax with Merleau-Ponty, a stage both implied in the logic of its own unfolding and for which the events to which we have referred were occasions.

Part III

*PHILOSOPHY
IS
PHENOMENOLOGY*

Chapter 9

The Meaning
of Philosophy

"Without doubt, I could not do better than to examine before you the function of the philosopher." Merleau-Ponty has discussed the nature of philosophy before, of course. But previously he made his contact with philosophy as he looked toward the ultimate implications of perception or language or history. The discussion tended to be structured by the problems arising in these areas so that it bore on the ability of the philosopher to emerge from the sensible or from history, perhaps by means of language. Now the phenomenon in question is to be philosophy itself; the behavior to be analyzed is not to be seeing or speaking or revolution but the practice of philosophers as the history of philosophy reveals it. With this phenomenology of philosophy and its attempt to appropriate the history of philosophy, Merleau-Ponty arrives by yet another path at that most radical point where philosophy takes itself as a problem. The duty of self-comprehension is, of course, traditional in philosophy and part of philosophy's essential drive for total comprehension. That the examination of philosophy should take the form of an analysis of behavior—activity and not doctrine, as we shall see, particularly in the case of Socrates—is obviously quite consistent with his phenomenological style. These two overlapping tendencies in the logic of his work converge with the trying events of the early fifties[1] to promote this reflection on philosophy that first (i.e., in *Eloge de la*

---

1. *Eloge* was written prior to the death of his mother but following the break with Marxism and Sartre.

philosophie) gives particular attention to the individual philosopher. Subsequent to *Eloge de la philosophie*, his editorship of the volume *Les Philosophes célèbres* gave him the opportunity to extend his examination of philosophy. In a series of brief essays he comments on the meaning of the history of philosophy, oriental philosophy, the relation of Christianity to philosophy, eighteenth-century rationalism, and the philosophical innovations of the nineteenth and twentieth centuries. After this, his most wide-ranging appraisal of philosophy, he returns to many of the themes to which he had given previous attention. In 1958, for example, he comments again on Husserl in a very valuable article "Le Philosophe et son ombre," attending not only to the traditional phenomenological themes but also to the priority of the sensible, which, he feels, emerged in Husserl's later work. His final published piece "L'Oeil et l'esprit" continues this return to the sensible. We must remember, of course, that *Les Aventures de la dialectique* was also written during this period, making for continuity with the preceding years and serving the advances that take place now by the secularization of Sartre and Marx.

PHENOMENOLOGY
AND THE HISTORY OF PHILOSOPHY

We can gain a useful perspective on *Eloge de la philosophie* as well as some sense of the distance traveled by Merleau-Ponty in the period since 1945 if we think back to the preface of *Phenomenology of Perception*. It asked, "What is Phenomenology?" and sought to answer its question by commenting one by one upon such basic phenomenological themes as description, reduction, intentionality, etc. This emphasized Merleau-Ponty's affinity with Husserl, of course, and most of the other philosophers introduced—Descartes, Kant, the Vienna circle, for example—were simply used to establish the intellectualist—empiricist alternatives against which he was defining phenomenology at that time. The contrast with these underscored the originality and value of phenomenology and set the stage for his answer to the question that the preface had posed. "What is Phenomenology?": Phenomenology is philosophy in its most authentic sense. *Eloge de la philosophie* endorses and prolongs this conclusion but without defending—or even explicitly *mentioning*—phenomenology or Husserl. Its question is "what is philosophy," and the philosophers who are introduced set precedents, not contrasts. Phenomenology is now at home in the history of philosophy, and as Merleau-Ponty examines the thinking of his predecessors at the Collège de France—Lavelle, LeRoy, and Bergson—he finds them anticipating its themes. His scrutiny of Bergsonian intuition, for example, discovers in it a primacy of perception on the part of a consciousness that is dynamic and self-developing and that generates meaning that remains behind it as its wake. He treats Bergson's philosophy as basically a philosophy of expression and adds that "what we call expression is only another formula for a phenomenon to which Bergson constantly returned and which is the retroactive effect of the true. The experience of the true cannot be prevented from projecting itself in the time that preceded it."

In addition to this conception of truth as sedimentation, Merleau-Ponty finds in Bergson—and also in both Lavelle and LeRoy—a precedent for a theme much more central to his discussion of the function of the philosopher: that of the ambiguity of consciousness. Speaking of that ambiguity as it is integrated in philosophical behavior, he says, "What makes the philosopher is the ceaseless movement leading from knowledge to ignorance and from ignorance to knowledge and a sort of rest in this movement." What he calls ignorance here is an aspect of that negative character of consciousness—a major dimension of its ambiguity—that essentially qualifies our relations to ourselves, to other persons, and to the truth, the three basic dimensions of philosophy of which he spoke when he said, "I think neither according to the true alone, nor according to myself alone, nor according to others alone, because each of these three needs the other two and it would be nonsense to sacrifice it to them. A philosophical life always takes its bearings on these three cardinal points." The negative character of consciousness qualifies these relations by imposing the rejection of absolute knowledge in our relation with the true (this is the *ignorance* of which he has spoken), by imposing *reserve* or secularization in our relation with others, and by imposing an awareness of finitude and incompleteness in our relations with ourselves. All of this Merleau-Ponty finds in Bergson, but it is from the career of Socrates, patron saint of philosophers, that he evokes these characteristics most impressively.

The turn to Socrates is a return to the *origin* of philosophy, but not simply because Socrates stands relatively close to the chronological beginnings of Western philosophy. Rather, it is because he represents philosophical *expression* at its purest, uncompromised even by having taken the fixed form of the written word. His is a philosophy that is *all* inquiry and relation, and its story is the best we have of the classic difficulties that these activities encounter. Socrates was loyal to his fellow citizens, refusing to flee the city to avoid either trial or execution. He was also loyal to the gods, to whom he made sacrifice. But he was loyal to himself as well, accepting both gods and city on his *own* terms and allowing no one to feel that his allegiance to either was blind and unquestioning. Underscoring first this distinctive presence—absence to other persons—Merleau-Ponty uses the familiar socratic term *irony* in its description: "Socratic irony is a distant but true relation with others. It expresses the fact that each is solely and irreducibly himself and yet sees himself in the other person. It attempts to loosen the bond between them in the interest of liberty." But if *irony* is a term for his relation with other persons, it is no less an attitude toward the *true* and toward *himself*. Continuing his discussion of irony, Merleau-Ponty quotes Socrates: "Each time that I reveal someone's ignorance . . . those present imagine that I know what he does not" and comments, "He does not know more than they. He knows only that there is no absolute truth and that it is by that gap that we are open to truth." *Irony, then,* is an appropriate name for the posture demanded of the philosopher. It is the attitudinal form of the negative consciousness. *Eloge de la philosophie* points out that Catholic theists fail of this posture because of their insistence upon an absolute Truth, God. Marxists fail too because they insist upon a future already known. Each at the same time tends to absolutize a particular human community: Church or Party.

Merleau-Ponty insists, however, upon the basically positive character of the philosophical endeavor that he has treated so much in negative terms. It was true, of course, with the most primitive giving of meaning by consciousness that "one must be able to withdraw in order to be capable of a true engagement, which is always an engagement in the truth." In this pattern irony is interpreted as an indispensable philosophical *detachment* from which follows not indifference but "a special type of action among men." Basically, this action is that of *expression* upon which he has insisted so much. Philosophy must speak the truth, but the truth it utters and defends is what it finds in the event. Above all does it go to the roots of the event to watch the truth take shape.

Here, Merleau-Ponty's assertions of the positive aspect of philosophical activity take up again the tone and sense of the preface to *Phenomenology of Perception*:

> Philosophy turns back toward the anonymous symbolic activity whence we emerge and toward the personal discourse that builds in us, which is ourselves. It scrutinizes the power of expression that other types of symbolizing restrict themselves to exercising. In contact with all the facts and experiences, it attempts to seize rigorously the fruitful moments where a meaning takes possession of itself. It retrieves and also pushes beyond every limit the becoming of truth, which both supposes and brings about the fact that there is just one history and just one world.[2]

The individual philosopher serves this becoming by his expression of world, self, and others. And it, in turn, penetrates him so that Merleau-Ponty's descriptions of philosophers and philosophies tend to turn persons and doctrines into activities and relations: in *Les Philosophes célèbres* he will call Descartes (who is being taken as an example of any important philosopher) "a hesitant discourse, affirming itself by experience and exercise, learning itself bit by bit . . . ," while in *Eloge de la philosophie*, now citing Martial Gueroult,[3] he says that the very core or center of a philosophy is "a developing meaning that constructs itself in accord with itself and in reaction against itself." These descriptions emphasize process and fit well the notion that meaning takes shape in successive presents. But if they declare the becoming of rationality, what room have they left for the *rationality* that becomes, for the stabilizing of meaning? Rationality, it will be remembered, was to be brought down to earth, not simply dissolved. Of course, the discourse, the activity that any philosopher *is*, does, as we see above, learn itself by exercise and experience; the developing meaning that is a philosophy does *construct* itself. If we call upon the habit or artistic style as a model of rationality, we can begin to make sense of established meaning in the particular philosopher and his efforts. A habit eliminates the "irrational"—that is, the practically unnecessary or cumbersome—gesture or movement in the interest of an integrated activity. A style makes for a distinctive coherence within a symbolic system that

---

2. *Eloge,* p. 78.
3. Gueroult is the author of many impressive studies in the history of philosophy and holds the chair of History of Philosophical Systems in the Collège de France.

structures the characteristic *expressive* behavior of the artist. This is well enough as far as it goes, and Merleau-Ponty feels that it can be extended to the historical institution as well. History too is to eliminate the *irrational* in the interest of a more livable life for the great number of mankind. But what can be said of philosophy? Taken in terms of its history, is there any elimination of the irrational in philosophy or should there be? Certainly there are few if any philosophical positions that have completely *disappeared*, and one doubts that Merleau-Ponty would be out to promote the disappearance of any.

This particular issue gets his attention in the various introductory sections that he wrote for *Les Philosophes célèbres* and that are gathered together in *Signes* under the title "Partout et nulle part."[4] He comments upon the variety in philosophy and upon the adventures in philosophizing that produced this. The model is still *expression*: philosophies are *languages* "that are not immediately translatable one into another," and the overall unity of philosophy is that of a landscape or a discourse whose unifying principle is only gradually disclosed and is never beyond some challenge. This center of interest can shift, of course, but within a whole where all philosophies have a place. Its foundation is a fundamental affinity among the situations of philosophers: "What makes Descartes present is that, amid circumstances now abolished and in the shadow of certain illusions of his time, he responded to these hazards in a way that instructs us in responding to our own, though these are different from his and so are our responses." The explicit contribution of each philosophy in the history of philosophy can obviously not be simply part of an explicit total system that would contain all philosophies.

THE DIMINISHING IMPORTANCE OF TIME

But then how is one to reckon with the *actual* content of the great philosophies? Merleau-Ponty calls them indestructible "because they established the landmarks [*bornes*]—reminiscence, Plato's ideas, Aristotle's physis, Descartes' evil spirit—through which posterity cannot cease to pass." Such is their *truth*, and as we see this preservation of the past in the present we are reminded again that Merleau-Ponty has

4. Cf. *Signes*, pp. 158–200. We shall cite "Partout et nulle part" from this text.

called truth sedimentation. He holds this relation with the past up as model for understanding the relation of philosophy with everything else: "This singular relation of philosophy with its past generally clarifies its relations with what is not philosophy and, for example, with personal and social history." As he continues, he brings the notion of *sedimentation* into line with the conception of *expression*: "Just as it lives off past doctrines, philosophy lives off everything that happens to the philosopher and to his time . . . . it transports it into the symbolic order." As we consider this seeming equivalence of sedimentation and expression, we must recall that, whatever the apparent weight of the term, *sedimentation* for Merleau-Ponty is not the mere accumulation of the past to structure an inert present. This would simply throw the source of meaning into the past where he has always refused to place it. Sedimentation, which he has called "the presence of all presents in our own," allows for the action of the present and even its initiative. We should also recall now that in the remark above where he offers us a model the model is not simply the *past* but the *relation of present and past* or perhaps even the *activity* of the present in relation to the past. But here, even if the priority of present over past is admitted, the present in question is still a *now* generating meaning and leaving it *behind* as a wake.[5] While there is nothing here as crude as a priority of the past, then, one wonders if we do not have what might be called the *priority of the backward glance*. It is quite noticeable that at this point in his career Merleau-Ponty's assertions about process have lost virtually all of that reference to the *future* that was part of them when he spoke of temporality in *Phenomenology of Perception*. Recall that in this work the present was treated as ecstatic, not simply leaving behind a wake but thrusting itself forward to open up a future: "the explosion or dehiscence of the present towards a future is the archetype of the relationship of self with self."

If we speculate on the reason for the shift of emphasis away from the perspective of the thrust toward the future and toward the perspective of the backward glance, the first thing that occurs is that in *Phenomenology of Perception* Merleau-Ponty was attending primarily to the relation of the individual consciousness with nature. Here the traditional threat would be a determinism operating either from past

5. Recall Merleau-Ponty's identification of expression with the *retroactive* effect of the truth in *Eloge*, page 42.

or present, and hence the affirmation of freedom and creativity necessitated a certain emphasis upon the future into which the subject might always escape or transcend the past and present. On the other hand when he treats of history and its institutions—philosophy included—the threat to freedom and creativity seems to be from a *future*: a political and social situation toward which everything is *necessarily* moving or an intellectual position, known in advance, that integrates every other position. This speculation, which makes the assertion of freedom and creativity the key to the variation in his emphasis, gains some support from the fact that in his final article, where he is obviously speaking again of the individual, he restores the tendency toward the future.[6] Quite evidently, the unknowability of the future that he has had to emphasize against both Marxists and rationalists has become very important as a result of his discussions of history. One must wonder whether it does not threaten, at least temporarily, the status of this essential component of time and history. One's uneasiness increases later when we watch him integrate into his vocabulary the term *discovery*, one with a strong orientation toward the future as a normal component of its meaning. By *discovery*—the *discovery* of subjectivity in philosophy is what is under discussion—is meant that "once introduced into philosophy, the subject would never again let itself be ignored." *Discovery* suddenly seems equal to sedimentation, taking the latter term in the quite passive sense, where it means accumulation.

Whatever is the case here—that is, even if we are correct about this priority of the backward glance—Merleau-Ponty sees Western philosophy faced with the heaviest pressures to revise its own conception of itself and sees it also in the actual process of carrying out that revision. These pressures have sprung from within and also from its relation with what is "outside," and, when he becomes precise about the change that they should bring about, he speaks of a revision of the theory of the concept. Western philosophy has been dominated by the concept, by its rigor, which has communicated itself into Western intellectual habits, and by the expectation of total and adequate intellectual possession of world and self that seems to haunt its pursuit. But this very demand for total possession necessitates attention to the philosophical positions that

---

6. "If creations are not acquired, it is not simply because, like everything, they pass; it is also because they have almost all of their lives before them." (*L'Oeil et l'esprit*, p. 227.)

have no such goal—oriental philosophies, for example, that witness a truth scattered about in the universe without attempting to systematize it, and Christian philosophies, always sensitive to a supernatural beyond human grasp. If it is to take seriously its own commitment to total inclusiveness, Western philosophy must cease to make such inclusiveness a possessing and allow it to be that *comprehension* that is simply the entering into a meaningful exchange with the positions in question. Expressing this now as a matter of revising the concept, he says that "our philosophical problem is to open up the concept without destroying it." The opened concept will not have to bear the entire burden of the unity of philosophy. There is an affinity among cultures, "a unity of the human spirit [that] already exists in the lateral relations of each culture with the others . . . ," that can serve as basis for the dialogue between Western and Oriental philosophy, just as the Christian experience of European philosophy can help ground the exchange of philosopher with Christian and as the affinity among philosophers— mentioned a moment ago when we spoke of Descartes—grounds their exchange.

Descartes' own time—which Merleau-Ponty calls the period of "Le Grand Rationalisme"—felt that it could ground philosophy in *being*, of which it had a total vision, and particularly in a creating God as "positive infinite." This was a privileged moment in philosophy as far as the sense of the unity of things and of disciplines is concerned, but it was also a period of innocence. Philosophical experience has since dispelled this innocence and come to know itself as a historical event. As a result the all-embracing agreements that rationalism affirmed— accords with evidence, with self, and with others—have been acknowledged as unstable. Philosophical thought is now seen to contain its great moments as memories from which it emerges to some extent by forgetting them but primarily by refusing to acknowledge that their expression exhausted, and thereby completed, its meaning. This transformation of philosophy with the abandonment of the notion that everything was clearly grounded in the "positive infinite" is further specified when Merleau-Ponty calls it the discovery of *subjectivity*. It is not that a doctrine of subjectivity is, in itself, a new thing. In fact he credits the Greeks with a highly developed conception of it. What is characteristic of philosophy since Descartes is that subjectivity is conceived in negative terms and that it has been placed at the center of philosophy, "charged with making the positive appear, assuming it and transforming it." The tone is Sartrian, and in fact at this point he cites with approval Sartre's conception of subject as negation needing the world and yet remaining foreign to it.

This reflection by Merleau-Ponty on the history of philosophy concludes with the assertion that *existence* and *dialectic* are the themes most characteristic of the philosophy of the last fifty years. By existence he means the being-in-the-world that was just discussed as negative subjectivity. As for dialectic, this is something that rises out of existence, and its first movement is the separation of reflection from the unreflective life of consciousness. It is evident that the conception of dialectic has become thoroughly domesticated in its relations with phenomenological existentialism as has that other Hegelian term *mediation*. Merleau-Ponty now treats mediation as the *recognition* of that self-possession and emergence from self to which he introduced us in *Phenomenology of Perception*. When he makes the guess about the future of philosophy that his general appraisal seems to require, we find a pair of negative assertions about the developments since Descartes that are to live on at the very center of philosophy: "it will never regain the conviction that it holds in the form of its concepts, the keys to nature, or history, and it will never renounce its radicalism, that search for presuppositions and foundations that has produced great philosophies."

What can be said of this from the point of view of philosophy's elimination of the irrational? We must realize, first of all, that the position "eliminated" does not completely disappear but remains as *memory* on the margin of philosophical activity, helping to structure its present. Thus the function of sedimentation is such that there can be elimination without total disappearance, and this seems to fit the facts rather well. We can also take note of the curious irony according to which the "irrational" element that the history of philosophy has most recently eliminated is *rationalism*. Its banishment testifies to the presence of another rationality in relation to which rationalism would have to be considered irrational. This inversion brings to mind the displacement of the meaning of *nature* that we observed during our discussion of *Phenomenology of Perception* and to which Merleau-Ponty himself returns in the article we shall consider next. To move to the very center of the question, however, it seems that what has been enduringly accomplished in philosophy is the recognition that the elimination of the irrational can never be completely achieved. What has been enduringly eliminated is the position that it can. This habit of challenging its own habits is to dwell in every philosophical *present*, and not only as its trailing memory. When he asserts that it *has* characterized the efforts of the great philosophers, he adds, of course, to the picture of the constancy of this distinctive *activity*. It doubtless animated Descartes himself, even though the explicit position he forged invited one to forget the original thrust that brought it into being. This forgetting is part of the play of sedimentation and part of the discovery that displaced rationalism. We can even say that it is part of the revised rationality. If we state the radicalism of philosophy in a positive rather than a negative way, it becomes expression again. It is sufficient for the existence of philosophy that the relation of philosopher and being should remain a problem—that is, "that the *être à être* subsist between being and he who, in every sense of the word, emerges from it, judges it, accepts and rejects it, transforms and finally leaves it."

RETURN TO THE SENSIBLE

After this meditation on the history of philosophy in its most general dimensions, Merleau-Ponty commented again on Husserl and on the themes—reduction, intentionality, and constitution—that Husserl had put at his disposal. The occasion was the centenary of Husserl's birth and an anthology of articles (*Edmund Husserl, 1859–1959*[7]) written by various persons associated with him. These include such figures as Binswanger, Levinas, Schutz, Fink, and Hocking. The impulse to compare what he does here with his management of those themes in the preface of *Phenomenology of Perception* is, of course, overwhelming. Here, as there, he declines the role of objective commentator and of disciple pure and simple in favor of "thinking through again . . ."[8] the themes Husserl had offered in his later writings. At the time of

---

7. We shall cite his contribution "Le Philosphe et son ombre" from *Signes*.
8. Cf. "Le Philosophe et son ombre," p. 202. It may be recalled that in the preface to *Phenomenology* Merleau-Ponty said that "A purely linguistic examination of the texts in question would yield no proof. . . . We shall find in ourselves, and nowhere else, the unity and true meaning of phenomenology. It is less a matter of counting up quotations than of determining and expressing in concrete form this *phenomenology for ourselves* which has given a number of present day readers the impression, on reading Husserl or Heidegger, not so much of encountering a new philosophy as of recognizing what they had been waiting for." (*Phenomenology*, Preface, p. viii.)

Phenomenology of Perception these later writings were unpublished, as we mentioned in our introduction. By 1958 they had been published by the Husserl Archives at Louvain. In "Le Philosophe et son ombre" he focuses primarily on *Ideen II* but also refers to *Umsturtz der Kopernikanischen Lehre* and to *Ideen III*.[9] He had cited the first two as unpublished in *Phenomenology of Perception*, though not the last. The commentary is remarkably dense, more so it seems to us than in anything else that he has done. We take this to reflect not only his great command of the themes in question but also a seriousness in this later discussion that gives "Le Philosophe et son ombre" a significant well beyond that of being a response to a centenary occasion. Its importance does not lie in his modification of previous positions, but rather in the fact that these are reaffirmed. He now operates with an even more highly developed descriptive capacity than before, and so the expression of the relation of consciousness with nature and with other people is most effective.

Beginning with the *reduction*, he sees Husserl's texts taking this move not only beyond the natural object—something that occurred in *Ideen I*—but also beyond absolute subject—which seemed to have the priority in that earlier work—to a pre-theoretical dimension from which these are both derived. In the process he distinguishes a pair of meanings for the term *natural* as it applies to intellectual attitudes, admitting that the transcendental attitude that places the philosopher in the presence of what is primitive is itself supremely "natural." The so-called natural attitude that phenomenology must break through is the *theoretical* attitude, canonized by natural science and intellectualism and still affecting the Husserl of *Ideen I*. What *Ideen II* and *Ideen III* break through to is the *sensible*, for whose philosophical rehabilitation Merleau-Ponty credits Husserl. *This* is the domain correlated with the natural—that is, primitive—transcendental attitude. It is "the being that touches me in my most secret recesses, but also the being that I reach in its unrefined, brute state, in an absolute of presence that includes the secret of the world, the others, and the true." The sensible is access to everything, then, and my body is my insertion in the sensible. It is gifted with the distinctive reflexivity that makes it both subject and object (when my hands touch I can feel myself feeling myself) and so

---

9. *Ideen II* and *Ideen III* are references to the second and third volumes of *Ideen zu einer Reinen Phänomenologie und Phänomenologischen Philosophie.*

allows it to transcend the distinction of subject and object. This is the mute contact with self that allows the body to be the condition for the appearing of the object, and in relation to whose endless perspectives I can see the possibility of another perceiving subject. Merleau-Ponty expands on this reflexivity now, making it the condition for the actual appearing of the other person: "My two hands are 'copresent' or 'coexistent' because they are the hands of one single body. The other person appears by extension of that copresence: he and I are like organs of a single intercorporeity."[10] The other self achieves even sharper relief when I perceive his perceiving other things—when I see, for example, that he sees the things that I am seeing. With this, my objects cease to be simply mine to become "in-itself," which here means to be an object for the intersubjectivity. Thus once more the remarkable versatility of the sensible: the object appearing leads me to the other person, and the other person's appearing leads me back to the object.

In my exploring of the sensible to which the reduction leads me, I may find myself solicited toward *nature*—phenomenal objects in their distinctive context—or toward the *intersubjective*. But never am I led toward one as unrelated to the other and never *yet*, under Merleau-Ponty's guidance, in a way that made their relation clear. Indeed, the persistent question of the relation between the social and natural remains a persistent question. The angle of attack is no less persistent: phenomenology must articulate what happens when we move from one of these levels to another, a move everyone makes regularly and that the sensible, in which we are immersed, invites. Merleau-Ponty goes to some pains to make it clear that this is not a movement in or out of solipsism. The self is not prior to others and to nature and consigned to the task of breaking out of itself to them: self, the other person, and nature take shape simultaneously. Prior to their doing this there is not a solipsist ego but rather generalized undistinctness with a primordial and impersonal consciousness woven into the sensible and awaiting utterance. The self holds all the intentional strands that must be followed into these areas:

---

10. Merleau-Ponty has in mind the experience of shaking hands with another person here. It might be claimed that he said as much in *Phenomenology* when he discussed the phenomenal being of the other person. This is possible. The least that can be said about his treatment of it here is that it is more dramatic with its assertion of intercorporeity.

since we *are* at the junction of nature, body, soul, and philosophical consciousness, since we live this, no problem is conceivable whose solution is not outlined in us and in the spectacle of the world. There should be a way to compose in our thought whatever is lived out as part of our lives.[11]

The subject holds these strands because it entered into the *constitution* of the meaning to which they lead. Constitution, the fundamental intentionality, is that *eliciting of meaning* from an original copresence of incarnate subjects in a single world. Beyond every explicit meaning, he says as he concludes, and gesturing again to the ultimate, there is "the articulation . . . of Being that is accomplished through [*à travers*] man."

BEING AND THE PRIMACY OF THE SENSIBLE

He speaks here of Being and capitalizes it. The integration of this term into Merleau-Ponty's vocabulary raises the obvious questions about whether it is another case of the domestication of traditional terms or concessions to the established philosophies he previously opposed. As is the case with most sets of philosophical alternatives, the response seems to be neither or perhaps both. He has already spelled out quite clearly his very central reservations about Descartes' "Le Grand Rationalisme," and although his increased attention to the pursuit of and confrontation with a philosophical ultimate resembles the classic pursuit of Being, still the negative character of consciousness is much too important to him for his quest to be considered Cartesian. Sartre is a far more likely point of comparison, and there are a number of remarks of a genuinely Sartrian flavor in this period. Even in *Eloge de la philosophie* he spoke of man whose central position in philosophy he acknowledges as "not a strength but a weakness at the heart of being . . . ," and in this echoes Sartre's assertions that it is through man that nothingness came into the world! The sound was also there in "Partout et nulle part" when he placed the negative subjectivity of contemporary philosophy "at the center of philosophy . . . charged with making being appear, with assuming and transforming the positive."

It is easy enough to appreciate a pressure in Merleau-Ponty's work to establish a more striking fundamental polarity, just as one can appreciate Sartre's need to ease the fierce polarity between Being and

---

11. "Le Philosophe et son ombre," pp. 223 and 224.

Nothingness. Sartre must assure us that the subject can be in effective contact with the world, while Merleau-Ponty needs to guarantee his effective *emergence* from the world. One might expect the two positions to slide toward each other as their work develops. To some extent they do, but Merleau-Ponty, for all of the regularity in his use of the term *Being* in later works, not only keeps alive his emphasis upon the sensible but seems to expand his conception of it to meet those greater demands to which his inclination to use the term *being* testifies and finally to couch in terms of the sensible his statement of fundamental polarity *around which*, it seems to us, his work was stabilizing. This is quite evident in the preface to *Signes* and merits a return to that brief piece. In it he remarks that his philosophy is devoted to "the unmasking of the *Being* in which we dwell."

Once again it is Being to which he attends, and again, as in the case of "Le Philosophe et son ombre," he places a compact and refined description of the sensible at the center of his meditation. Now, however, the relation of the social and nature is on his mind and he turns much more to the nature of language and to its relation to the sensible than he did in the recent comment on Husserl. His pages include valuable observations on the nature of ideas, but more than anything else they move from the sensible toward what he calls

> the fundamental thought. Fundamental because it takes no other as its vehicle. . . . In principle it rests on nothing else and is, if you wish, an abyss. That means that it is never *with* itself, that we find it on the basis of things thought, that it is openness, the other invisible extremity of the axis which anchors us in things and ideas.[12]

Should he not call this extremity *nothingness*, then, and accept the Sartrian statement of the root polarity? "Rather than speaking of being and nothingness it is preferable to speak of the visible and the invisible." The trouble with nothingness is that it is unrestricted negation, and so, though it can apply generally to all being, it is completely undifferentiated and cannot be the source of explicit meanings. To use his words again: "the differences between near and far, the relief of being, would be effaced. . . . Without another dimension from which it would have to distinguish itself, what we have called 'verticality'—the present— would mean nothing." This integrates the *invisible* with the dimension

---

12. *Signes*, Preface, p. 29.

of time in which Merleau-Ponty has located the function of giving meaning. The brief descriptive remarks that follow suggest a relation of invisible with visible equivalent to the relation that *Phenomenology of Perception* indicates between the immobile and mobile, which is, in turn, the same fundamental interpenetration without loss of integrity that reigns in the order of present, past, and future. Beyond asserting his preference for this over Sartre's alternatives, Merleau-Ponty does not add to the description of the polarity in the preface to *Signes*. At the same time he does present *other* expressions for the dialectic in which consciousness finds itself: the private and the public, the event and its meditation, word and thought, and the question is open as to the exact meaning of his emphasis on the visible and the invisible. "L'Oeil et l'esprit" extends his reflections on this polarity.

THE VISIBLE AND THE INVISIBLE

"L'Oeil et l'esprit" was the last of Merleau-Ponty's works published during his lifetime, though it was written, one gathers, at the same time as the preface to *Signes*.[13] It is composed of five sections, in which a variety of material, most of it quite familiar, is brought to bear on the issue of visibility.[14] Because much of the material is familiar, the article seen as his last manages a recapitulation of his position that it could not have seriously intended. It also extends his reflection on the sensible somewhat beyond previous positions.

Merleau-Ponty does not comment directly on the title of this article, but on reading it one is drawn back to a remark by Brunschvicg that

---

13. "L'Oeil et l'esprit," as we mentioned, was published in *Art de France*, 1961, No. 1, and again in *Les Temps Modernes*, 1961, No. 184–85, the special issue commemorating Merleau-Ponty. We shall cite it from the latter. It should be noted, though, that the preface to *Signes* straddles "L'Oeil et l'esprit" in time of composition: The date given for the composition of the latter is July–August, 1960, while the preface is dated February *and* September, 1960. Apparently he completed the first part of the preface to *Signes*, then read Sartre's introduction to *Aden Arabie*, and added the last fifteen pages as response. The date of Sartre's introduction to *Alden Arabie*—March, 1960—seems to harmonize with this view.

14. Section One, for example, restates his attitude toward the sciences; Section III discusses Descartes' conception of vision, restating the intellectualist position on sensation, though with special emphasis on vision. Sections II and IV conduct phenomenologies of vision, painting, and the visible in ways similar to those conducted in *Phenomenology* and in his article on Cézanne.

he quoted in "Lecture de Montaigne."[15] Commenting on the Cartesian theory of sensation, Brunschvicg says that "the eye does not see itself ... but the spirit [*l'esprit*] alone knows ... the eye and itself." Merleau-Ponty conceives their relation quite differently, of course. If the eye does not exactly see itself, the person with vision does see himself. Added to the fact that I can feel myself feeling, this results in expanding the reflexivity of the body and helping make sensation a yet more worthy correlate of being. In its most telling portions the article is a hymn in praise of vision: "Vision is the encounter ... of all the aspects of Being," in which painting is read as a prolongation of the power of vision and thus "a central operation that contributes to defining our access to being."

"Our eyes," he says, "have the gift of the visible." Things are visible because they strike echoes in me. Their visibility is accomplished in my seeing them just as my vision is accomplished in their being seen. There is, in short, a system of exchange between self and world where their mutual exteriority yields to a polarized interiority. The form taken by the presence of the visible—by the concrete relation "seeing-seen"—is the *image*, and Merleau-Ponty treats it very briefly but according to its full "relationality." It is at once the seeing and the being seen of the visible object, partaking of the "duplicity of sensation" that we saw a moment ago as the reflexivity of the body.[16]

If the eye, whose seeing is invisible, has the gift of the visible, the painter transforms and extends this gift by making public—that is, visible—the very seeing that fulfills the seen: "Painting awakens and carries to its ultimate point a delirium that is vision itself since to see is to *have* at a distance, and painting extends this bizarre possession to all the aspects of being that must, somehow, become visible to enter into it." Notice that the extension of vision, the making public of the seeing, lies in making visible those aspects of the visible that are not ordinarily seen. What are these features of being that painting "sees"? Line, color, light, shadows, reflections: all of which, Merleau-Ponty says, normally make themselves forgotten in favor of the thing that one

---

15. "Lecture de Montaigne," *Signes*, pp. 250–66.
16. It would be interesting to speculate, on the basis of Merleau-Ponty's few remarks here, about the manner in which his conception of imagination would differ from Sartre's. It is easy to say that it would emphasize less the extreme opposition of the imagining and what is imagined. One suspects, along the same line, that for Merleau-Ponty even the object *present* is sufficiently "absent"—that is, at a distance—for an image to function in the consciousness of it. If so, this would bring imagination into *perception*.

sees. The artist must recover them and their manner of constituting a thing seen: "the questioning of the painter aims in every case at that secret and feverish genesis of things in our body." *His* vision is "continuous birth." Carrying this theme to a descriptive climax, he trades upon the fact that the French term for the fundamental agitation of the artist—*inspiration*—can also be used to mean inhalation and says that "there is truly *inspiration* [inhalation] and *expiration* [exhalation] of Being: respiration in Being."

The genetic character of these remarks carries us back to those in *Phenomenology of Perception* to the effect that the body animates the world as the heart does the organism, that the subject of sensation is *born into* an environment, and that the body is the condition for the being of objects. For Merleau-Ponty the analysis of painting is an opportunity in addition to that provided by the analysis of sensation—or at least extending it—to explore the perceptual constitution of phenomena.[17] "L'Oeil et l'esprit" returns—with additional descriptive impact, it is true—to the revision of the dimensions of sensibility that *Phenomenology of Perception* promoted—revision wherein depth, for example, ceased to be a kind of length to become the most primitive simultaneity of things[18] and color became a fundamental dimension rather than an outer envelope of the visible thing. It quickly reaches even beyond this: the ability of painters to shift their approach and to sketch well or to be good sculptors is, he says, "the proof that there is a system of equivalences, a logos of lines, lights, colors, relief, masses; a manifestation without concept of universal being." He underscores the non-conceptual character by calling art an "inarticulate cry." The analogy with the basic system of equivalences existing among the senses is evident, and one would have expected this, given the rooted-

---

17. One can wonder, given the striking character of his descriptions of painting, why he did not make more frequent and important use of them. The fact is that he usually subordinated them to other issues. In the article on Cézanne, for example, remarkably rich descriptions are controlled by the problem of the relation of the artist's life and its effect on his work. In "Le Langage indirect et les voix du silence" the problem dominating his use of painting was that of language. Why did he not free it more from such questions and simply follow its lead as he did with sensation? Probably because he was not a painter.

18. "Depth . . . is the experience of the reversibility of dimensions, of a global locality where everything is at once, of which height, breadth, and distance are abstractions, of a voluminousness that one expresses in a single word when he says that a thing is there." ("L'Oeil et l'esprit," p. 216.)

ness of painting in vision to which he leads back the discussion as the article reaches its climax. It does so when it defines vision as "the means given me to be absent from myself, to assist from within at the splitting of being at the end of which only can I close in on myself." The description is almost identical with those remarks in *Phenomenology of Perception* that describe the subject as time: time "exists only when a subjectivity is there is to disrupt the plenitude of being in itself, to adumbrate a perspective and to introduce non-being into it."

What does "L'Oeil et l'esprit" suggest about this final period in Merleau-Ponty's thought? The *invisible* is certainly an equivalent, in his system of equivalents, for what he previously called the *present*. The peculiar style of his emphasis on it now—that is, the use of a more concretely visual-sensible term instead of the more embracing and seemingly more versatile term *present*, or presence—points to his turning back toward the reflection upon the relations of consciousness with nature. Sartre mentions Merleau-Ponty's contemplating a book on nature in about 1958 and guesses that "L'Oeil et l'esprit" was part of it.[19] In an important sense this speaking of the visible and the invisible tends to sharpen or intensify the polarity he previously expressed as presence and world. He tends to pair vision, which *is* the invisible in question, with *Being*. One can ask if this narrows being or expands vision and arrive at the usual answer: both. If being is what can be visible, its visibility must be taken as one of those *total parts* that we met when we learned that existence was sexual. As for the sensibility, the effect of "L'Oeil et l'esprit" is to expand it to equal that full and unanticipated wealth of the visual model where the sensible seems to reveal the presence-absence that one normally attributes to thought. The attention to vision again accents the *genesis* of meanings and seems capable of restoring the *future* dimension of time, which we saw Merleau-Ponty neglect as he considered history. His final word, the one with which the article closes, points to that very dimension. We take the liberty of repeating it: "If creations are not acquired, it is not because, like everything else, they pass; it is because they have almost all of their lives before them."

---

19. As our own manuscript is completed we learn of the publication of the manuscript upon which Merleau-Ponty was working at the time of his death. The title is *Le Visible et l'invisible* (Paris: Gallimard, 1964), and the text has been established by his friend Claude Lefort. It runs to 187 pages and is accompanied by 121 pages of Merleau-Ponty's work notes as well as valuable comments by Lefort.

Epilogue

MAN AND THE ENLARGEMENT OF REASON

Merleau-Ponty enlarges reason at the expense of the irrational. He begins with nature and consciousness, the permanent structure of being, and the lucid self-possession that are the foundation of classic rationality and finds them rooted in being-in-the-world—that is, in a moving dynamic *presence*. This presence is itself an operation without a model from which meaning issues: it is the possibility of situations, the *power of expression*. The fact that it lies elsewhere than in consciousness or in nature is enough for it to be taken as irrational. Is not its incorporation into reason by its being placed at the center of philosophy an *enlargement* of reason? And with this does not reason comprehend its own genetic instance and so accomplish one of the most precious hopes of philosophy? Critics remind us, however, that with *this* particular comprehending, reason incorporates into philosophy the incompleteness of things and the obscurity of finite consciousness. They protest that the operation without a model terminates in no position beyond which there may not lie a further position and that its very march cannot be conceived as method. Near the end of "L'Oeil et l'esprit" Merleau-Ponty lends their complaints an accurate and vehement rhetoric: "Is this reason's highest accomplishment: observing the ground as it slips away beneath our feet, pompously calling interrogation what is simply a state of continual stupor, calling research what is a wandering in a circle, calling Being something that never completely is?" Such is, in truth, the dark side of enlarged reason. It can—and must—be balanced off by calling attention to the freedom and creativity of this enlarged reason and to the fact that the incompleteness and obscurity in the human situation deserve a place in the inventory of our experience, not simply as *de facto* obstacles and limitations, but also as the correlate of our doing and our making.

This freedom and creativity, however, does not permit—much less demand—chaos, and Merleau-Ponty's option against the traditional concept and essence is not an option against the coherence of what is but for another reading of that coherence. Experience has its reference points—things, the world, other persons and institutions—all constituting a "material a priori." And it is *here*, in dealing with these, that we find out what the very words *to know, to be certain,* and *to be true* mean. But here our knowing has always been at ease with their incompleteness and its own, our certitudes with their instability and the future, our truth with process and obscurity. If the concept and the essence as traditionally understood cannot cohabit comfortably in this way with their contraries, then they are untrue to themselves as features of men and the human situation.

Enlarged reason is a humanized reason. Its categories are modeled on the gesture, on the style, and on presence. It speaks of behavior, affinities, systems of equivalence, and institutions where structure and process, stability and a future, are at peace. Such is its rationality, the intelligibility with which its intelligence is at grips. There is, we think, a development by means of a phenomenology of imagination that can strikingly extend its range, allowing it many of the privileges once accorded only to idea and concept, without rupture with the familiar and the human from which phenomenology must draw its strength. Nothing is more characteristic of the style and the behavior of Merleau-Ponty than this adherence to the human.

Index

Painting
  as expression of reality, 161–62
  and meaning, 86
  and the visible, 263–65
Pavlov, Ivan, and higher behavior, 35–38
Perception
  and environment, 131
  in infants, 46–47
  preconscious, 12, 62, 150
Perspectivism. *See* Profile-object
Phenomena, meaning of, 8
Philosophy
  and absolute comprehension, 254–55
  Christian, 190–02
  and relationship with its past, 252–53
  themes of, 256
Praxis
  historical, 216–17, 223
  as symbolic activity, 194
Profile-object, 51–52
  capacity of, to solicit consciousness, 114
  perspectivism of, 55–57

Reduction, 116, 167
  meaning of, 12
  naive, 29, 51
  and transcendental attitude, 9
Ricoeur, Paul, on Merleau-Ponty's work, 130

Scheler, Max, 4–5, 198
Science, and phenomenological method, 62–63
Sedimentation, 136, 253
  and language, 158–66
Signification, philosophy of, 130–32

Socrates, 249–50
Speech
  and body deficiency, 81, 85
  as expressive intention, 120
Structure
  for consciousness, 50
  as perceptual involvement, 93
  presented by perception, 60
  See also Form
Subjectivity
  discovery of, 254
  negative, 255–56

Terror
  as dimension of human condition, 205
  and historical contingency, 204
Thought, and speech, 156
Time
  as establishing permanence, 121
  and perception, 97
  and priority of the present, 127–28
  as subjectivity, 125–30, 138
  and its transcendence, 127
  See also Consciousness
Transcendence, 116–19, 122–23, 132
Trotsky, Leon
  as example to Merleau-Ponty, 210, 218–19
  and "permanent revolution," 219
  See also Humanisme et terreur
Truth
  effectiveness of, 122–23
  as establishing coherence, 165–66
  in political order, 216
  as sedimentation, 166

Vitalism, and behavior, 45–46

A 7
B 8
C 9
D 0
E 1
F 2
G 3
H 4
I 5
J 6